AF735491

Training Correctional Staff to Recognize Criminal Thinking

Ashley B. Batastini • Ashley C. T. Jones •
Kaylee Cook

Training Correctional Staff to Recognize Criminal Thinking

In the Act

Springer

Ashley B. Batastini
Swinburne University of Technology
Centre for Forensic Behavioural Science
Melbourne, SA, Australia

Ashley C. T. Jones
University of Southern Mississippi
Hattiesburg, MS, USA

Kaylee Cook
University of Memphis
Memphis, TN, USA

ISBN 978-3-031-88403-0 ISBN 978-3-031-88404-7 (eBook)
https://doi.org/10.1007/978-3-031-88404-7

© The Editor(s) (if applicable) and The Author(s), under exclusive license to Springer Nature Switzerland AG 2025

This work is subject to copyright. All rights are solely and exclusively licensed by the Publisher, whether the whole or part of the material is concerned, specifically the rights of translation, reprinting, reuse of illustrations, recitation, broadcasting, reproduction on microfilms or in any other physical way, and transmission or information storage and retrieval, electronic adaptation, computer software, or by similar or dissimilar methodology now known or hereafter developed.
The use of general descriptive names, registered names, trademarks, service marks, etc. in this publication does not imply, even in the absence of a specific statement, that such names are exempt from the relevant protective laws and regulations and therefore free for general use.
The publisher, the authors and the editors are safe to assume that the advice and information in this book are believed to be true and accurate at the date of publication. Neither the publisher nor the authors or the editors give a warranty, expressed or implied, with respect to the material contained herein or for any errors or omissions that may have been made. The publisher remains neutral with regard to jurisdictional claims in published maps and institutional affiliations.

This Springer imprint is published by the registered company Springer Nature Switzerland AG
The registered company address is: Gewerbestrasse 11, 6330 Cham, Switzerland

If disposing of this product, please recycle the paper.

Competing Interests The authors have no competing interests to declare that are relevant to the content of this manuscript.

Contents

About the Authors

Ashley B. Batastini is an Associate Professor in the Centre for Forensic Behavioural Science at Swinburne University of Technology, located in Melbourne, Australia. She earned her doctorate in Counseling Psychology at Texas Tech University after completing a pre-doctoral internship at Western State Hospital in Tacoma, Washington. She received her Master of Science degree in Psychology with a focus in Forensic Psychology from Drexel University and her Bachelor of Science degree in Psychology from the University of Pittsburgh. Her work focuses on developing novel intervention strategies for higher-risk populations and improving access to appropriate interventions at various stages of criminal legal involvement. Dr. Batastini has authored or co-authored over 50 peer-reviewed publications related to topics such as the psychological effects of administrative segregation, barriers to employment for people with criminal records, violence risk assessment, and the efficacy of telepsychology in assessment and treatment. She has also authored or co-authored numerous book chapters related to the treatment of justice-involved persons and is the lead developer of *Stepping Up, Stepping Out: A Mental Health Treatment Program for Inmates in Restrictive Housing*.

Ashley C. T. Jones, Ph.D., is an Assistant Professor at the University of Southern Mississippi. She completed her pre-doctoral internship and a postdoctoral fellow in forensic psychology at Utah State Hospital in Provo, Utah. Dr. Jones earned her Master of Science degree in Psychology from Arizona State University and her doctorate in Counseling Psychology from the University of Southern Mississippi. Her research focuses on the use of technology to increase access to forensic and correctional services and understanding its impact on treatment and court proceedings. Dr. Jones was the recipient of two competitive dissertation grants from the American Psychological Foundation and the American Academy of Forensic Psychology, and received the Outstanding Graduate Student Award given by the Criminal Justice Section of Division 18 (Psychologists in Public Service) of the American Psychological Association.

Kaylee Cook, Ph.D., is a Postdoctoral Fellow specializing in substance use treatment at the Federal Medical Center in Fort Worth, Texas, where she completed a pre-doctoral internship. She earned her doctorate in Counseling Psychology from the University of Memphis. Prior to graduate school, she worked as a teacher and aided in a program evaluation in a state prison. Additionally, while in her doctoral training, she has gained experience providing mental health services and competency evaluations in a forensic and correctional setting. Her research interests focus on program evaluation of correctional interventions and re-entry post-release, specifically employment-related barriers. She was a recipient of the APA Division 18 (Psychologists in Public Service) Criminal Justice Section Outstanding Graduate Student Award, as well as an inaugural recipient of APA Division 18 Criminal Justice Section's Gavel Award.

List of e-Resources

Materials for Training Implementation

1. *ITA* Training Announcement Flyer
2. *ITA* PowerPoint slide deck
3. *ITA* Trainee Attendance Sheet (see also Appendix 2.1)
4. *ITA* Movie Clip Practice Guide (optional time-permitting) (see also Appendix 4.1)
5. *ITA* 3-Step Desktop Reference (see also Appendix 4.2)
6. *ITA* Criminal Thinking Rewind Thought Log (see also Appendix 4.3)
7. *ITA* Staff Intervention Log (see also Appendix 4.4)
8. *ITA* Practice Scenarios (see also Appendix 6.1)
9. *ITA* Knowledge Acquisition Quiz Answer Sheet (for trainees) (see also Appendix 6.2)
10. *ITA* Knowledge Acquisition Quiz Answer Key (for trainers) (see also Appendix 6.3)
11. *ITA* Evaluation of Trainee Engagement Form (see also Appendix 6.4)
12. *ITA* Completion Certificate (see also Appendix 6.5)
13. *ITA* Training Evaluation Form (see also Appendix 6.6)

Supplemental Appendices: Optional Measures for Evaluation

14. *Attitudes Toward Correctional Staff*
15. *Attitudes Toward Prisoners Scale (ATP)* (see also Appendix 2.2)
16. *Psychological Inventory of Criminal Thinking Styles—Simplified Version (PICTS-SV)*
17. *Self-Efficacy-12 (SE-12)*
18. *Stigma Toward Prison Records Questionnaire (STPPR)* (see also Appendix 2.3)
19. *Work Stress Scale*
20. *Burnout Assessment Tool (BAT)*

Chapter 1
Overview and Preparation

Rationale

The literature on correctional treatment is quite clear: interventions aimed at reducing behavioral misconduct and criminal activity are substantially more successful when they focus on empirically supported, changeable risk factors (see Bonta & Andrews, 2016). Among the most predictive of these factors are criminal thinking styles or antisocial cognitions (Walters, 2012; Walters & Lowenkamp, 2016). Importantly, criminal thinking styles often do not involve explicit thoughts about crime; rather, they are distortions in how one interprets the world that justifies or supports a criminal lifestyle (Yochelson & Samenow, 1976; Walters, 2013). Sometimes, however, these types of thoughts can be less obvious, involving less serious offenses. Think about a time you may have called off sick for work when you weren't actually sick or sped down the highway. By faking illness for a day off, you may have put heavier workloads on your co-workers and increased risks to their safety with fewer staff on duty. It's one thing to take allotted personal or sick days when needed; it's another to create unnecessary stressors for your colleagues who are likely spread thin to begin with. Similarly, driving recklessly down the highway puts you, your passengers, and other motorists in harm's way. Your decisions led to behaviors that violated rules and other people's well-being. The more often and more frequently people engage in criminal thinking, the more likely they are to get in serious trouble including being arrested or incarcerated.

> **Important:** Criminal thinking is a category of thoughts that help justify behaviors that violate rules or other people's well-being.

Supplementary Information The online version contains supplementary material available at https://doi.org/10.1007/978-3-031-88404-7_1.

© The Author(s), under exclusive license to Springer Nature Switzerland AG 2025

A. B. Batastini et al., *Training Correctional Staff to Recognize Criminal Thinking*, https://doi.org/10.1007/978-3-031-88404-7_1

Criminal thinking describes errors in judgment and decision-making that represent general irresponsibility. These errors are typically not recognized by the person engaging in them, but nonetheless lead to antisocial behaviors and often serious undesirable outcomes. Therefore, a common goal of many evidence-based programs used by correctional departments is to help incarcerated or otherwise justice-involved persons better recognize these maladaptive thinking patterns and adjust their decision-making in favor of more productive choices (see Batastini et al., 2018 for a review).

Criminal thinking can be changed (Walters, 2003; Gaspar et al., 2019). One of the more popular programs used in the United States for changing criminal thinking is *Thinking for a Change* (*T4C*; Bush et al., 1997), with 31 states currently offering *T4C* training (National Institute of Corrections [NIC], 2023). Other well-known and efficacious programs that specifically target antisocial cognitions include *Reason and Rehabilitation* (Ross et al., 1988; Tong & Farrington, 2006) and *Moral Reconation Therapy* (Little & Robinson, 1988). Several available programs also incorporate techniques for reducing criminal thinking among other treatment targets (e.g., Morgan et al., 2018; Batastini et al., 2020; Folk et al., 2016). Programs that use cognitive-behavioral techniques to reduce criminal thinking can subsequently reduce recidivism by about 20% to as high as 55% compared to control and comparison groups (Landenberger & Lipsey, 2005; Lipsey et al., 2001, 2007; Lowenkamp et al., 2009; Wilson et al., 2005). Criminal thinking-focused programs can also result in the reduction of institutional misconduct (Walters, 2017), thereby contributing to a safer correctional environment.

Criminal thinking can be changed.

In the Act (ITA) is a novel training program that teaches correctional staff (primarily security and unit staff) brief and effective strategies to promptly address instances of criminal thinking that occur beyond the view of mental health providers—that is, in their daily life within the institution. Correctional or custodial officers in particular are a prime group to contribute to systemic intervention efforts designed to reduce criminal thinking when it happens. Not only do they spend the most time with incarcerated persons, but they are also often the first staff to respond to their needs or conflicts. Thus, these staff are in an advantageous position to provide in-the-moment education and redirection to help incarcerated persons modify criminal thinking. In fact, in the context of mental health treatment, experts argue that correctional officers are ideal for providing supportive counseling and skills training to people who are incarcerated to ***supplement*** programming initiatives (Anthony & Carkhuff, 1977; Dvoskin & Spiers, 2004). Most treatment programs focused on reducing criminal thinking currently do not involve correctional officers as essential change agents in their implementation. That's where this training comes in! However, this training is geared toward any type of correctional employee who routinely encounters incarcerated individuals in less therapeutic contexts (e.g., during brief cell-front rounds, on-unit interactions). It may be especially useful for those who are newer to the carceral environment and/or have fewer skills or experiences to effectively address problem behaviors.

As criminal thinking is engrained over years of life experience, the process of unlearning these thinking errors requires significant practice with *cognitive restructuring* (a fancy psychology term for changing the way you think about things or interpret events). Practicing cognitive restructuring across settings is likely to be superior to practicing in isolated situations such as when incarcerated clients are in the treatment room with a clinician and/or among peers in a treatment group. In fact, it has been demonstrated that when skills are practiced outside of sessions (e.g., via homework) the likelihood of success for justice-involved individuals improves (Morgan & Flora, 2002; Morgan et al., 2012). That is, the more clients practice and are encouraged to adjust their criminal thinking in their real-world environment, the more likely they are to experience maximal change.

However, it has been suggested that the extent to which programs targeting criminal thinking work may generally be overestimated, as existing studies have been primarily concerned with overall effects (i.e., looking at program participants as a group) rather than more nuanced differences among individuals or subgroups of program participants (Lester et al., 2020; Kravitz et al., 2004). Recidivism and/or misconduct rates following participation in cognitive-behavioral programs may be more accurate, and potentially decrease, with further individualization of treatment content. *ITA* improves the individualization of treatment by promoting even swifter and more frequent redirection of specific instances of criminal thinking. *ITA* also allows for client-focused criminal thinking interventions to become systemic programs—creating a unified responsibility among staff to facilitate change and hold incarcerated persons accountable.

All staff, no matter their credentials, will not only be able to redirect incarcerated persons "in the act," but will also have the skills to respond proactively and in a manner consistent with how these clients are taught to self-correct in treatment. Training modules are designed to generalize across variants of criminal thinking treatment protocols (e.g., T4C, MRT) rather than accompany a specific program. That is, the skills learned through this training will "fit" with most cognitive-behavioral programs in which reducing criminal thinking is a primary aim. Additionally, *ITA* is intended to complement other types of trainings that are becoming more prevalent for correctional staff, such as those that teach mental health sensitivity, trauma-informed practices, and gender responsiveness (Covington & Bloom, 2007; DeHart & Iachini, 2019; Kubiak et al., 2017; Parker, 2009). The inclusion of security and unit staff in *ITA* is especially necessary given the extensive amount of time they spend interacting with incarcerated persons daily. Appropriately managing immediate (i.e., in the moment) expressions of criminal thinking may prevent the direct behavioral (sometimes violent) consequences of these cognitive processes, improve institutional milieu, and lead to more permanent changes. While the skills taught in this training may not work every time or even most of the time, it is worth learning and applying them if just one instance of violence is avoided. Further, the more often these skills are implemented on a unit, the more normalized and expected they become. Shifting the culture of the prison environment takes time and persistence.

Perceptions of Program Acceptability

Data from initial implementations of *ITA* suggest overall favorability among trainees who completed the program. In developing and refining program curriculum and materials, the training was implemented with two samples of trainees. The first implementation was conducted with a group of 15 mental health and educational staff employed in a large metropolitan adult detention center in the United States. Trainees were mixed gender, but majority were women (11 women; 4 men). Some trainees were students completing practical field hours. The average total score on the training evaluation form (see Chap. 6 appendix 6.6 or e-Resource 6.6) for this first implementation was 123.58 (standard deviation[1] [SD] = 15.32) out of a possible 140.[2] In further delineating perceptions, trainees reported positive opinions regarding the specific learning objectives (average = 17.80 out of 20 max), program content (average = 41.57 out of 48), the trainer (average = 48.64 out of 52), and how the training was generally administered (average = 16.54 out of 20).

The second implementation was conducted with a group of 54 correctional officers and frontline staff employed by an Australian adult correctional services department over the course of 2 days (28 trainees in Day 1 and 26 trainees in Day 2). Trainees were also mixed gender but were majority men (38 men; 18 women). Thirty-four trainees were within their first 12 months of employment; other trainees ranged in experience from 3 to 30 years. The average total score on the training evaluation form for this sample was 119.95 (SD = 14.64) out of 140. Trainees likewise reported generally positive opinions regarding the specific learning objectives (average = 16.63), program content (average = 39.94), the trainer (average = 47.84), and how the training was administered (average = 15.42).

Across both samples, only 27 trainees provided written feedback in the open-ended question on the training evaluation form. Constructive feedback tended to focus on wanting more real-world examples, some complaints about content repetition, and feeling the skills might be more difficult to implement on the job than in the training session. Notably, in the U.S. pilot, less time was available for Module 5 due to excess content. Slides were revised and reduced to allow more time for practice exercises as intended. Additional revisions to the slides, this user's manual, and the appendices/e-Resources were also made after both the U.S. and Australian implementations to improve the flow/organization of the training and help minimize common concerns (e.g., recommending trainers explain the purpose of repetition,

[1] Standard deviation is a measure of variability in scores relative to the average score for the group. A low standard deviation means that most people's scores were close to the average; therefore, the average score is a good representation of how most people felt. A higher standard deviation means that individual scores were more spread out from the mean and that the average is less representative of how people felt.

[2] Note that *ITA* evaluation form scores were converted from a range of 1–5 to a range of 0–4 for ease of interpretation.

normalizing that practice scenarios cannot fully capture how events unfold on the unit). Overall, however, most people who included qualitative feedback believed it would be a useful training, especially for newer officers. Example comments included:

- *I definitely feel like the course is relevant, tasteful especially for new staff. I feel like this training aligns with current practice, but our de-escalation training does cover a lot of this already, but maybe just reinforces it.*
- *[It was] beneficial to learn a little about programs prisoners undertake. Allows staff to better communicate in difficult situations with examples of how to possibly deal with them.*
- *Very effective information session that could be useful to other officers. Especially those in new corrections, content was very relevant and engaging.*
- *I believe this does benefit the new officers in terms of tactical communication with the prisoners.*

Structure and Outline

Use of the Train-the-Trainer Model

For the best outcomes, implementation of *In the Act* should follow a train-the-trainer (T3) model, which involves two key steps. First, it is strongly suggested that *ITA* program developers be retained to train upper-level security or unit staff on the basic principles of the training program (e.g., empirical foundation, modular structure) and demonstrate how to teach go-to skills for recognizing and correcting criminal thinking. Second, trained upper-level or senior staff will then train frontline staff with access to consult with the *ITA* development team. Once upper-level, senior staff are properly trained, your facility then has the freedom to conduct multiple trainings throughout the year on a schedule conducive to your facility's needs or rate of staff turnover. There is no need to continue hiring consultants or trainers. This capability is particularly important in correctional settings where staff turnover can be high (Kiekbusch et al., 2003; Taylor & Cooper, 2008), and new staff orientations may take place as routinely as once a month. Research on the effectiveness of T3 implementation models shows success across relevant disciplines (mental health, Frank et al., 2021; law enforcement, Molinaro et al., 2019). Other studies support the fact that T3 models increase the number of staff members trained, the number of consumers who benefit from programs (Becan et al., 2019), and dramatically reduce training expenses (Baxter & Harrison, 2000). The structure of T3 programs also makes it cost-effective (Fig. 1.1).

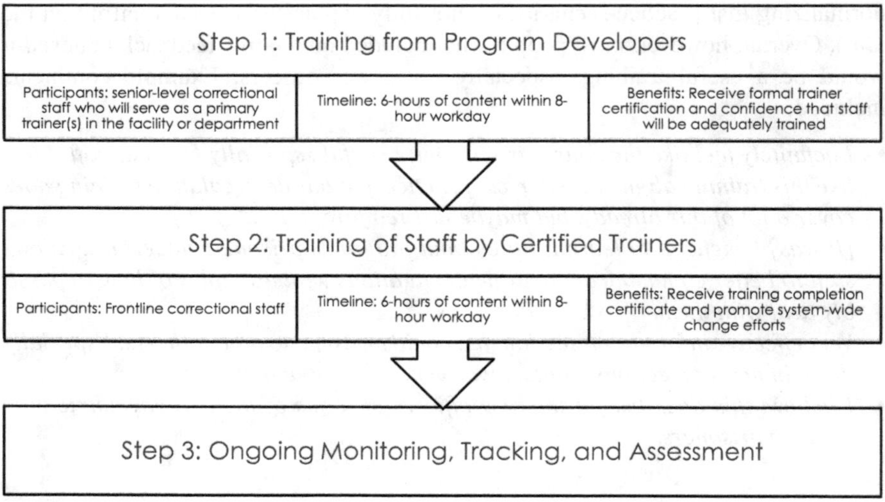

Fig. 1.1 Process of train-the-trainer

Step 1: Training from Program Developers

Training correctional trainers (i.e., senior supervisory staff) is conducted over a 6-h (full day) workshop using PowerPoint presentations, handouts, skill development exercises, case examples, and role plays designed to maximize retention of material and skill development. The use of interactive examples and hands-on demonstration provides a novel and memorable experience for new trainers, thereby increasing their ability to translate information effectively to their staff. In this way, the T3 model is focused not only on the content itself, but also on teaching high-quality instructional methods and managing challenging student/staff behaviors (e.g., resistance, participants who are slower to grasp material). The training slides and accompanying notations provided within this workbook provide instructional content from the perspective of a new instructor. However, training from the program developers is recommended to get your department started. Executive correctional staff can schedule a trainer certification session by contacting the *ITA* program developers. Contact information is available on the Springer International website.

Step 2: Training of Staff by Certified Trainers

When delivered to front-line correctional staff, *ITA* is also a 6-h (full day) training that incorporates educational/didactic components with interactive, hands-on practice and demonstration of acquired skills led by a qualified trainer at the facility.

However, it is highly recommended that at least two qualified trainers co-facilitate the training day. It can be both physically and mentally straining to stand in front of a group of people—no matter how large or small—for 6 full hours talking, answering impromptu questions, guiding discussions, monitoring trainee behavior, handing out training materials, etc. Co-facilitation can not only reduce the fatigue that comes with running a training of this nature, but it can also provide varied perspectives and anecdotal examples, help change up the energy in the room, model healthy collaboration and teamwork, and show there's some consensus regarding the need to learn these skills (it's not just one person telling them to make these adjustments in their workday). Further, co-facilitators can rely on each other to problem-solve issues that come up during the training and debrief after the day has concluded. Keep in mind that effective co-facilitation requires some planning before the training day such as who will present which parts of the training, strategies for maintaining trainee engagement, or how the practice exercises will be implemented. It also helps if the co-facilitators have a good rapport. A weird vibe between facilitators will be felt by trainees and will likely overshadow the content being delivered.

The five training modules are summarized below and in their intended order of administration.

Module Overview

Module 1: Your Role in Change (30–45 min). The primary goal of this brief module is to increase staff buy-in regarding their role in supporting prosocial change among incarcerated persons and why this task cannot be the sole responsibility of mental health staff. This module begins with a facilitated discussion about existing attitudes toward incarcerated persons and their ability to change through structured treatment programs. Measuring related attitudes using surveys like the Attitudes Toward Prisoners (ATP; Melvin et al., 1985) scale or the Stigma Toward People with Prison Records (STPPR; Shi et al., 2022) scale (see Chap. 2 appendices 2.2 and 2.3 or e-Resources 2.2 and 2.3) to assess participants' attitudes is recommended.

Staff impressions about ITA and its usefulness are expected to be largely negativistic or, at best, ambivalent. Trainers must be accepting and understanding of dismissive and/or skeptical attitudes from trainees at this stage but should be careful not to condone their beliefs. In other words, do not perpetuate negative perceptions about people in prison or who are otherwise under correctional supervision. Similarly, do not join trainees in commiserating about how bad the inmates are; instead, you could say something like: "I understand why you might feel that way" or "This is a tough population to work with and I know we've all had challenging or disappointing experiences when trying to help them." Trainees at this stage may also diverge into discussing other barriers of their jobs such as feeling unsupported by upper management or not having enough resources to do their jobs to the best of their ability (e.g., short-staffed, low pay). Trainers can validate these feelings and show empathy for the realities of this work without allowing the discussion to deviate into a "bitch" session. Trainers can redirect the conversation by noting this training will not solve many of these deeper-rooted concerns, but it is intended to give trainees some simple skills to use that may build less adversarial relationships with the people in their custody and hopefully reduce some of the stress in their workday. Skeptical or dismissive attitudes will be further challenged in Module 2. The emphasis in Module 1 is buy-in, which can be accomplished by: (1) acknowledging the everyday workplace struggles and burnout experienced by frontline staff and (2) outlining the direct and indirect benefits of uniting with and supporting their mental health colleagues who are leading program implementation efforts. Benefits center on the personal safety and well-being of individual staff, their co-workers, the incarcerated persons they manage, and the communities they are committed to protecting.

Module 2: What Helps (45 mins to 1 h). This empirically guided module is designed to teach trainees about the intervention models and techniques that are most successful in producing behavioral changes and reducing recidivism. The module begins with an overview of the Risk-Needs-Responsivity model (RNR; Bonta & Andrews, 2016) and other relevant treatment variables such as the need for intensive, structured, long-term, cognitive-behavioral programs and reliance on social learning (Wooditch et al., 2014; Bonta & Andrews, 2007). Given the importance of criminal thinking and antisocial attitudes to criminal risk, this broader overview leads into a more detailed discussion about the definition and historical context of criminal thinking and its relationship to disruptive behavior. The dimensional nature of criminal thinking is emphasized, and trainees are asked to consider times in which they, too, have engaged in thinking errors to avoid responsibility or blame. The occurrence of criminal thinking in the context of other presenting concerns or characteristics, such as mental illness, cognitive impairment, gender, or age, is also discussed. Finally, trainees learn about direct response strategies that are likely to escalate already tense staff-inmate interactions.

Module 3: Addressing Criminal Thinking (1.5 h). This module orients trainees to the underlying cognitive-behavioral framework and how evidence-based treatment programs use this general framework to address and help reduce instances of criminal thinking. Trainees are briefly introduced to several existing programs commonly used for correctional clients; however, we recommend consulting and collaborating with program providers in your facility so this portion of the module can be appropriately tailored. Slides may be added or substituted as needed to illustrate how the specific program used in your facility teaches incarcerated persons about the concept of criminal thinking and how to identify and subsequently correct it. Such collaboration will ensure correctional staff are using similar terminology, common metaphors, slogans, mnemonics, and other unique learning tools. Matching the way staff respond to expressions of criminal thinking during their day-to-day interactions with the way concepts are presented in treatment will enhance learning through consistency and repetition. Examples of criminal thinking specific to in-custody settings, go-to corrective responses (i.e., quick, back-pocket options), and how to manage adverse reactions to redirection efforts are reviewed. Most notably, this module introduces trainees to a three-step model for addressing criminal thinking that is referenced throughout the remaining training modules. More details about the three-step model are provided below (see Fig. 1.5). This module also highlights the importance of communicating criminal thinking events with other unit staff and clinicians for continuity of care purposes. We provide instruction on how to track/document such events. Suggestions for documentation are offered in Chap. 4 appendix 4.4 or e-Resource 4.4 with the understanding that documentation procedures will ultimately be determined by institutional policy.

Module 4: Specific Populations (1.5 h). Although the prevalence of criminal thinking and its association with criminal activity or institutional misconduct has largely shown to generalize across various justice-involved populations (Walters et al., 2009; Wilson et al., 2014), certain subgroups warrant additional consideration. This module focuses on several specific populations (i.e., those with serious mental illness, cognitive/neurological impairment, youth, and women) for whom criminal thinking may be uniquely expressed and for which effective responding depends on a more nuanced knowledge of the research. Trainees learn to recognize less obvious signs of criminal thinking among these groups and respond to expressions of criminal thinking with sensitivity to group-based responsivity factors. For those with serious mental disorders, there is often an inclination to excuse poor behavior as a direct result of their illness. While no one should ever be blamed for having a mental illness, they can be redirected regarding decisions that lead to poor symptom management (e.g., medication non-compliance). Older incarcerated persons and those with cognitive and neurological deficits will likely need more repetition with simplified and/or nonverbal feedback. For incarcerated youth, developmental limitations can be barriers to motivation and skill acquisition, similarly requiring unique strategies to reinforce information. Incarcerated women and other minority gender identities are especially likely to benefit from a trauma- and gender-informed communication style (Taylor et al., 2018) when challenging criminal thinking; for example, statements with victim-blaming undertones must be avoided.

Keep in mind that there are many other subgroups for which special considerations might be relevant; however, a training of 6 h does not allow sufficient time to go into detail about everyone or every group. Think of Module 4 as a set of four examples. Trainers could also tie other groups into their discussions of these special considerations as appropriate and if time allows. For example, many considerations for cisgender[3] women also apply to transgender[4] persons (e.g., higher rates of victimization and discrimination, different personal hygiene or medical needs; Dalzell et al., 2024; Campbell et al. 2023). Trainers may also emphasize issues of racism, cultural identity, and/or intersectionality;[5] for example, that people of color or Indigenous persons may experience unique frustrations or agitation related to systemic or individual forms of discrimination. Across subgroups (even those not explicitly covered in the training), Module 4 emphasizes that, even when there are genuine external factors that can be used to justify the way someone thinks or behaves, some degree of responsibility for their current situation and how they respond to that situation can be taken.

Module 5: Putting It into Practice (1.5 h). This final module includes practical hands-on training to demonstrate and facilitate skill development. The module begins with a scripted trainer-led demonstration using a volunteer trainee from the audience in the role of the incarcerated person. During this first stage, trainers are in the role of the staff member and model appropriate responses to expressions of criminal thinking. Stage 2 involves a trainee-led demonstration with two volunteers: one in the role of the incarcerated person and one as the staff member. Trainers will assume more of an observer perspective in Stage 2 to help guide the exercise and engage the audience. In the final stage, participants break into pairs or small groups to act out assigned role-play scenarios. If the training group is relatively small, trainers may have all pairs act out their scenarios in front of the entire group so their peers and the trainer can provide constructive feedback (e.g., what did they do well, what other response options might they have considered). However, if the training group is too large for this approach, trainees can take turns acting out their scenarios within their respective break-out group; trainers should then float between groups to provide direct supervision to ensure trainees are navigating the scenarios effectively. For larger training groups, multiple trainers or a trainer's assistant are recommended. Regardless of approach, each trainee should play the role of the staff member at least once. Trainers must attend to both the content and tone of these mock interactions. Trainees' attention and participation in Module 5 should be weighted more heavily than other training activities on the Evaluation of Trainee Engagement Form (e-Resource 11).

As discussed further below, trainees are often hesitant to engage in role-play exercises; they can feel silly, awkward, or not a true reflection of reality. The fact of the matter is: role plays are unrealistic, and they can't do justice to the complex and

---

[3] A term used for people whose biological sex (i.e., male, female, intersex) matches their gender identity.

[4] A term used for people whose biological sex does not match their gender identity, such as a person with male sex chromosomes identifying as a woman.

[5] When a person has multiple historically marginalized characteristics or identities that can expose them to compounded experiences of discrimination or oppression. The term was originally used to describe the experiences of Black women in the United States who encounter both racism and sexism (Crenshaw, 1989).

unpredictable interactions people experience on their units. That being said, they offer one of the best ways to practice skills within a structured educational setting. Trainers can acknowledge that real-world attempts at redirecting criminal thinking are unlikely to go as smoothly; however, the goal of these role plays is to increase trainees' recollection of the three-step model, ability to recognize opportunities to apply the three-steps, and confidence in implementing them. Other trainees may feel anxious about performing in front of or with their peers. Hopefully, trainers have worked to establish trust and cohesion throughout the training day, which can minimize performance anxiety, but it may help to emphasize no one is here to judge anyone and everyone is on the same playing field—everyone is learning.

Following the hands-on activities of Module 5, participants will take a written knowledge acquisition quiz. A pass score of 75% or better is recommended (e-Resource 10). The knowledge acquisition quiz should be completed successfully for trainees to pass the course and receive their certificate of completion. Trainees who earn less than 75% should, at a minimum, be asked to review their materials independently and demonstrate a rational understanding of the correct answer (i.e., what makes this answer the correct one?). During initial pilot testing of *ITA* with 14 trainees, the average total quiz score was 85.27% (standard deviation of 14.42) with a score range of 56–94% (only 1 trainee did not pass). The knowledge quiz provided in this workbook reflects a slightly modified version based on feedback from this pilot (i.e., some items were reworded due to low correct response rates). Using the modified quiz, trainees from the Australia sample earned an average score of 88.56% (SD = 10.01). The most difficult question was #7, with 30% of trainees getting this question wrong.

Trainers are also encouraged to rate each trainee's level of engagement using the Evaluation of Trainee Engagement Form (see Chap. 6 appendix 6.4 or e-Resource 6.4). This can be challenging to do when the training group is large, especially if there is only one trainer for the day; it's almost impossible to teach content, engage with trainees, and monitor individual behavior throughout the course of the day. But, when feasible, having data on trainee engagement could be useful for later evaluations of post-training success. For example, the extent to which skills were/are used on the unit may be related to how well staff attended to the training. Further, if engagement ratings are low, it may provide the trainer with important feedback about the need to improve engagement next time. While there is no official cut-off score for this evaluation form, it is recommended that ratings of 2 or less on any domain be discussed with the trainee privately.

Whether trainees need to retake the training course based on their quiz score or level of engagement is ultimately at the discretion of the trainer. However, any consequences of poor or inadequate participation should be made transparent at the outset of the training session. Trainees will also have an opportunity to provide their feedback about the training and the trainer using the Training Evaluation Form (see Chap. 6 appendix 6.6 or e-Resource 6.6).

Proposed Training Day Schedule

Time	Activity
8:00 am–8:10 am	Welcome and introduction to training
8:10 am–8:40 am	Module 1
8:40 am–9:40am	Module 2
9:40 am–9:50 am	Break
9:50 am–11:20 am	Module 3
11:20 am–12:20 am	Lunch
12:20 pm–1:50pm	Module 4
1:50 pm–2:00 pm	Break
2:00 pm–3:30 pm	Module 5
3:30 pm–4:00 pm	Closing remarks, proficiency quiz, and training evaluation forms

Step 3: Ongoing Monitoring, Tracking, and Assessment

Facilities are strongly encouraged to develop a systematic plan to evaluate the acceptability and impact of *ITA* after implementation. Evaluation of desired outcomes may provide useful information about how trainers could improve their approach or teaching style to increase trainee engagement, whether reasonable modifications to the training curriculum are warranted (e.g., increased emphasis on individuals with serious mental illness), the extent to which staff are applying the skills in practice, how often training certification may need to be renewed, and the specific ways in which the training is benefitting the institution (e.g., decreased misconduct, less time in segregation, increased participation in mental health programming, improved staff well-being). It is further recommended that evaluations become routine such that impacts are assessed on an ongoing basis. Ongoing evaluation is important given the high rate of turnover among staff, trainers, and individuals in custody, which may create shifts in the institutional culture. *ITA* is expected to have positive impacts on staff and incarcerated persons individually, as well as the overall safety of the institution.

Proper evaluation requires tracking and measuring outcomes both *before* and *after* front-line correctional staff participate in *ITA*. If possible, facilities may want to designate a program evaluation coordinator to help compile and analyze data related to the delivery of *ITA*. If your facility is unable to allocate staff resources to program evaluation or does not have any staff with adequate expertise in data collection or statistical procedures, consider partnering with a research-active university (in the United States, a Carnegie Designated R1 or R2 university is recommended). Often, researchers in psychology, public health, education, and/or criminal justice and criminology departments have interests in correctional program implementation and evaluation. In most cases, these researchers are interested in disseminating findings through academic outlets (e.g., journals, professional conferences) rather than monetary compensation, making a partnership of this nature cost-effective. A 2017 article in *Corrections Today* (the mainstream publication for the American Correctional Association) highlighted the mutual advantages of collaborations between correctional and academic institutions (Hallundbaek, 2017; see also Batastini et al., 2018).

Outcomes can be measured in three general ways: (1) examining data already collected by the institution such as electronic records or administrative reports, (2) building new variables into existing data collection mechanisms, and (3) administering self-report surveys or questionnaires. Further, there are multiple levels or perspectives from which to examine outcomes including trainers, trainees, incarcerated persons, mental health staff, administrators, unit staff, and the institution more broadly. Facilities can also determine when and how often to collect and review data. For example, a program evaluation may compare information obtained 3 months before the initiation of *ITA* to 3 months and 6 months after *ITA*. Perhaps outcomes are examined on a yearly basis. For adequate comparison, data points measured before the training should be measured the same way after the training. For example, if you use the Attitudes Toward Prisoners (ATP) scale pre-*ITA* to examine trainee's beliefs, the ATP should be used again post-*ITA*. It would not be a good idea to start with the ATP then switch to the Stigma Toward People with Prison Records (STPPR) at later timepoints. Figure 1.2 provides suggested outcomes as they may be useful to the evaluation of *ITA*. A combination of methods will offer the most comprehensive assessment of *ITA* within your correctional environment.

The self-report measures listed in Fig. 1.2 with an asterisk (*) are non-proprietary and can be found in the e-Resources, along with information on how to score and interpret them. However, these are not the only measures that may have relevance for assessing the impacts of *ITA*. For example, the Maslach Burnout Inventory (MBI, Maslach et al., 1997) is a popular tool for measuring burnout even among correctional staff but is proprietary and may cost money to use within your institution. In some cases, it may be best to create a rating form or tracking spreadsheet that can uniquely accommodate how information is or can be collected at your facility.

Orientation to the Trainer Workbook and Accompanying Slides

Understanding the Cognitive-Behavioral Framework

Most of the time, we get the best glimpse into someone's thought processes through their behaviors—or the way they act. The behaviors they choose are products of their internal decision-making. But sometimes our internal decision-making isn't perfect or simply doesn't serve us in the best ways.

Consider someone who is depressed. Their thought processes cause them to paint the world in a more negative light; they see themselves more negatively (e.g.,

In the months before ITA	Immediately before *ITA*	Immediately after *ITA*	In the months after *ITA*
Frequency of inmate behavioral incidents	Trainee attendance*	Trainee knowledge acquisition quiz*	Frequency of behavioral incidents
Frequency of assaults against staff	Trainee demographic data (e.g., age, gender, assigned unit, years of experience)	Training evaluation form*	Frequency of assaults against staff
Frequency of staff misconduct/write-ups	Trainee attitudes toward people in custody (using the ATP* or STPPR*)	Trainee attitudes toward people in custody (using the ATP* or STPPR*)	Frequency of staff misconduct/write-ups
Segregation unit census	Trainee burnout measure (using the Work Stress Scale* or Burnout Assessment Tool)	Trainee burnout measure (using the Work Stress Scale* or Burnout Assessment Tool)	Segregation unit census
Incarcerated persons' engagement in mental health programs addressing criminal thinking	Incarcerated persons' attitudes toward correctional staff and environment (using Attitudes Toward Correctional Staff*)	Trainee perceptions of self-efficacy or ability to communicate with incarcerated people (using the SE-12*)	Incarcerated persons' engagement in mental health programs addressing criminal thinking
	Criminal thinking errors of incarcerated persons (using the PICTS-SV*)		Trainee burnout measure (using the Work Stress Scale* or Burnout Assessment Tool)
	Trainee perceptions of self-efficacy or ability to communicate with incarcerated persons (using the SE-12*)		Trainee reported use of *ITA* skills
			Mental health and/or unit staff observations of changes in incarcerated persons' behavior
			Criminal thinking errors of incarcerated persons (using the PICTS-SV*)
			Incarcerated persons' attitudes toward correctional staff (using the Attitudes Toward Correctional Staff*)

*Form or measure included in e-Resources

Fig. 1.2 Suggested outcomes

lowered self-esteem) and think other people see them as bad, weak, or undeserving of love. Because of these thoughts, they tend to socially withdraw or engage in other dangerous behaviors (e.g., self-harm, substance misuse). The same is true with criminal thinking—it leads people to paint the world a bit differently. For example,

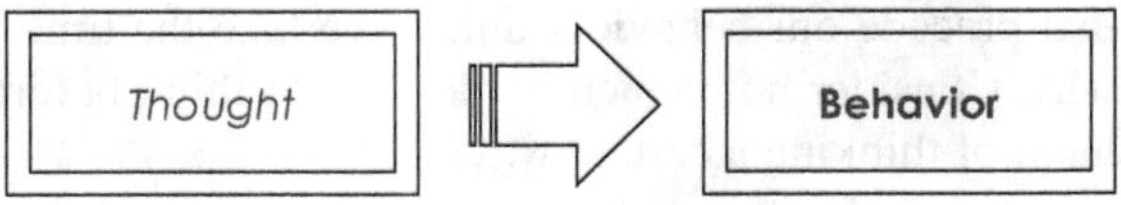

Fig. 1.3 Basic cognitive-behavioral link

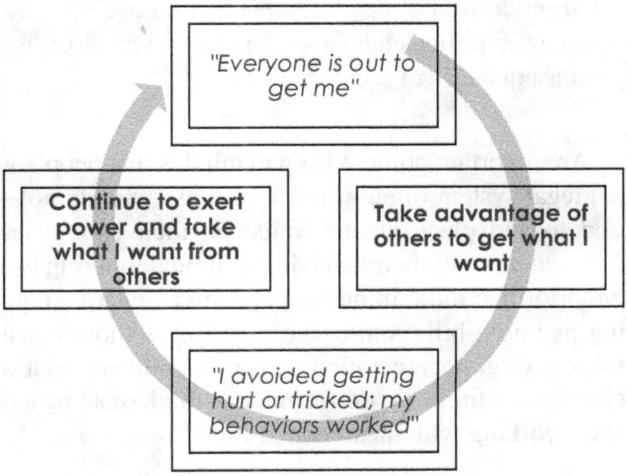

Fig. 1.4 Example of the criminal thinking cognitive-behavioral cycle

many people who rely on criminal thinking see the world as manipulative, greedy, or owing them something (maybe because they were abused or grew up in a disadvantaged neighborhood). They may, in turn, behave in a manipulative manner to "beat others to the punch." People who feel society owes them something for their pain and suffering may come across as entitled or narcissistic. Keep in mind, this is just one example. Not everyone who engages in criminal thinking will present this way. The idea that thoughts drive behaviors is the underlying theory used in cognitive-behavioral therapies, including those that focus on reducing behaviors rooted in criminal thinking (Fig. 1.3).

The consequences of behaviors (or what happens as a result of the behavior) can reinforce a way of thinking. Let's look at the depression example again. Because someone who is depressed spends more time alone, they may have fewer friends or have a more difficult time making friends. Such results reinforce the thought that no one wants to be around them or that they're undeserving of support. In other words, their own behaviors produce a self-fulfilling prophecy. See how this thought-behavior connection can become a cycle? This can happen with criminal thinking, too. For example, when an individual with a high level of criminal thinking gets what they want (e.g., money, drugs, power, respect) after committing a crime or otherwise behaving in ways that violate others' rights or well-being, it might reinforce the idea that they can avoid certain problems by "taking aim first." When criminal thoughts continue to be reinforced, the connection between these thoughts and undesirable behavior becomes a cycle that's difficult to stop (see Fig. 1.4). The more thought processes are reinforced, the more likely they are to become what cognitive-behavioral clinicians call "automatic thoughts," meaning these thoughts occur almost without thinking. For most of us, we often aren't aware of the thoughts that precede our behaviors unless we take the time to analyze what happened and why. Consider how much harder it is to think before you act when you've made a habit of thinking a certain way.

> **Important:** The cognitive-behavioral cycle for those high on criminal thinking is complicated by a tendency to favor short-term needs over the long-term consequences of their behavior.

An important point to keep in mind is that people who get caught up in the criminal legal system often differ from those who do not—they tend to pay more attention to and place greater value on their shorter-term needs than the long-term consequences of their behavior. Criminal thinking is often maintained because people prioritize more immediate, positive rewards (e.g., making a quick buck, avoiding paying a bill, getting the next fix) without considering the eventual, negative fall-out (e.g., incarceration, loss of significant relationships, job termination, foreclosure/eviction). No doubt you can think of some examples from your own experience working with incarcerated folks!

Behavioral Examples of Criminal Thinking in Prison

- *Continually placing sick call requests for mental health services when they are not in crisis or needing intensive care. This could be preceded by the thought, "If I wear them down, maybe they'll move me somewhere where I can finally get some peace and quiet!"*
- *Cheeking medications to stash or sell. This could be related to thoughts such as "I can't trust nobody and I certainly won't be trusting these doctors—these meds are what's fucking me up" or "I gotta keep up my reputation of having the power and respect in here so I can survive this hell hole."*
- *Throwing bodily fluids on an officer. This might be rooted in a thought like, "The only way I've ever been able to get people to pay attention to me is by doing something drastic."*

> **Important:** Repetition and practice are the keys to changing thoughts.

Notice these examples range in severity and dangerousness, but they all show irresponsibility, violation of rules, and disregard for the impact of their choices on others (from potentially overwhelming mental health staff to spreading infectious diseases). We also understand that some instances of criminal thinking will require serious consequences. However, the intention of the *ITA* training program is to begin reducing both the frequency and severity of criminal thinking so there is less need for punitive interventions. Further, when criminal thinking is identified and addressed directly, people will begin to see patterns in their behavior, how their own thoughts keep them stuck in the same cycle of negative consequences, and practice new ways of thinking. Be advised, this process takes time. The people you are working with have learned, developed, and used these thought processes (sometimes with positive outcomes) for a very long time; it will take a lot of correction to make a new style of thinking the norm. Trainees may need to be reminded of this fact throughout the training day.

It is worth noting that people generally do not like to be corrected about the way they think. How would you feel if someone told you that your thinking is all wrong? However, once these redirections become routine, the people in your custody will come to expect them. You may even find some people will begin self-correcting their thoughts about a situation before you have the chance! Repetition is key.

Overview of the Three-Step Model

A three-step formula to identifying criminal thinking errors with your clients is the primary intervention strategy taught in *ITA* (see Fig. 1.5). The model is easy to remember and can be applied similarly to various types of scenarios and individual needs. The three steps are based on a cognitive-behavioral framework in that they foster an analysis of the thoughts (i.e., criminal thinking) underlying inappropriate or unhelpful behaviors and, through this analysis, help individuals restructure these thoughts and adjust their behavior. The model encourages validation of the individual's perspective in the process of targeting problematic behavior. In doing so, the model helps correctional staff maintain composure and understanding as they're interacting with people in custody.

The first part of the model requires some reflection on the staff's part before initiating contact with the individual. When staff encounter a situation in which they recognize a criminal thinking error (or a behavior that appears to be rooted in criminal thinking), they should ask themselves the following questions:

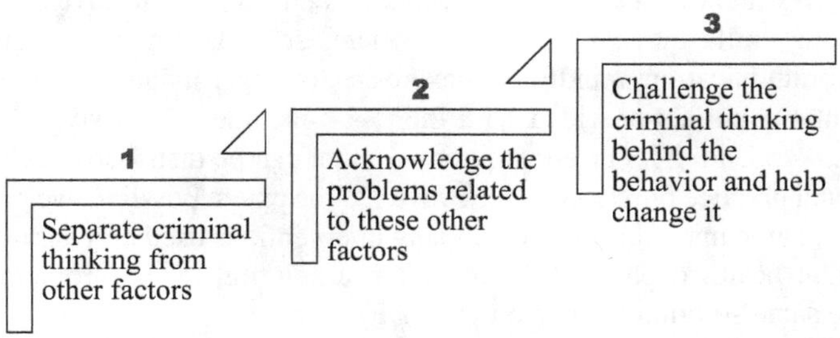

Fig. 1.5 The three-step model for addressing criminal thinking

(1) *What criminal thinking error could be at play here? How is the error being used to justify the person's current behavior?*
(2) *What other factors could be contributing to the situation? For example, are there conditions on the unit, genuine needs or characteristics of the person, or relationship dynamics that could be impacting their decision-making?*
(3) *How can I help them meet their needs in another way? This doesn't mean giving in to the person or getting them what they wanted. It may mean offering them a compromise, directing them to use coping skills they learned in treatment, or simply giving them a listening ear.*

Helping someone meet their needs doesn't mean giving in to them.

Answering these questions doesn't need to take more than a minute or two and trainees will be taught how to quickly think through these questions during the training session. Once the staff member has an idea in their mind about how the criminal thinking can be separated from other factors and what solutions might be possible, they can then use this material to talk to the individual in a direct and effective manner.

In the second step, the staff member will first acknowledge the problem(s) the person is experiencing because of factors *not* associated with the criminal thinking. This uses the concept of *validation*! For example, maybe the person has a genuine medical or mental health need that's causing distress, or they're upset because someone violated their privacy or property. This step may seem too "therapy-like" or unimportant but taking a moment to demonstrate understanding and compassion may reduce the likelihood of a negative reaction and increase the likelihood the person will actually listen when prompted to correct their thinking and behavior. Oftentimes, incarcerated individuals expect staff to immediately point out what they did wrong. Think about a time when someone showed you a little empathy before asking you to change something about yourself compared to someone who started off by attacking or criticizing you.

In the final step, the staff member will calmly label the person's criminal thinking for what it is, state how the person's thought process (or associated behavior) is ineffective, and offer alternative ways to approach the situation from both a cognitive (rethinking) and behavioral (reacting) lens. When in doubt, staff can ask the person to help identify alternative thoughts or behaviors themselves, which may involve using skills they've learned elsewhere, such as cognitive restructuring, assertive communication, mindfulness exercises, or anger management techniques. Supplemental materials provided with this book include a CBT-style thought log (see Chap. 4 appendix 4.3 or e-Resource 4.3) that can be distributed to individuals for additional practice or reflection. However, to the extent possible, we recommend using the resource materials that accompany interventions used by your own institution's mental health department. Remember, a solution to the problem may not involve the same solution the person originally wanted.

A Desktop Reference of the three-step model is also provided in Chap. 4 appendix 4.2 or e-Resource 4.2. Bring copies to the training session for each of your trainees. This reference can be placed in their office, control units, or even in their uniform pocket for a quick reminder.

Tips and Tricks for Interacting with Trainees

There will be trainees, and sometimes entire classes, who have trouble "buying into" the program or the need for a training like *ITA*. The tone of *ITA* encourages a shift from the traditional, adversarial relationship between correctional staff and the people in custody. It requires staff to balance this sort of "helping role" with ensuring individual and institutional safety, rather than leaving all the therapeutic work to mental health professionals. Correctional institutions are moving away from this siloed approach of mental health support toward more effective and collaborative ways of running penal institutions; nonetheless, some trainees will be resistant to embracing some or all aspects of *ITA*. Trainees are likely to vary in how open they are to learning the techniques in *ITA*, ranging from total engagement to outright disagreement and hostility. Trainees may make statements about how "pointless" training is because inmates "will do whatever they want anyways." Earlier parts of the training curriculum (see Module 1) are intended to address some of this resistance by encouraging an honest discussion about attitudes toward people in prison and emphasizing the benefits of being a change agent; however, as the trainer, you will likely need to develop your own ways of countering resistance. Be prepared to do so throughout the training day. Below are some examples of both obvious and implied resistance from trainees, as well as techniques that may be helpful in addressing resistance during class.

Getting and Maintaining Buy-In from Trainees

Your initial strategies to increase trainee buy-in and prevent resistant behavior can be employed before the training even begins or early in the training day. First, a facility may consider advertising the training well in advance and in multiple ways (e.g., posting flyers in communal places throughout the facility, sending email reminders). Seeing frequent advertisements may increase curiosity and interest. This chapter includes a modifiable flyer to help you spread the word (see e-Resource 1.1). All you need to do is insert the time, date, and location. In addition, it could be beneficial to ask people in higher authority positions (like supervisors or team leads) or popular staff members (like long-time employees or frontline staff with great reputations) to discuss their enthusiasm about the training with other staff in the days or weeks leading up to the training.

On the day of the training, some facilities may choose to have someone in an administrative role like a warden, lieutenant, or superintendent sit in on the training and observe the course. If not, consider inviting someone whose presence will help demonstrate to trainees that supervisory and administrative staff support the training materials and the trainer. Trainees may also be less likely to engage in disruptive behaviors if a "higher up" with a good level of respect is present, especially if the trainer is not an employee at the institution or not well known to trainees.

Trainers can encourage positivity and participation from trainees throughout the day by modeling a positive, enthusiastic attitude. For example, trainers can model professionalism by silencing their cell phone at the beginning of the day and inviting others to do the same. When trainees make comments or tell stories that support the need for *ITA* training, trainers should respond positively and make connections between their story and the training material. An example of this conversation might look like this:

> Trainee: "This reminds me of when I had an inmate threaten to slit their throat with a razor during a shakedown. Everyone kept yelling at them and calling for psych to respond. I just walked up to them and said, 'you and I both know that ain't gonna solve your problems. You'll end up in medical, then psych, for who knows how long. Let me help you instead.' They actually handed the razor over and let us take them to psych where they got meds and were back on the unit within the week."
>
> Trainer: "Wow, that sounds like a really intense situation. And all the officers involved responded how they were trained to—everyone did a good job—but it was communicating with the person in custody and helping them to see the faulty logic in their thinking that eventually persuaded them to stand down. That's exactly what we want to do here—teach you all how to recognize that faulty logic not just in crisis situations but in everyday behavioral disruptions too, so you can encourage the people you oversee to make better choices, avoid more infractions, and get back to their lives."

As mentioned earlier, some trainees may have an eye-roll reaction to trainings like *ITA* because skill development components, such as pretend verbal exchanges or role plays, feel oversimplified or disingenuous. Concerns about the feasibility of enacting *ITA* skills "in the real world" are valid. Trainings cannot capture the range of emotional, behavioral, or situational factors that influence how an interaction will unfold. Remember, training exercises are more about developing good memory recall for intervention strategies, recognizing when to intervene, and building confidence in implementing interventions rather than replicating real-life situations. Recognizing the simplified nature of this training early may also reduce resistance by creating a shared understanding and setting expectations. It could be helpful to say something like this:

> You're totally right. Trainings like this one tend to simplify what you deal with every day. Even the best trainings can't represent all the complexities and challenges you face working in the pods or units. We work with people who test our boundaries and act in unpredictable ways. We also deal with changing environments and expectations. The reality is—trainings have to balance effective learning with feasibility. We can't predict what it will look like when you actually test out these new skills and we can only accomplish so much in the time we have. When learning something new, we have to start with the basics. Your skills will evolve and expand as you get more comfortable applying them, and as you learn to modify your approach to suit certain people or settings.
>
> So, think of today's activities as the jumping off point; the goal today is to commit new skills to memory, have a better sense of when they might be useful, and increase your confidence in redirecting criminal thinking. If we were to train immediately 'on the ground,' it

would be more difficult to retain what we're talking about because so much is going on. Practicing skills in a controlled environment like this will make it easier for you to translate these skills to more complex situations later on. We're also not naïve enough to think our skills will work every time or with every person. But, we're adding more tools to the toolbox, as the saying goes.

It's common for motivation and buy-in to wax and wane over the course of the training day or in the weeks and months following the training as staff learn to implement the skills in their daily work. Think about someone in your custody who started making good progress. Then, you come into work the next day and an officer leaving her shift tells you that person was caught smoking in their cell. Or you see that person get mad and attack another staff member. It's frustrating watching someone throw away all the hard work they put in. When people seem to "fall off the wagon," it's easy to feel betrayed and grow hardened, thinking that all inmates are the same and everyone will mess up eventually.

Trainees will likely bring up similar frustrations or ask why *ITA* is useful when "inmates will just act up anyways" regardless of what staff say or do. When comments like these are made, it presents an opportunity for the trainer to recognize trainees' experiences and how discouraging it can feel to work in a correctional environment. The trainer can then share some of the ways in which they maintain an optimistic perspective and find the motivation to come to work every day hoping to make a positive difference in people's lives. Remember: if only one person changes their ways, it could have massive impacts, such as saving someone's life, preventing sexual exploitation, or reuniting a child with their parent. Don't worry too much about people's reactions to the training; Module 1 is specifically designed to increase buy-in and prevent resistance, so you'll have some additional guidance in the slide deck annotations and presenter notes.

Think about: What motivates you to do this job? What strategies do you use when you feel deflated or burnt out?

If only one person changes their ways, it could have massive impacts.

Strategies for Recognizing and Minimizing Resistance

Although Module 1 is intended to mitigate resistance, it may not be enough to eliminate it. Resistance to training can appear both subtly and overtly during the training session and can include nonverbal and verbal signals. Staff who have difficulty understanding the benefits of the program may frequently offer counterpoints or undermine the trainer's statements with anecdotes or skeptical views; for example, "I actually read an article the other day about how these countries with 'soft' prisons have more violent crimes than places like us. We're just headed downhill too, I guess." Others may sit at the back of the room, avoid looking at the presentation, scroll through social media, lean back in their chair and take a nap, or contribute very little to discussions. Resistant trainees may look and act differently, but similar strategies can be used to deal with various forms of resistance during the training day.

Managing resistant trainees ideally starts at the beginning of the day. There are ways to establish a positive tone that sets the stage for the rest of the day. Expressing empathy for the trainees' positions, workplace challenges, and showing a genuine interest in improving the quality of their work environment can help. These statements can convey authenticity, concern, and mitigate suspicions that the so-called higher-ups don't understand what work life is like for frontline staff, or that the training is intended to punish staff for poor work performance. One strategy is to acknowledge that it's a big request to ask staff to adjust the way they do their job, then following up with a statement about how confident you are this training will ultimately make their lives easier. Here's an example:

> We ask you all to do a lot every day. Your jobs aren't easy, and I'm grateful to have such a dedicated group of staff here. I realize asking you to come in and learn a new way of doing things is a tall order, but I wouldn't be here with you if I didn't believe it could make a difference in the way our facility is run. Thank you for being here and giving me your attention today.

It may also be helpful to explain to trainees that negative staff perceptions and low workplace cooperation are major contributors to an unpleasant work climate (Leung & Snape, 2012). *ITA* is intended to alter staff members' perspectives about the capacity for people in custody to change and promote staff cohesion regarding intervention strategies to reduce criminal thinking. Learning the skills taught in *ITA* could improve workplace morale and cooperation among staff as well as between staff and those under their supervision and care.

It is possible—and encouraged—to address resistance throughout the training as close to when it occurs as possible. In fact, openly discussing trainee resistance during the training will be more beneficial than ignoring it or immediately turning to punitive strategies (like kicking a trainee out of the training). Research suggests several techniques (often called change-talk) that can help achieve buy-in from clients with mental health, substance use, and justice involvement when they are resistant to change (Bani-Yaghoub et al., 2018; Farbring & Johnson, 2008; Hampson et al., 2015; Haque & D'Souza, 2019). These strategies can work with resistant trainees, too! Some key techniques can be remembered using the following acronym:

P.A.C.E.

- *Work in* ***partnership*** *with the resistant trainee. Ultimately, everyone's goal is the same: to maintain the safety and security of the facility. Helping to rehabilitate people in custody protects those inside and outside the prison walls.*
- ***Accept*** *the trainee's stance and point of view. Using empathy and compassion can help with this. Note that acceptance is more about* <u>*understanding*</u> *someone's perspective, not agreeing with it or allowing it to persist.*

- *Use **compassion** when talking with trainees. This will help the trainee feel you are not against them or assuming they are bad at their job.*
- ***Evoke** strong feelings or memories from trainees, particularly those that show their current strategies are not as effective as the trainee would like them to be. For example, encouraging someone to think of a time their response triggered a negative outcome.*

The key is to meet the trainee where he or she is at currently. Trainers can show they understand the trainee's point of view without reinforcing it. It is important to get the trainee to see that their current strategies can be supplemented or enhanced to be more effective. However, don't tell the trainee this explicitly or explain how; rather, ask them questions that prompt reflection about their past and current experiences so they can come to this conclusion themselves. But, be careful not to allow one or a few trainees to dominate and derail the group with their skepticism. You have a lot of content to get through, so you don't have time to continually challenge resistance. As the trainer, you need to strike a balance between working to achieve buy-in and knowing when to move on.

Important: Don't let a small number of trainees take over the group with their toxic behavior; know when enough is enough.

So far, we've talked mostly about trainee resistance from the point of view that it's worthless or a waste of time because inmates don't ever change. However, some trainees may express negative attitudes about the training because they find the term "criminal thinking" to be labeling, stigmatizing, or demoralizing. Help these trainees understand that criminal thinking is not about labeling the person; it's about labeling their thoughts. In the first author's experience, teaching justice-involved people to view their behaviors through the lens of criminal thinking can actually help them detach from the "criminal" label. That is, it's not something inherent to them as a person or a character flaw. Rather, it's how they think that leads to criminal or immoral decisions and—good news—their thinking can be changed! As discussed earlier, thoughts can be molded and solidified through experiences including trauma. Using the term "criminal thinking" doesn't eliminate the origin of these thoughts, like trauma or neglect in childhood. These experiences are not the person's fault. So, why not use a different term? Because these thoughts ultimately contributed to the commission of criminal behavior. Calling this type of thinking something other than "criminal" diminishes the seriousness of its consequences and minimizes the sense of urgency to change.

As the day progresses, when trainees make comments that appear to be resistant (e.g., are argumentative, undermining, or sarcastic), you have a choice in how to respond to each statement. For example, to address a trainee who is making off-handed, sarcastic comments to their neighbor, you could ignore the first instance or two of the behavior. As the training goes on, this person might change their tune. However, for repeated comments or a generally argumentative approach, you may choose to acknowledge the behavior verbally, either in the moment as the training is ongoing, or individually with the disruptive trainee during a scheduled break. Remember your tone of voice is just as (if not more) important than what you say. Try to maintain a neutral but caring tone; you likely won't improve buy-in if your tone is belittling or scolding. Here's an example:

> Your remarks about the training material are starting to distract the group from today's goals. If you'd like to discuss a concern with me, we can do so individually on a break or at the end of the day. Though, I think if you used your time wisely today you might be able to find something beneficial about being here.

A similar approach with more severe consequences may be warranted for especially disruptive behavior or comments that devolve from questions or criticisms to insults and grievances:

> It seems you're frustrated with this training or with being here today. I understand this is new and we're asking you to do some things that may be challenging, but disrupting the training is not an appropriate way to respond. I ask that you either keep your remarks to yourself or leave the training and speak with your supervisor.

If, after a verbal warning, the trainee continues to engage in disruptive behavior, requesting that they leave the training session is warranted. This can be done one-on-one during a scheduled break or lunch hour to minimize disruptions among the group, but it may become necessary to do this in the moment to maintain control over the training session and prevent others who are taking the training seriously from growing frustrated with their co-worker's repeated disruptions.

Finally, it could be useful to remind trainees their participation and engagement factor into whether they will be awarded a completion certification at the end of the day.

Keeping Your Cool

ITA trainers may also feel frustrated when the training day doesn't go as planned, or when encountering staff who express negative attitudes about the training or the people they supervise. Because criminal thinking is so engrained, it might take a long time for a person in custody to get the hang of the skills needed to change it—which of course can wear down frontline staff. It's expected that staff will want to give up at times or go back to older, more punitive ways of responding to poor behavior. This can be exhausting as a trainer, as there are only so many ways you can explain the material or encourage people. While you can teach trainees how to support people in changing criminal thinking, you cannot force staff to implement the skills—or be happy doing it!

When frustrations toward trainees bubble, find an appropriate outlet to release them. Acting hostile toward those who work for or with you is not an appropriate outlet. Instead, talk calmly with a trusted peer or supervisor about how you can handle the situation better the next time, get in a good workout at the gym, or do something ultra-relaxing when you get home from work to decompress. You may even need to practice restructuring your own thoughts just like you're teaching others to do with criminal thinking! Try some of these or come up with your own go-to reframes.

- *Letting this get to me will only stress me out and ruin my day.*
- *I know there was a time when I had trouble changing my perspective—they'll get there too.*
- *I knew I might feel frustrated at times, but I won't give up. Maybe next time it will "click."*

Addressing Burnout and the Importance of Self-Care

Administrative and training staff who work in corrections know firsthand it can be exhausting trying to make changes in a correctional environment. Penal systems have operated similarly for a long time, and it takes a while to get staff on board with new ideas or procedures. This can wear on instructors, supervisors, and those implementing change. If you have or had young children, recall the irritation you felt repeating requests to brush their teeth or do their homework. At times you may have simply given up and did the chore for them or let them deal with the consequences later. Or, maybe you lost your cool and yelled at them a little louder than you intended. Now, think of a time when you tried to help someone you cared about. Maybe you supported an aunt who was working toward sobriety, or a friend who was trying to reenter the job market after a long leave of absence. You may have found yourself giving them suggestions and resources to help them get better or improve their chances of success. Sometimes they might accept these suggestions while other times they might blow them off. After a year of this, what happens to you on the inside? You might get annoyed or lose hope they'll make progress (in other words, you are burnt out).

Self-care can be a remedy for burnout. The term "self-care" is tossed around a lot and many employees in correctional environments may blow it off as silly or unnecessary, but research shows routine self-care and healthy coping skills can mitigate burnout in high-stress jobs like emergency room personnel, law enforcement, and even corrections (Abellanoza et al., 2018; Farnese et al., 2017; McDonald et al., 2022). Notably, in one study, corrections officers reported even higher levels of burnout than nurses (Harizanova & Stoyanova, 2020). Self-care can include any activity that results in relaxation or in-the-moment enjoyment for a person. These activities are most effective when they focus on several of the eight dimensions of wellness (see Fig. 1.6) and leave a person feeling refreshed and more prepared for the next workday or week (Brice et al., 2013; Gill et al. 2016; Swarbrick et al., 2016). Some examples were listed in the previous section. Regular self-care is good for everyone, but especially important—almost necessary—for people who work in high trauma-risk environments and/or those who care for other people with little gratitude in return (like nurses, first responders, therapists, and teachers). For some staff, practicing good self-care could be the difference between a lengthy, fulfilling

Emotional	Knowledge and skills to identify and cope with personal feelings
Physical	Attention to physical aspects such as nutrition, exercise, substance use, and disease prevention
Occupational	Focus on satisfaction in one's job or carrer
Social	Wellness in social interactions and relationships
Spiritual	Finding meaning and purpose in life (does not have to be associated with religion)
Intellectual	Stimulation of brain health through thought-provoking mental exercises
Environmental	Activities that involve improving one's environment; could be immediate (in the home) or larger-scale (eco-friendly practices)
Financial	Knowledge and skills to be and feel financially secure

Fig. 1.6 The eight dimensions of wellness

career and one filled with chronic stress, burnout, and a premature career exit (Griffin et al., 2010; Lambert et al., 2015). Some of these facts about burnout and how burnout relates to the objectives of *ITA* are included in Module 1.

For more information on promoting wellness, we recommend consulting the Substance Abuse and Mental Health Services Administration (SAMHSA)'s guide to community action, a part of their Wellness Initiative: https://store.samhsa.gov/sites/default/files/d7/priv/sma16-4957.pdf.

Encouraging self-care and promoting its importance throughout the training session (even beyond Module 1) may help trainees develop better solutions when they eventually become frustrated with those in their custody or supervision. Gently remind trainees of their duties as staff to manage their own emotional reactions while continuing to offer quality care and security. Offer some of the same tips outlined earlier, like getting in some physical exercise on their lunch break to release energy or respectfully voicing frustrations to a peer or supervisor who can help problem-solve. You can also encourage trainees to adopt a "mantra" or go-to thoughts to say to themselves or journal about later. It might get them through a frustrating moment without blowing up. Here are some examples:

- *These are people who struggle to think and act prosocially, so setbacks and slip-ups are expected.*
- *I did my best to point out a criminal thinking error, that's all I can do right now. I can try again another time.*
- *Getting pissed off and yelling is just going to make the situation worse and model bad behavior.*

Some tips and reminders about self-care are included in Module 3.

Signs and Symbols

To help you navigate the Trainer Workbook, several icons are used to designate how information is to be presented or when supplemental materials are needed.

Check It Off: The clipboard icon is where you'll find a list of materials you'll need for a given module.

Ask the Audience: The lightbulb brain icon will let you know about a critical thinking question you can pose to trainees.

Hand It Out: The paper and pencil icon indicates when a topic has a handout to distribute to trainees.

Act It Out: These speech bubbles tell you when a scenario should be role-played.

Show Your Stuff: This icon appears when there is a trainee evaluation component.

Navigating the PowerPoint Slide Deck

A copy of the PowerPoint slide deck is accessible in the online supplemental materials associated with this book. [Online resources are available at https://doi.org/10.1007/978-3-031-88404-7_2]. Some slides may need to be modified, such as the agenda for the day, to accommodate the logistics or procedures of your institution. Trainers may also add or replace slides in Module 3 to more specifically describe the criminal thinking program used in their facility. However, most slides should largely remain as is to ensure standardization with the training protocol; any changes should be made with discretion and clear intent. Presenter view/mode is recommended when starting the slideshow so you can easily see notations and prompts as you are speaking. Notes appearing within quotation marks and bold-faced should be said out loud to trainees. Trainers may alter the wording or word order of statements to fit their own style of speaking, but the core content of the slide must still be presented. Notes appearing within brackets and italicized are like stage directions for actors; they are not meant to be spoken to the audience, but help trainers move more smoothly through the information on the slide. Here's an example of what you might see in the slide notes:

"I'm excited to spend the day with you all and teach some new and easy skills you can use to make your daily interactions less stressful! Since we'll be together all day, let's take some time to get to know each other. I'll go first."

Say this part out loud and modify to fit your personal style as needed.

[Tell a little about you, your background, how long you've been working in corrections, etc.]

Trainer "stage directions"—this prompts an action from you.

It is highly recommended trainers familiarize themselves with the slide-by-slide annotations in the trainer workbook and keep a copy of the workbook near them during the training session so they know when to prompt discussions, distribute handouts, initiate role-play exercises, and other activities. Trainers may engage the audience in discussions that are not explicitly prompted in the workbook or slide notations but should be mindful of time constraints. Spontaneous discussions are great for learning, but they must be facilitated with good time management.

Each module is associated with various supplemental materials, most of which are included as appendices within each respective chapter or can be found in an online e-Resources folder accessible with the purchase of this book. Other materials, such as blank notepaper or a whiteboard will need to be provided by the training facility. Trainers may elect to distribute all relevant source materials at the outset of the training (e.g., as a training packet or binder) and reference materials as the training progresses. Alternatively, trainers may wish to hold onto materials and distribute each one to the group when it appears within the slides. If materials are not distributed during the training, trainees should be clearly informed about how and where to access them.

References

Abellanoza, A., Provenzano-Hass, N., & Gatchel, R. J. (2018). Burnout in ER nurses: Review of the literature and interview themes. *Journal of Applied Biobehavioral Research, 23*(1). https://doi.org/10.1111/jabr.12117

Anthony, W. A., & Carkhuff, R. R. (1977). The Art of Health Care Trainer's Tips. Human Resource Development Press.

Axboe, M. K., Christensen, K. S., Kofoed, P., & Ammentorp, J. (2016). Development and validation of a self-efficacy questionnaire (SE-12) measuring the clinical communication skills of health care professionals. *BMC Medical Education, 16*. https://doi.org/10.1186/s12909-016-0798-7

Bani-Yaghoub, M., Elhomani, A., & Catley, D. (2018). Effectiveness of motivational interviewing, health education and brief advice in a population of smokers who are not ready to quit. *BMC medical research methodology, 18*(1), 52. https://doi.org/10.1186/s12874-018-0511-0

Batastini, A. B., Hill, J. B., Repke, A., Gulledge, L. M., & Livengood, Z. K. (2018). Approaching correctional treatment from a programmatic standpoint: Risk-Need-Responsivity and beyond. In Ternes et al. (eds) The Practice of Correctional Psychology. Springer. https://doi.org/10.1007/978-3-030-00452-1_13

Batastini, A. B., Lester, M. E., Morgan, R. D., & Atterberry, E. (2020). Stepping Up, Stepping Out: A program description and preliminary findings. *Psychological Services*. https://doi.org/10.1037/ser0000430

Baxter, K. & Harrison, D. (2000). A simple cost benefit analysis for an ergonomics "Train-The-Trainer" program. Presented at the *Proceedings of the IEA 2000/HFES 2000 Congress*. Retrieved at https://journals-sagepub-com.lynx.lib.usm.edu/doi/pdf/10.1177/154193120004400701

Becan, J. E., Crawley, R. D., & Knight, D. K. (2019). Using a train-the-trainer model to promote practice change among agencies serving justice-involved youth. *Federal Probation, 83*(3), 47-53.

Bonta, J., & Andrews, D. A. (2007). Risk-need-responsivity model for offender assessment and rehabilitation. *Rehabilitation, 6*(1), 1-22.

Bonta, J., & Andrews, D.A. (2016). *The psychology of criminal conduct* (6th ed.). Routledge. https://doi.org/10.4324/9781315677187

Brice, G. H., Swarbrick, M. A., & Gill, K. J. (2013). Promoting wellness of peer providers through coaching. *Journal of Psychosocial Nursing and Mental Health Services, 52*(1), 41-45. https://doi.org/10.3928/02793695-20130930-03

Bush, J., Glick, B., & Taymans, J. (1997). *Thinking for a Change: Integrated Cognitive Behavioral Change Program*. National Institute of Corrections.

Campbell, W. L., Miller, S. L., Boyd, S. E., Farmer, D. D., & Olezeski, C. L. (2023). Incarcerated While Transgender. In *The History and Future of Correctional Psychology* (pp. 189–215). Springer International Publishing. https://doi.org/10.1007/978-3-031-37480-7_10

Covington, S. S. & Bloom, B. E. (2007). Gender-responsive treatment and services in correctional settings. *Women and Therapy, 29*(3/4), 9-33.

Crenshaw, K. (1989). Demarginalizing the intersection of race and sex: A black feminist critique of antidiscrimination doctrine, feminist theory and antiracist politics. *University of Chicago Legal Forum, 1*(8), 139–167

Dalzell, L. G., Pang, S. C., & Brömdal, A. (2024). Gender affirmation and mental health in prison: A critical review of current corrections policy for trans people in Australia and New Zealand. *Australian and New Zealand Journal of Psychiatry, 58*(1), 21–36. https://doi.org/10.1177/00048674231195285

DeHart, D., & Iachini, A. L. (2019). Mental Health & Trauma among Incarcerated Persons: Development of a Training Curriculum for Correctional Officers. *American Journal of Criminal Justice, 44*(3), 457–473. https://doi.org/10.1007/s12103-019-9473-y

Dvoskin, J. A. & Spiers, E. M. (2004). On the role of correctional officers in prison mental health. *Psychiatric Quarterly, 75*(1), 41-59.

Farbring, C. Å., & Johnson, W. R. (2008). Motivational interviewing in the correctional system: An attempt to implement motivational interviewing in criminal justice. In H. Arkowitz, H. A. Westra, W. R. Miller, & S. Rollnick (Eds.), *Motivational interviewing in the treatment of psychological problems*. The Guilford Press.

Farnese, M. L., Barbieri, B., Bellò, B., & Bartone, P. T. (2017). Don't abandon hope all ye who enter here: The protective role of formal mentoring and learning processes on burnout in correctional officers. *Work, 58*(3), 319-331. https://doi.org/10.3233/WOR-172628

Folk, J. B., Disabato, D. J., Daylor, J. M., Tangney, J. P., Barboza, S., Wilson, J. S., Bonieskie, L., & Holwager, J. (2016). Effectiveness of a self-administered intervention for criminal thinking: Taking a Chance on Change. *Psychological Services, 13*(3), 272-282. https://doi.org/10.1037/ser0000079

Frank, H. E., Becker-Haimes, E. M., & Kendall, P. C. (2021). Therapist training in evidence-based interventions for mental health: A systematic review of training approaches and outcomes. *Clinical Psychology, 27*(3). https://doi.org/10.1111/cpsp.12330

Gaspar, M., Brown, L., Ramler, T., Scanlon, F., Gigax, G., Ridley, K., & Morgan, R. D. (2019). Therapeutic outcomes of Changing Lives and Changing Outcomes for male and female justice involved persons with mental illness. *Criminal Justice and Behavior, 46*(12), 1678-1699. https://doi.org/10.1177/0093854819879743

Gill, K. J., Zechner, M., Zambo Anderson, E., Swarbrick, M., & Murphy, A. (2016). Wellness for life: A pilot of an interprofessional intervention to address metabolic syndrome in adults with serious mental illnesses. *Psychiatric Rehabilitation Journal, 39*(2), 147–153. https://doi.org/10.1037/prj0000172

Griffin, M. L., Hogan, N. L., Lambert, E. G., Tucker-Gail, K. A., & Baker, D. N. (2010). Job involvement, job stress, job satisfaction, and organizational commitment and the burn-out of correctional staff. Criminal Justice and behavior, 37(2), 239-255. https://doi.org/10.1177/0093854809351682

Hallundbaek, H. (2017). Art for a change: Innovative reentry program shows off practical implications. Corrections Today, 79(1), 56–61.

Hampson, M. E., Hicks, R. E., & Watt, B. D. (2015). Exploring the effectiveness of motivational interviewing in re-engaging people diagnosed with severe psychiatric conditions in work, study, or community participation. American Journal of Psychiatric Rehabilitation, 18(3), 265-279. https://doi.org/10.1080/15487768.2014.954158

Haque, S. F., & D'Souza, A. (2019). Motivational interviewing: The RULES, PACE, and OARS. Current Psychiatry, 18(1), 27-28.

Harizanova, S., & Stoyanova, R. (2020). Burnout among nurses and correctional officers. *Work, 65*(1), 71–77. https://doi.org/10.3233/WOR-19305910.3233/WOR-193059

Kiekbusch, R., Price, W., & Theis, J. (2003). Turnover predictors: causes of employee turnover in sheriff-operated jails. *Criminal Justice Studies, 16*(2).

Kravitz, R. L., Duan, N., & Braslow, J. (2004). Evidence-based medicine, heterogeneity of treatment effects, and the trouble with averages. *Milbank Quarterly, 82*(4), 661-687.

Kubiak, S. P., Covington, S., & Hillier, C. (2017). Trauma-informed corrections. In Springer and Roberts (Eds.), *Social work in juvenile and criminal justice systems* (4th ed., pp. 92-104). Charles C. Thomas Publisher, LTD.

Lambert, E. G., Barton-Bellessa, S. M., & Hogan, N. L. (2015). The consequences of emotional burn-out among correctional staff. *Sage Open, 5*(2), 1-15. https://doi.org/10.1177/2158244015590444

Landenberger, N. A. & Lipsey, M. W. (2005). The positive effects of cognitive-behavioral programs for offenders: A meta-analysis of factors associated with effective treatment. *Journal of Experimental Criminology, 1*, 451-476.

Lester, M. E., Batastini, A. B., Davis, R., & Bourgon, G. (2020). Examining differences in treatment response among male incarcerated persons. *Criminal Justice & Behavior, 47*(7), 829-847. https://doi.org/10.1177/0093854820915740

Leung, A.S.M. & Snape, E. (2012). Hostile work environment: "Is it just me or is it chilly in here?". In Reilly, N., Sirgy, M., Gorman, C. (eds.) Work and quality of life (pp. 375-394). International Handbooks of Quality-of-Life. Springer. https://doi.org/10.1007/978-94-007-4059-4_20

Lipsey, M. W., Chapman, G. L., & Landenberger, N. A. (2001). Cognitive-behavioral programs for offenders. *Annals of the American Academy of Political and Social Science, 578*, 144-157.

Lipsey, M. W., Landenberger, N. A., & Wilson, S. J. (2007). Effects of cognitive-behavioral programs for criminal offenders. *Campbell Systematic Reviews, 6*. https://doi.org/10.4073/csf.2007.6

Little, G. L. & Robinson, K. D. (1988). Moral Reconation Therapy: A systematic step-by-step treatment system for treatment resistant clients. *Psychological Reports, 62*, 135-151.

Lowenkamp, C. T., Hubbard, D., Makarios, M. D., & Latessa, E. J. (2009). A quasi-experimental evaluation of Thinking for a Change. *Criminal Justice and Behavior, 36*(2), 137-146. https://doi.org/10.1177/0093854808328230

Maslach, C., Jackson, S. E., & Leiter, M. P. (1997). Maslach burnout inventory. Scarecrow Education.

McDonald, M. A., Yang, Y., & Lancaster, C. L. (2022). The association of distress tolerance and mindful awareness with mental health in first responders. *Psychological Services, 19*(Suppl 1), 34–44. https://doi.org/10.1037/ser0000588

Melvin, K. B., Gramling, L. K., & Gardner, W. M. (1985). A scale to measure attitudes toward prisoners. *Criminal Justice and Behavior, 12*(2), 241-253. https://doi.org/10.1177/0093854885012002006

Molinaro, P. F., Fisher, R. P., Mosser, A. E., & Satin, G. E. (2019). Train-the-trainer: Methodology to learn the cognitive interview. *Journal of Investigative Psychology and Offender Profiling, 16*(1), 32–43. https://doi.org/10.1002/jip.1518

Morgan, R. D., & Flora, D. B. (2002). Group psychotherapy with incarcerated offenders: A research synthesis. *Group Dynamics: Theory, Research, and Practice, 6*(3), 203–218. https://psycnet.apa.org/doi/10.1037/1089-2699.6.3.203

Morgan, R. D., Flora, D. B., Kroner, D. G., Mills, J. F., Varghese, F., & Steffan, J. S. (2012). Treating offenders with mental illness: a research synthesis. *Law and Human Behavior, 36*(1), 37. https://psycnet.apa.org/doi/10.1037/h0093964

Morgan, R. D., Kroner, D. G., & Mills, J. F. (2018). *A treatment manual for justice involved persons with mental illness: Changing lives and changing outcomes*. Routledge/Taylor & Francis Group.

National Institute for Corrections. (2023). *Thinking For A Change usage map*. https://info.nicic.gov/t4c/node/39

Parker, G. F. (2009). Impact of a mental health training course for correctional officers on a special housing unit. *Psychiatric Services, 60*(5), 640-645.

Ross, R. R., Fabiano, E. A., & Ewles, C. D. (1988). Reasoning and rehabilitation. *International Journal of Offender Therapy and Comparative Criminology, 32*(1), 29–35. https://doi.org/10.1177/0306624X8803200104

Schaufeli, W. B., Desart, S., & Witte, H. D. (2020). Burnout Assessment Tool (BAT)—Development, Validity, and Reliability. *International Journal of Environmental Research and Public Health, 17*(24). https://doi.org/10.3390/ijerph17249495

Shi, L., Silver, J. R., & Hickert, A. (2022). Conceptualizing and measuring Public Stigma Toward People With Prison Records. Criminal Justice and Behavior, 49(11), 1676–1698. https://doi.org/10.1177/00938548221108932

Swarbrick, M., Gill, K. J., & Pratt, C. W. (2016). Impact of peer delivered wellness coaching. *Psychiatric Rehabilitation Journal, 39*(3), 234-238. https://doi.org/10.1037/prj0000187

Taylor, P. & Cooper, C. (2008). 'It was absolute hell': Inside the private prison. *Capital & Class*. Retrieved from https://doi.org/10.1177/030981680809600101

Taylor, K., McDonagh, D., & Blanchette, K. (2018). Assessing and treating women offenders. In Ternes, Magaletta, & Patry (eds) *The Practice of Correctional Psychology*, 103-126. https://doi.org/10.1007/978-3-030-00451-4

Tong, L. S. J. & Farrington, D. P. (2006). How effective is the "Reasoning and Rehabilitation" programme in reducing reoffending? A meta-analysis of evaluations in four countries. *Psychology, Crime, & Law, 12*(1), 3-24. https://doi.org/10.1080/10683160512331316253

Walters, G. D. (2003). Changes in criminal thinking and identity in novice and experienced inmates: Prisonization revisited. *Criminal Justice and Behavior, 30*(4), 399–421. https://doi.org/10.1177/0093854803253137

Walters, G. D. (2012). Criminal thinking and recidivism: Meta-analytic evidence on the predictive and incremental validity of the Psychological Inventory of Criminal Thinking Styles (PICTS). *Aggression and Violent Behavior, 17*(3), 272–278. https://doi.org/10.1016/j.avb.2012.02.010

Walters, G. D. (2013). Applying CBT to the criminal thought process. In R. C Tafrate & D. Mitchell (Eds.), *Forensic CBT: A handbook for clinical practice* (pp. 104-121). Wiley Blackwell.

Walters, G. D. (2017). Effect of a brief cognitive behavioural intervention on criminal thinking and prison misconduct in male inmates: Variable-oriented and person-oriented analyses. *Criminal Behaviour and Mental Health, 27*(5), 457-469. https://doi.org/10.1002/cbm.2028

Walters, G. D., Deming, A., & Elliott, W. N. (2009). Assessing criminal thinking in male sex offenders with the psychological inventory of criminal thinking styles. *Criminal Justice and Behavior, 36*(10), 1025-1036. https://doi.org/10.1177/0093854809342200

Walters, G. D., & Lowenkamp, C. T. (2016). Predicting recidivism with the Psychological Inventory of Criminal Thinking Styles (PICTS) in community-supervised male and female federal offenders. *Psychological Assessment, 28*(6), 652–659. https://doi.org/10.1037/pas0000210

Williams, M. M., Rogers, R., & Hartigan, S. E. (2020). The validity of the PICTS-SV and its effectiveness with positive impression management: An investigation in a court-mandated substance use treatment facility. *Criminal Justice and Behavior, 47*(1), 80–98. https://doi.org/10.1177/0093854819879733

Wilson, A. B., Farkas, K., Ishler, K. J., Gearhart, M., Morgan, R., & Ashe, M. (2014). Criminal thinking styles among people with serious mental illness in jail. *Law and Human Behavior, 38*(6), 592-601.

Wilson, D. B., Bouffard, L. A., & Mackenzie, D. L. (2005). A quantitative review of structured, group-oriented, cognitive-behavioral programs for offenders. *Criminal Justice and Behavior, 32*(2), 172-204. https://doi.org/10.1177/0093854804272889

Wooditch, A., Liansheng, L. T., & Taxman, F. S. (2014). Which criminogenic need changes are most important in promoting desistance from crime and substance use? *Criminal Justice and Behavior, 41*(3), 276-299. https://doi.org/10.1177/0093854813503543

Yochelson, S. & Samenow, S. E. (1976). *The Criminal Personality: The Change Process*.-1985-Xvi, 578 S. Aronson.

Chapter 2
Introduction and Module 1 Guide

Introduction to the Training

Materials:

1. *Trainee Attendance sheet (Appendix or e-Resource 2.1)*
2. *PowerPoint Slides 1-10 (presenter mode is recommended)*
3. *Whiteboard or large writing pad*

The annotations below are intended to help you prepare for the content and discussions related to each slide. Remember, there are also presenter notes within the PowerPoint slide deck to help you along in real time.

Supplementary Information The online version contains supplementary material available at https://doi.org/10.1007/978-3-031-88404-7_2.

© The Author(s), under exclusive license to Springer Nature Switzerland AG 2025

A. B. Batastini et al., *Training Correctional Staff to Recognize Criminal Thinking*, https://doi.org/10.1007/978-3-031-88404-7_2

Slide 1 This slide shows the title of the training. Say "good morning," welcome everybody for joining you today, and give a brief introduction about yourself and your position within the agency. You may save a more in-depth personal introduction for Slide 3. This would also be a good time to pass around the attendance sheet.

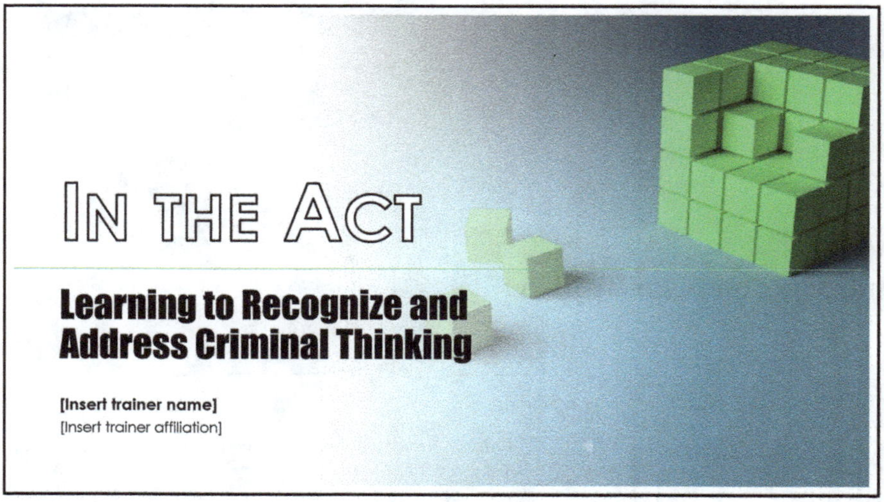

Slide 2 This slide outlines the agenda for the day. You may need to adjust the agenda in the PowerPoint slides to accommodate the work schedule of your agency. Let trainees know about any expectations for breaks, rules for leaving the room while in session, and that their attendance and participation for the entire day is required for completion.

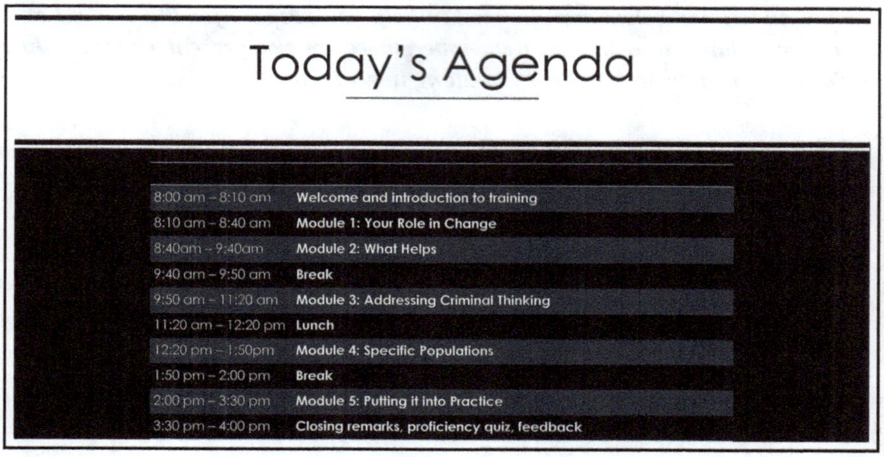

Slide 3 Go around the room and ask your trainees to introduce themselves. You may select icebreaker prompts for trainees to answer such as a "fun fact," how long they have been working in corrections, what they hope to get from this training, or what they like most about their job. We also recommend emphasizing your excitement to be with them today and your interest in sharing new skills.

Slide 4 This slide summarizes the two overarching purposes of the training: (1) to create a unified responsibility across the institution and (2) build continuity between everyday staff interactions and psychological programming. You may need to empathize with trainees who view this as "just another mandatory training" and encourage them to think about what they hope to learn (rather than focusing on what they already know or don't believe they need to know).

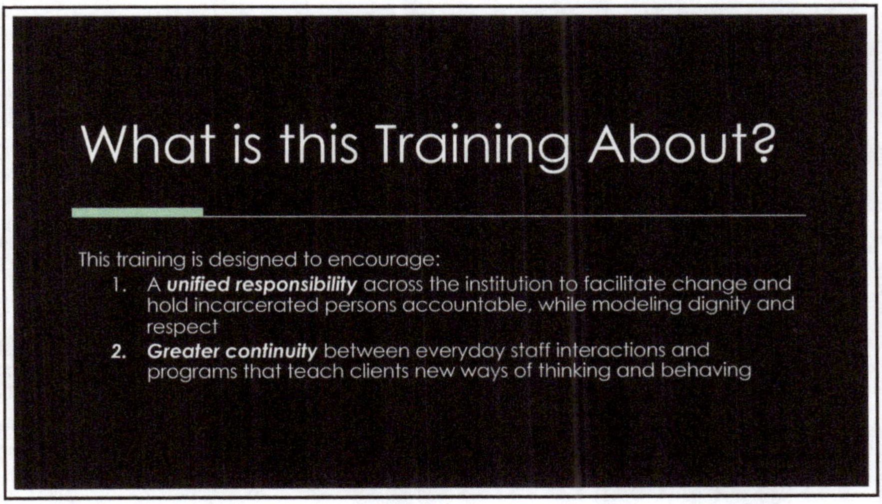

Slide 5 Although correctional and security officers are the intended audience for this training, it is possible other types of staff will be in attendance including but not limited to staff in education, mental health, social work, clerical, culinary, religious or spiritual services, booking and release, etc. You may also have people with a wide range of experiences in corrections from old timers to people fresh out of school or making a career change. This slide helps frame the training and is intended to make all staff feel welcome and relevant.

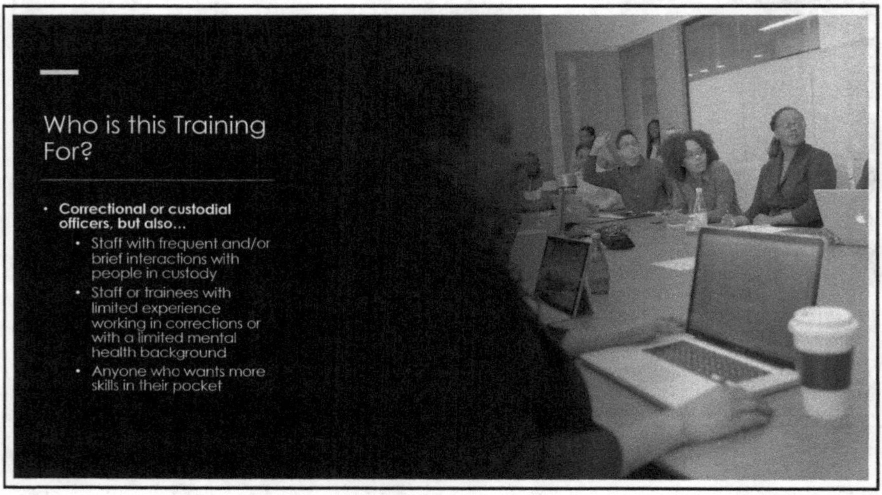

Slide 6 Read the primary goal of the training and emphasize that staff who are not already mental health providers will not be expected to become mental health providers. This training is insufficient to give trainees the necessary expertise to practice counseling or psychotherapy. They should instead view themselves as teammates to mental health staff. Some custody staff may hold the perception that mental health staff are "too soft on inmates." It may be helpful to explain these staff share the same goals of institutional safety and reducing disruptive behavior. They have just been trained to use different approaches.

Slide 7 This is the first time trainees see a definition of criminal thinking. The concept of criminal thinking will be fleshed out as the training progresses, and it may be worth reminding trainees to pay extra close attention to this definition. It's worth committing to memory!

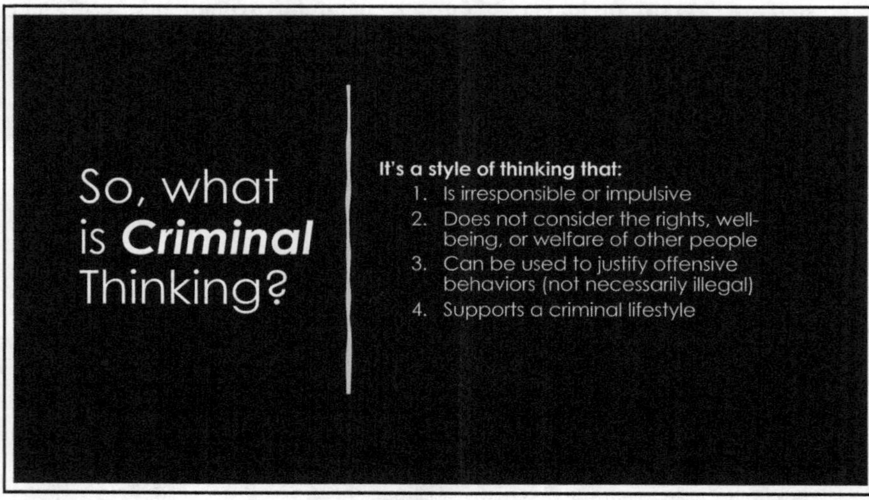

Slide 8 This slide depicts a cartoon of a so-called normal brain and a criminal brain. It is intended to help reinforce the concept that people in custody often think differently than other people. And thinking can be changed! Although the cartoon uses a dichotomous categorization that could be taken as "good vs. bad," it is not intended to support labeling people in this way. It's merely driving home a point through simplicity.

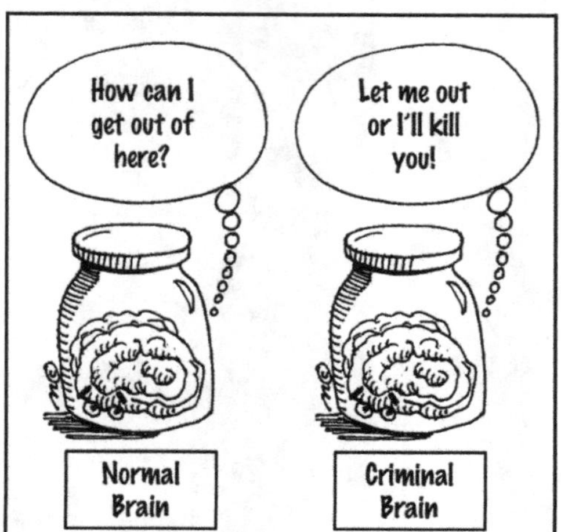

Slides 9 and 10 These two slides emphasize the scope of the training. They help manage trainees' expectations by acknowledging that violence and rule violations will nonetheless persist given the nature of correctional facilities and who is housed there. The skills they will learn today are both reductive and complementary, meaning they can help reduce problems within the institution and be used alongside other interventions including punitive sanctions.

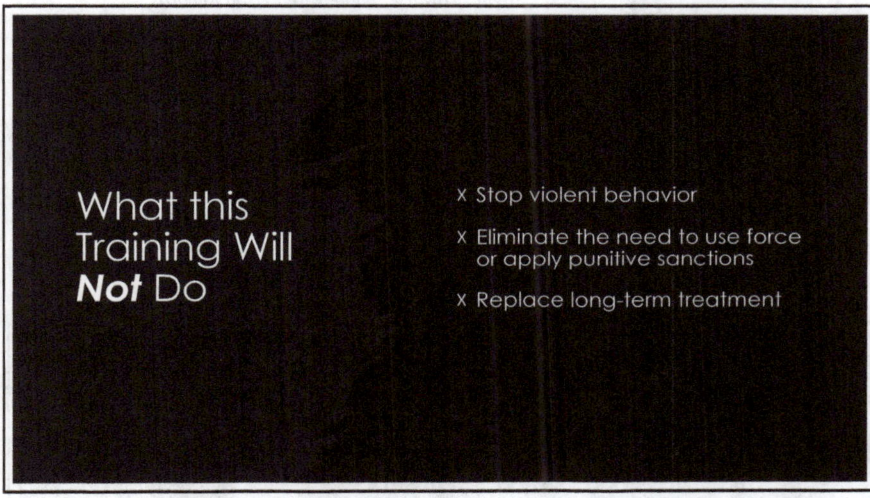

Module 1. Your Role in Change

Materials:

1. *PowerPoint Slides 11-27*
2. *Whiteboard or large writing pad*
3. ***Optional:** Attitudes Toward Prisoner Scale or Stigma Toward People with Prison Records (Appendices or e-Resources 2.2 and 2.3)*

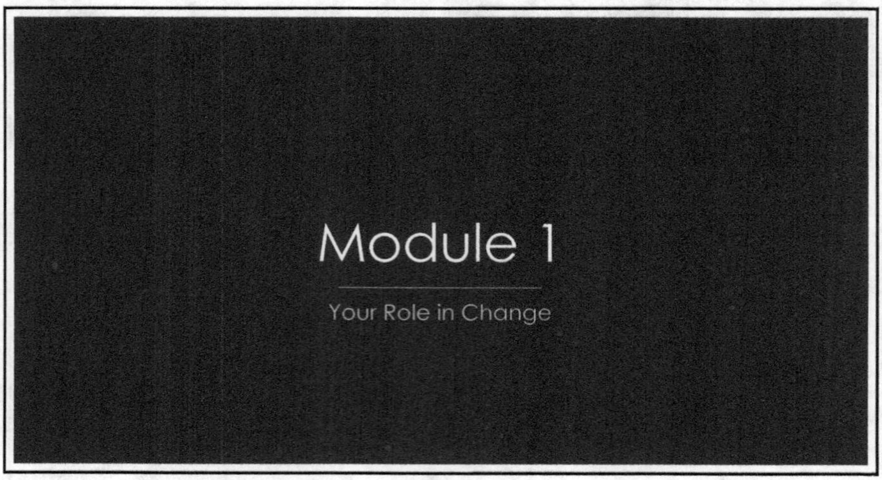

Slide Annotations

Slide 12 Spend some time gauging trainees' perceptions and biases about people in custody. The statements on this slide were pulled directly from a rating scale called the Attitudes Toward Prisoners (ATP) scale. This would be a good place to distribute the ATP or the Stigma Toward People with Prison Records (STPPR) scale and have trainees tally up their total score. The STPPR is similar to the ATP scale in that it captures negative attitudes toward people living in prison, but there are fewer items. Either one would provide trainees a general overview of how they tend to perceive "inmates."

Slide 13 These are several sample items from the Attitudes Toward Prisoners scale. If you don't ask trainees to complete the ATP, you can review each statement and ask trainees to raise their hand if they ever had similar thoughts. If trainees completed the ATP, you can ask them to raise their hand if they endorsed any of these views on the questionnaire. This is not a place to shame trainees for their views or attempt to modify their views; the exercise is intended to show how common these beliefs are among staff (often for good reason). As trainees learn more about criminal thinking and how to intervene, their beliefs should become less absolute.

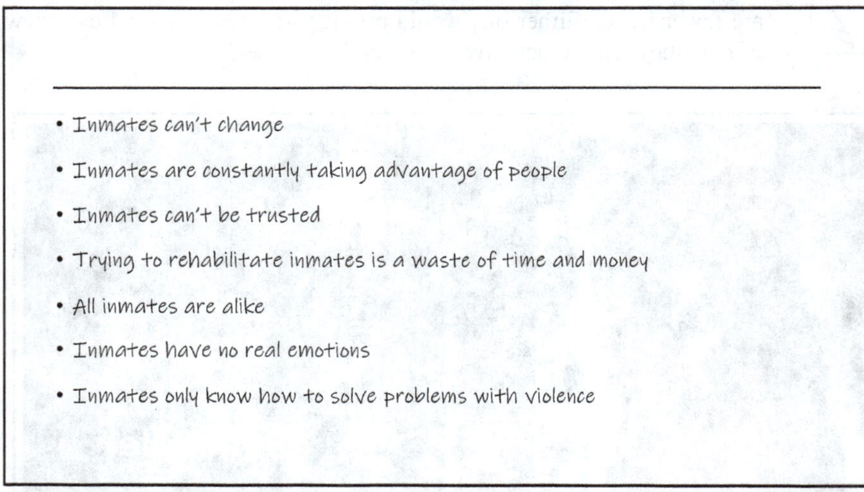

Slide 14 This slide summarizes the results of a study comparing correctional officers' attitudes about prisoners to those of other prison staff. For more details about this study, see Kjelsberg et al. (2007). The full reference appears at the end of this chapter.

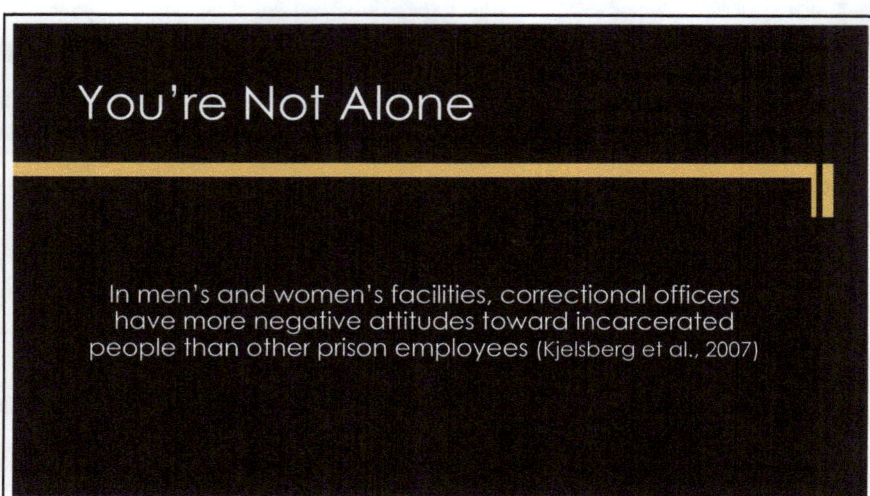

Slide 15 Here you'll emphasize that criminal thinking can be changed, but it will be a long-term process. Trainees shouldn't expect to change criminal thinking with one interaction…or even a few. You could reinforce this idea by asking trainees to share a time when they were challenged to change their mind about something/someone or tried to quit a bad habit (e.g., smoking, nail biting). Or, a time when they tried to change someone else's mind or helped them stop a bad habit (e.g., their children, a spouse). Ask them to reflect on how difficult the change process was and what they had to do to make the change permanent.

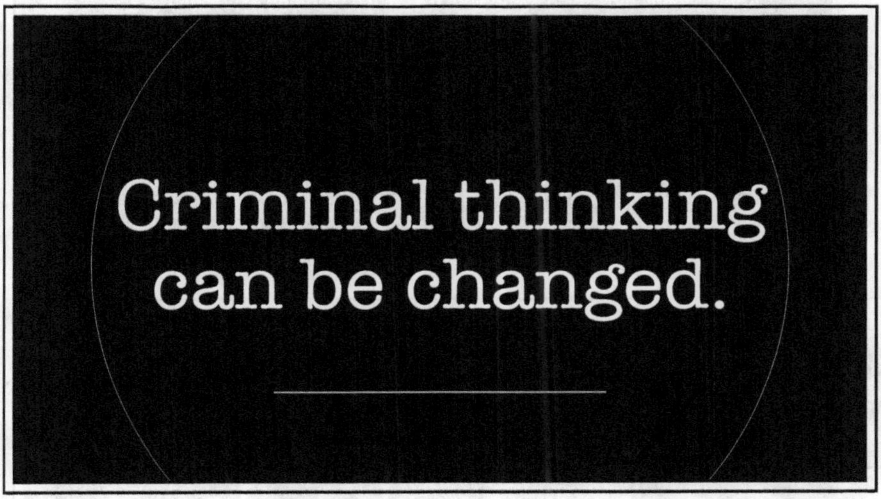

Slide 16 The benefits of addressing criminal thinking may take some time to sink in, so don't worry if trainees are not yet resonating with these points. The connection will become clearer as the training progresses.

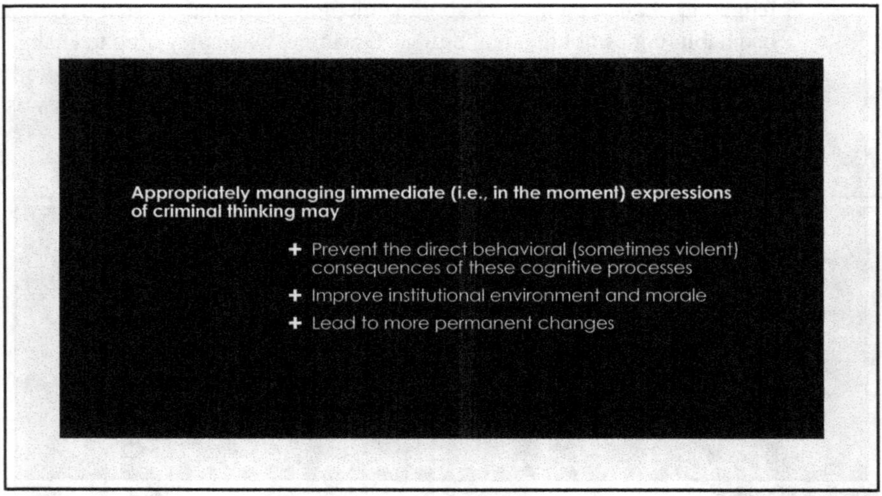

Slide 17 Here you will transition to focus more explicitly on the role of all staff, and especially custody staff, in the process of change.

Slide 18 You may ask trainees to share other reasons why they are so important to the change process. Because correctional officers and custody staff are already tasked with many high-stakes demands, you may receive some pushback from trainees about having even more pressures placed on them. Reiterating they are learning to be part of a broader mental health team (not taking on the job of a mental health provider) and that learning these new skills may reduce burdens in the long run may mitigate concerns or frustrations.

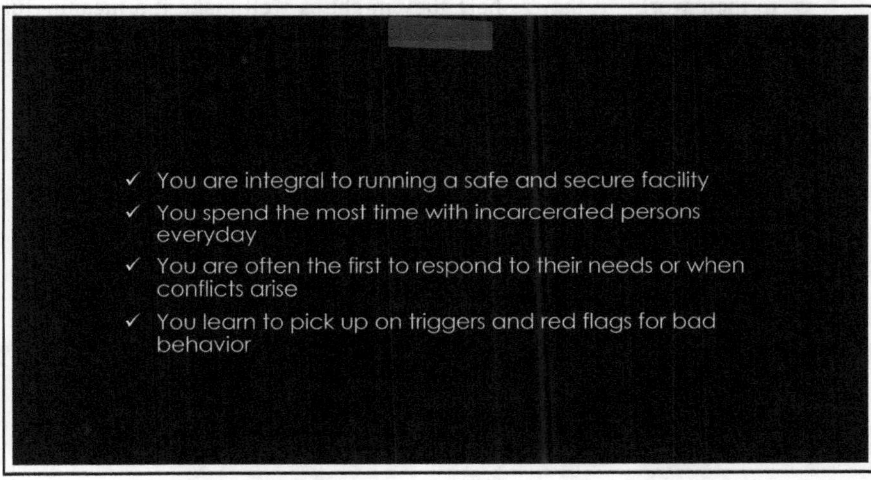

Slide 19 Read this slide with emphasis! Trainees should start feeling some level of commitment to the process of change and pride when thinking about how impactful they can be. Their good work not only benefits the institution, but it has the potential to reach into the communities incarcerated people reenter once released. You could ask trainees to share why they chose this career path in the first place or what mark they hope to leave. And/or share what keeps you motivated to work in corrections. If trainees focus on getting the job for money or because they simply needed a job, encourage them to think about how they can add purpose to their work—if they're here they might as well make it a meaningful experience!

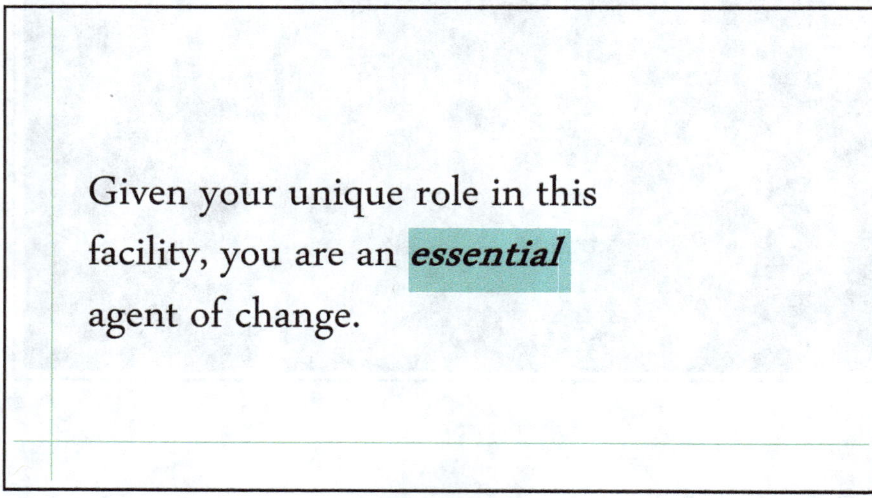

Slide 20 This slide lists a few benefits of being an agent of change. Emphasizing this role is not just about helping those in custody manage their behavior, but about making their day-to-day life as an employee at the institution more manageable. If you have time, have trainees consider other benefits. This is another place where trainees may express frustration about having to do or learn more stuff. Reassure trainees they will be sharing the responsibility with many other agents of change and the skills discussed today are designed to be easily integrated into their work.

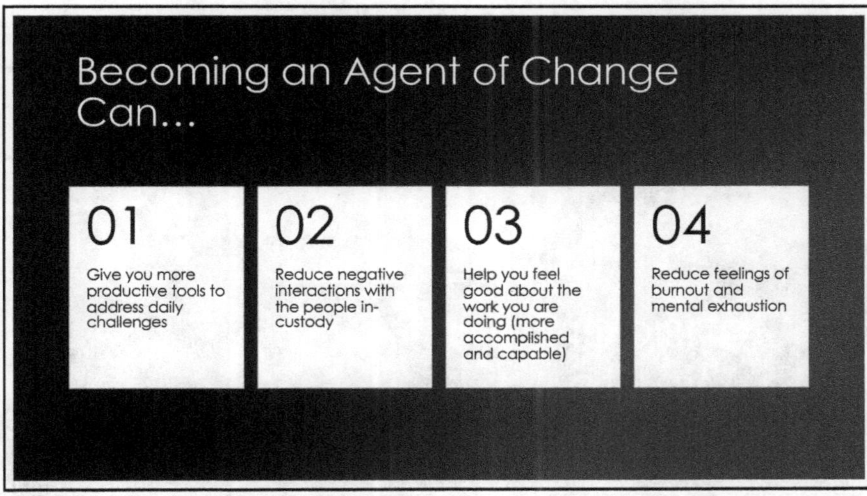

Slide 21 This slide gives space to recognize that correctional work is immensely challenging, both physically and mentally. However, this slide is not intended to facilitate a venting session. Redirect the conversation if trainees begin to story-tell or "trash talk." Instruct them to focus on general themes such as safety concerns, feeling helpless about controlling how people act, etc. Having trainees reflect on the factors that make their job hard may create a sense of community among trainees and help bolster buy-in for learning new and simple techniques to prompt change.

Slide 22 This slide gives a sense of solidarity. You should get a lot of head nods on this one!

Slide 23 Because it's so challenging to work in a correctional institution, there is a much higher risk of burnout and associated consequences. This slide highlights some research on correctional officer burnout and how it compares to other professions. Full references for Morgan and Flora (2002), Jaegers et al. (2020), Harizanova and Stoyanova (2020), and Forman-Dolan et al. (2022) can be found in the reference list at the end of this chapter. After you review the research, you'll ask trainees to talk about what burnout looks like for them; what signs or symptoms do they experience. You can even offer a simple or silly example of your own workplace behavior when you're stressed or in a bad mood (e.g., "My coworkers know when my door is closed, I'm probably cranky. If they knock, they risk getting their head bit off!").

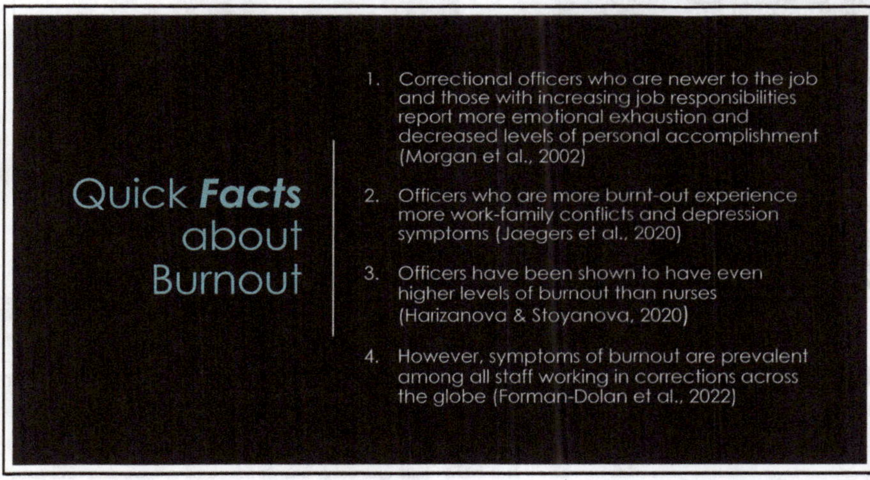

Slide 24 Whether the result of burnout or preconceived notions about incarcerated people being "bad" or "less than," responding in a hostile way toward people in custody can have serious consequences. The study by Ellison and Gainey (2020; see references list) illustrates that an antagonistic style can lead to staff victimization and increased concerns about being harmed on the job. So, even if staff feel incarcerated people deserve to be treated poorly, it is not in their best interest to do so!

Slide 25 This slide drives home the message that this training is just as much for the benefit of your trainees as it is for the people in custody.

Slide 26 This slide encourages trainees to reflect on more positive interactions with the people in their custody. If trainees have a hard time generating examples, have a few of your own ready to share. The discussion is intended to balance out any negative feelings; it's not meant to sugarcoat the experience and real dangers of working in a correctional institution. We know it's not rainbows and butterflies! Being able to identify at least some rewarding interactions may instill hope that the skills they'll learn today might make a difference.

Slide 27 Hopefully trainees are beginning to show some motivation to learn about criminal thinking and how to address it so they can have a better work experience and contribute to positive change.

Appendices

Appendix 2.1: Trainee Attendance Sheet

Date of Training: ____/____/____ Trainer Name: ____________________

IN THE ACT ATTENDANCE SHEET

Trainee Name	Employee ID	Department/Unit	Immediate Supervisor	Certificate given?

Appendix 2.2: Attitudes Toward Prisoners Scale

Please indicate the level to which you agree with each statement by circling a number on the five-point scale (0 = Strongly Disagree, 4 = Strongly Agree).

	Strongly disagree	Somewhat disagree	Undecided	Somewhat agree	Strongly agree
*1. Prisoners are different from most people**	0	1	2	3	4
2. Only a few prisoners are really dangerous	0	1	2	3	4
*3. Prisoners never change**	0	1	2	3	4
4. Most prisoners are victims of circumstance and deserve to be helped	0	1	2	3	4
5. Prisoners have feelings like the rest of us	0	1	2	3	4
*6. It is not wise to trust a prisoner too far**	0	1	2	3	4
7. I think I would like a lot of prisoners	0	1	2	3	4
8. Bad prison conditions just make a prisoner more bitter	0	1	2	3	4
*9. Give a prisoner an inch and he'll take a mile**	0	1	2	3	4
*10. Most prisoners are stupid**	0	1	2	3	4
11. Prisoners need. affection and praise just like anybody else	0	1	2	3	4
*12. You should not expect too much from a prisoner**	0	1	2	3	4
*13. Trying to rehabilitate prisoners is a waste of time and money**	0	1	2	3	4
*14. You never know when a prisoner is telling the truth**	0	1	2	3	4
15. Prisoners are no better or worse than other people	0	1	2	3	4
*16. You have to be constantly on your guard with prisoners**	0	1	2	3	4
*17. In general, prisoners think and act alike**	0	1	2	3	4
18. If you give a prisoner your respect, he'll give you the same	0	1	2	3	4
*19. Prisoners only think about themselves**	0	1	2	3	4

	Strongly disagree	Somewhat disagree	Undecided	Somewhat agree	Strongly agree
20. There are some prisoners I would trust with my life	0	1	2	3	4
21. Prisoners will listen to reason	0	1	2	3	4
*22. Most prisoners are too lazy to earn an honest living**	0	1	2	3	4
23. I wouldn't mind living next door to an ex-prisoner	0	1	2	3	4
*24. Prisoners are just plain mean at heart**	0	1	2	3	4
*25. Prisoners are always trying to get something out of somebody**	0	1	2	3	4
26. The values of most prisoners are about the same as the rest of us	0	1	2	3	4
*27. I would never want one of my children dating an ex-prisoner**	0	1	2	3	4
28. Most prisoners have the capacity for love	0	1	2	3	4
*29. Prisoners are just plain immoral**	0	1	2	3	4
*30. Prisoners should be under strict, harsh, discipline**	0	1	2	3	4
*31. In general, prisoners are basically bad people**	0	1	2	3	4
32. Most prisoners can be rehabilitated	0	1	2	3	4
33. Some prisoners are pretty nice people	0	1	2	3	4
34. I would like associating with some prisoners	0	1	2	3	4
*35. Prisoners respect only brute force**	0	1	2	3	4
36. If a person does well in prison, he should be let out on parole	0	1	2	3	4

How to determine your score

1. *For items with an asterisk (*) at the end, give the score the opposite of what you indicated. In other words, if you circled a 1, your new score is 5 (and vice versa), 2 is scored as a 4 (and vice versa), and 3 remains the same. Indicate your new score next to these items.*
2. *Add up all your scores on each item.* _________
3. *Mark your score on the number line below. This is the range of possible scores.*

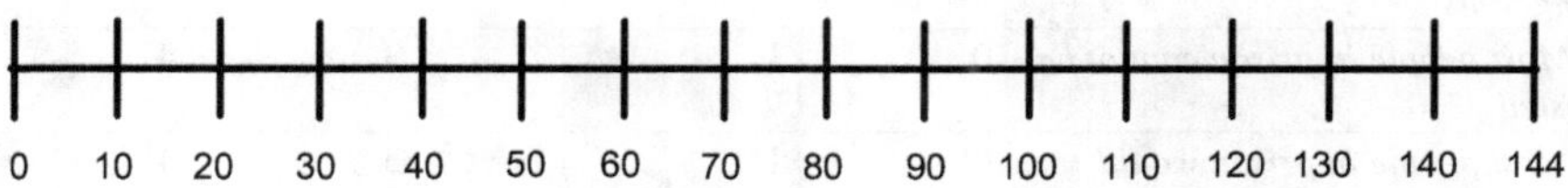

4. *Where your score is on the number line tells you how you view people who are incarcerated. Scores between 0 and 72 suggest more negative perceptions of incarcerated individuals. Scores between 72 and 144 suggest more positive perceptions.*

Appendix 2.3: Stigma Toward People with Prison Records

Please indicate the level to which you agree with each statement by circling a number on the five-point scale (0 = Strongly Disagree, 4 = Strongly Agree).

	Strongly disagree	Somewhat disagree	Unsure	Somewhat agree	Strongly agree
1. Most people in prison are dangerous	0	1	2	3	4
2. Most people in prison cannot be trusted	0	1	2	3	4
3. Most people in prison would commit more crimes if they were released	0	1	2	3	4
4. People in prison are cold and mechanical, like robots	0	1	2	3	4
5. People in prison lack self-restraint, like animals	0	1	2	3	4
6. People in prison are unsophisticated	0	1	2	3	4
7. Most people in prison committed crimes because they have little to no self-control	0	1	2	3	4
8. Most people in prison committed crimes simply because they have bad moral character	0	1	2	3	4
9. Most people in prison committed crimes simply because they are selfish people	0	1	2	3	4
10. Most people in prison committed crimes because they are just too lazy to get a job to earn money	0	1	2	3	4
11. I would be afraid to be around someone who had been in prison	0	1	2	3	4
12. I would be upset if a person who had been in prison moved into my neighborhood	0	1	2	3	4
13. I feel disgusted by people who are in prison	0	1	2	3	4
14. I would not want to work with a person who had been in prison	0	1	2	3	4
15. I would not want to live near a person who had been in prison	0	1	2	3	4
16. I would not want to be friends with a person who had been in prison	0	1	2	3	4
17. I would never be willing to date a person who had been in prison	0	1	2	3	4

How to determine your score

1. *Add up your scores on each item.* __________
2. *Mark your score on the number line below. This is the range of possible scores.*

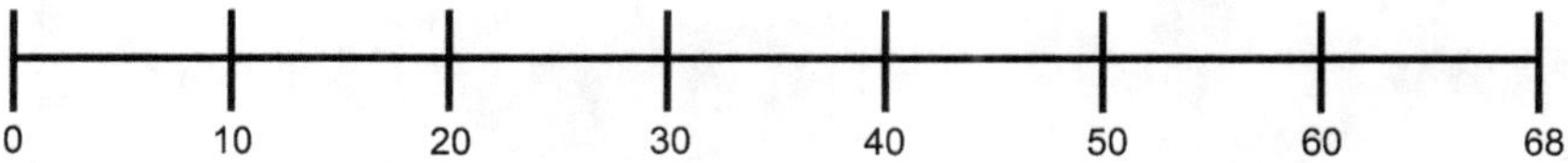

3. *Where your score is on the number line tells you your opinion of those with a criminal record. Scores below 34 suggest more positive perceptions of those with a criminal record. Scores of 34 and above suggest more negative perceptions.*

References

Ellison, J. M., & Gainey, R. (2020). An opportunity model of safety risks among jail officers. *Journal of Criminal Justice*, *66*, 101632. https://doi.org/10.1016/j.jcrimjus.2019.101632

Forman-Dolan, J., Caggiano, C., Anillo, I., & Kennedy, T. D. (2022). Burnout among professionals working in corrections: A two stage review. *International Journal of Environmental Research and Public Health, 19*(16), 9954. https://doi.org/10.3390/ijerph19169954

Harizanova, S., & Stoyanova, R. (2020). Burnout among nurses and correctional officers. *Work, 65*(1), 71–77. https://doi.org/10.3233/WOR-193059

Jaegers, L. A., Vaughn, M. G., Werth, P., Matthieu, M. M., Ahmad, S. O., & Barnidge, E. (2020). Work–family conflict, depression, and burnout among jail correctional officers: A 1-year prospective study. *Safety and Health at Work, 12*(2), 167-173. https://doi.org/10.1016/j.shaw.2020.10.008

Kjelsberg, E., Skoglund, T. H., & Rustad, A. (2007). Attitudes towards prisoners, as reported by prison inmates, prison employees and college students. *BMC Public Health,* 7, 1-9. https://doi.org/10.1186/1471-2458-7-71

Morgan, R. D., & Flora, D. B. (2002). Group psychotherapy with incarcerated offenders: A research synthesis. *Group Dynamics: Theory, Research, and Practice, 6*(3), 203–218. https://doi.org/10.1037/1089-2699.6.3.203

Chapter 3
Module 2 Guide

Module 2. What Helps

Materials:

1. *PowerPoint Slides 28-61*
2. *Whiteboard or large writing pad*

The annotations below are intended to help you prepare for the content and discussions related to each slide. Remember, there are also presenter notes within the PowerPoint slide deck to help you along in real time.

Supplementary Information The online version contains supplementary material available at https://doi.org/10.1007/978-3-031-88404-7_3.

© The Author(s), under exclusive license to Springer Nature Switzerland AG 2025

A. B. Batastini et al., *Training Correctional Staff to Recognize Criminal Thinking*, https://doi.org/10.1007/978-3-031-88404-7_3

Slide 28 This is a transitional slide introducing the Module 2.

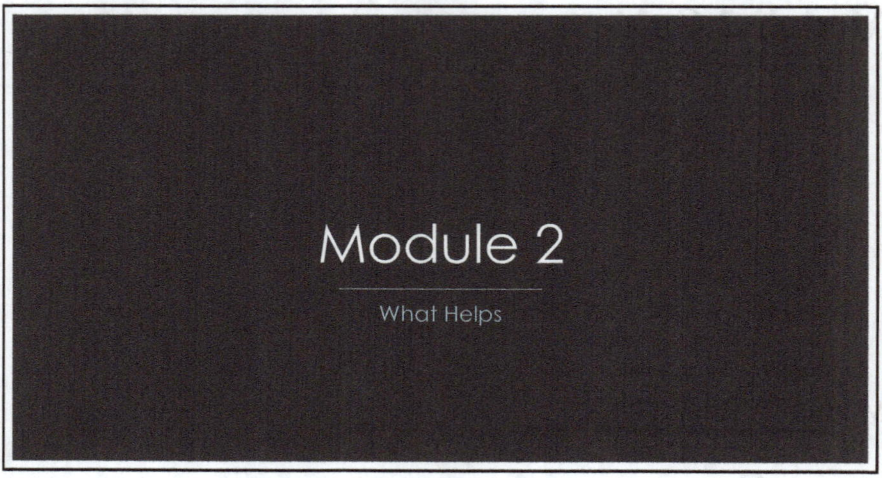

Slide 29 This slide introduces trainees to the current gold standard model for case planning and treatment in correctional environments. The Risk-Needs-Responsivity model (or RNR) is not the only model, but it is the most researched and most applied across the United States and Canada in both in-custody institutions and community corrections. You may already be familiar with it. The slides that follow will get into more detail about each principle. Criminal thinking, the concept at the center of this training, is part of the Risk and the Needs principles so it's an integral part of reducing someone's risk of further criminal behavior.

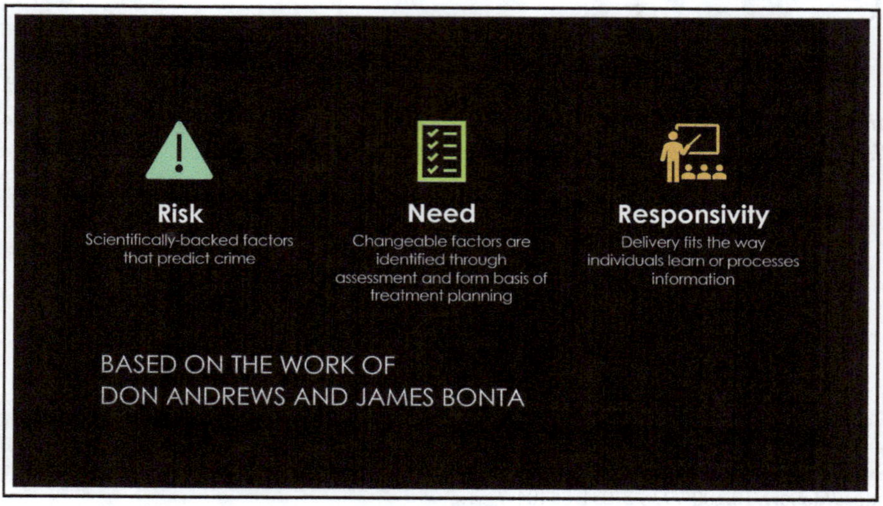

Slide 30 This slide begins the discussion of the Risk principle of RNR.

Slide 31 Here, you'll prompt trainees to think about the top eight risk factors for criminal behavior. These have been dubbed "the Central 8" and have the most predictive power. In other words, while other factors may help predict crime, these are the ones that have the biggest impact. If you have the materials, you may choose to write trainees' responses on a whiteboard. Spend about a minute collecting responses.

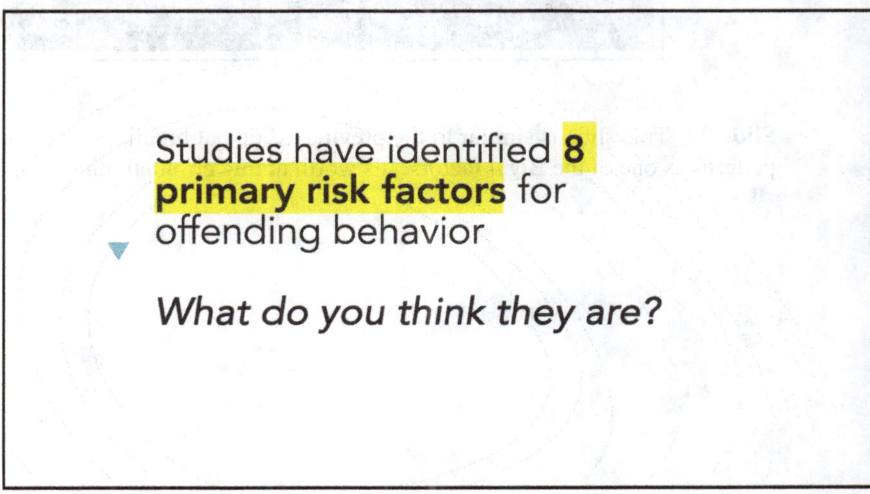

Slide 32 This slide includes an animation. The box surrounding The Big 4 will appear with an additional mouse or keyboard click. Ask trainees for their reaction to

the factors on the list. Is it what they expected? You may also point out any risk factors that trainees accurately identified when prompted during the previous slide. Remember: just because a factor isn't on the list doesn't mean it has nothing to do with criminal behavior, but the Central 8 (and especially the Big 4) are the most influential. Often people expect mental illness to be on this list and may become insistent it should be there. At this point, you can tell trainees that, for some people in your facility, mental illness is an issue. However, mental illness is not linked to dangerousness for the large majority of people. The relationship between mental illness and crime will be discussed later in the training.

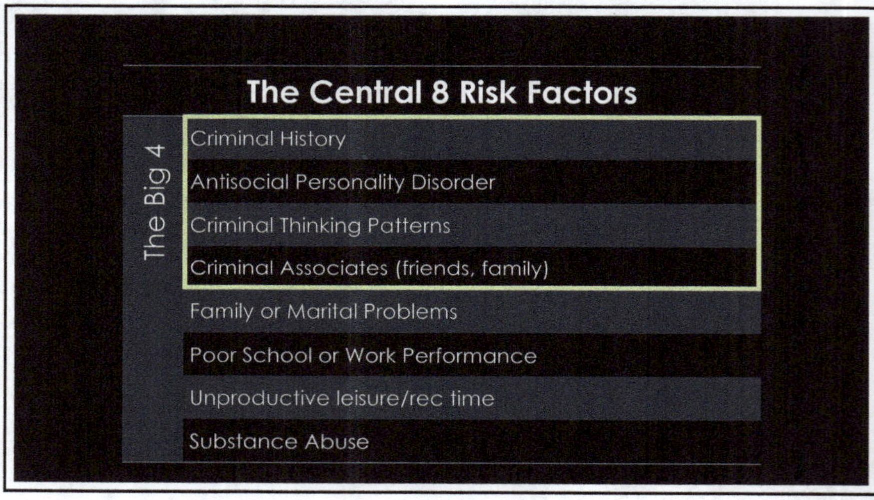

Slide 33 This slide is similar to the previous slide but highlights criminal thinking patterns as one of the Big 4 factors. It's worth noting criminal thinking also contrib-

utes to other criminogenic needs such as decisions to use illicit substances, whom people choose to hang out with, or using violence to control a romantic partner.

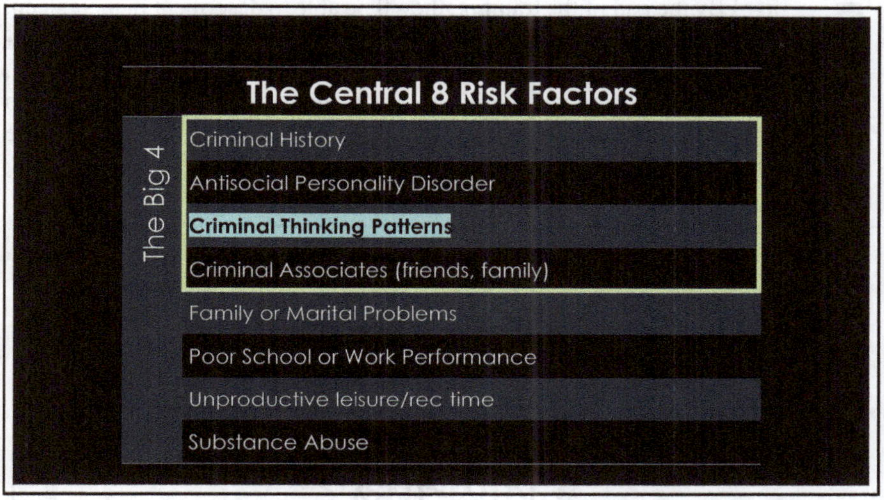

Slide 34 This isn't a real pop quiz, so no one needs to panic! This is simply a good spot to review the concept of criminal thinking and make sure everyone is on the same page. If trainees seem nervous, tell them you'll talk through it as a group, and no one gets shamed for wrong answers. The goal is to learn.

Slide 35 Ask trainees to recall what they know about criminal thinking from your earlier discussion. Remind trainees it's ok if they forgot some components. Many of them only learned about criminal thinking moments ago! By the end of the training, they'll be able to describe it in their sleep. Reinforce any correct or partially correct answers. For example, if someone says it's a way of thinking about crime, you could say, "That's close, but it's a little broader than just thinking about crime." You don't have to get into every detail of criminal thinking on this slide; the next few use True/False questions to highlight the key components.

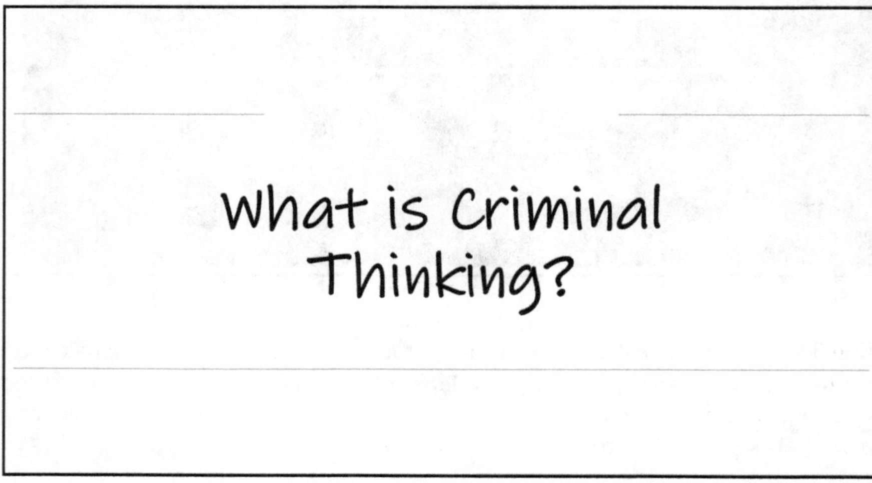

Slides 36–39 For slides 36 through 39, you'll first read the question, pause for trainees to provide their response, then click the mouse or keyboard to reveal the correct answer. Reinforce trainees for correct responses.

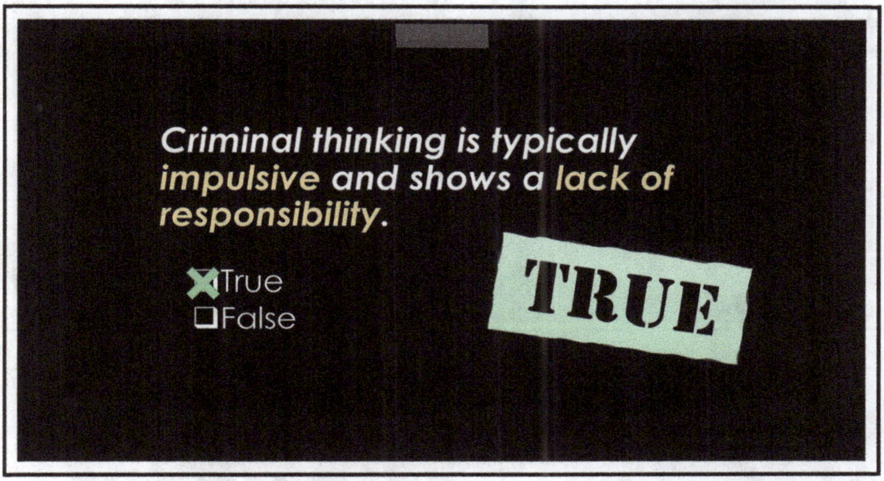

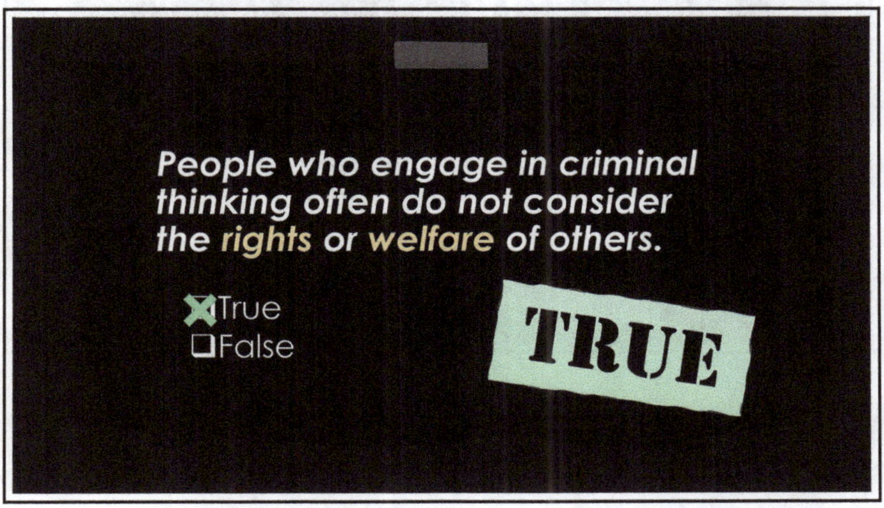

Criminal thinking always leads to illegal behaviors.
True
False
FALSE

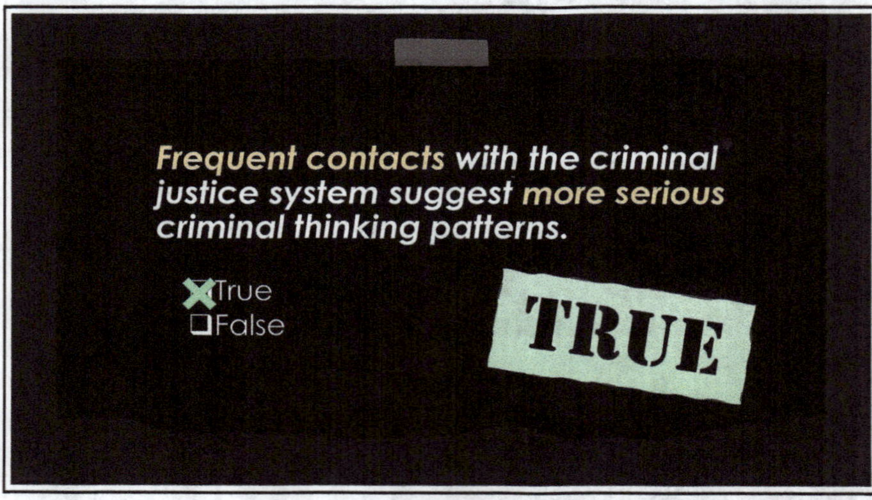
Frequent contacts with the criminal justice system suggest more serious criminal thinking patterns.
True
False
TRUE

Slide 40 This slide simply reiterates the importance of criminal thinking and, by extension, the importance of trainees' participation in helping to address criminal thinking.

Slide 41 This slide begins the discussion of the Need principle.

Slide 42 The Needs principle is about converting the changeable risk factors (also called "criminogenic needs" into targets for treatment and understanding that more needs equate to more intensive services. So, someone with four criminogenic needs will need more services for a longer period of time than someone with two criminogenic needs.

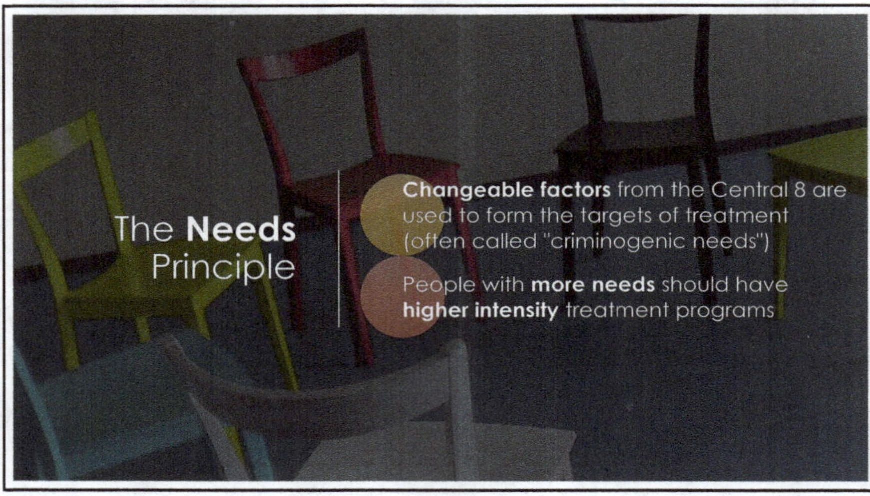

Slide 43 What makes criminal thinking so relevant to discuss and address is that it's both a major risk factor and a criminogenic need, meaning it contributes significantly to whether someone will engage in criminal behavior, but it can be worked on through appropriate interventions. It may help to remind trainees that criminal thinking also plays a role in maintaining other criminogenic needs.

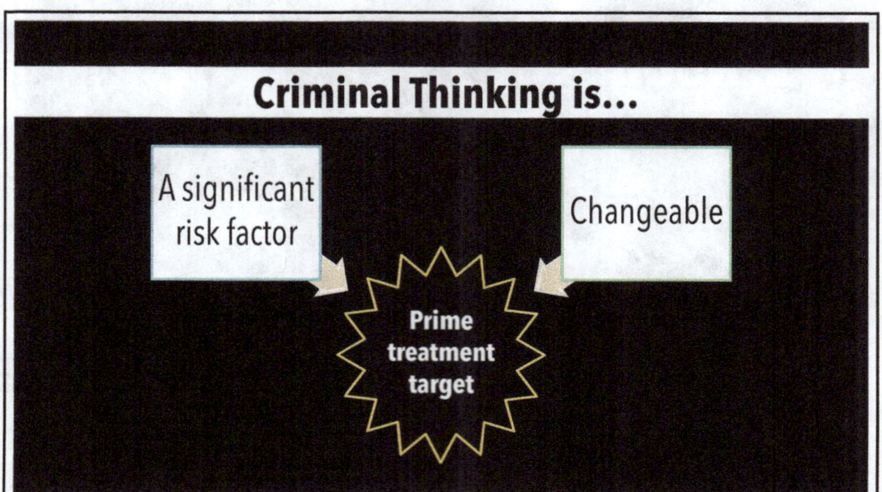

Slide 44 By helping to address criminal thinking in people's everyday lives in the institution, correctional staff (your trainees) are increasing the intensity of services. They are forcing the people in their custody to continually monitor their thinking and practice new and more helpful ways of approaching problems.

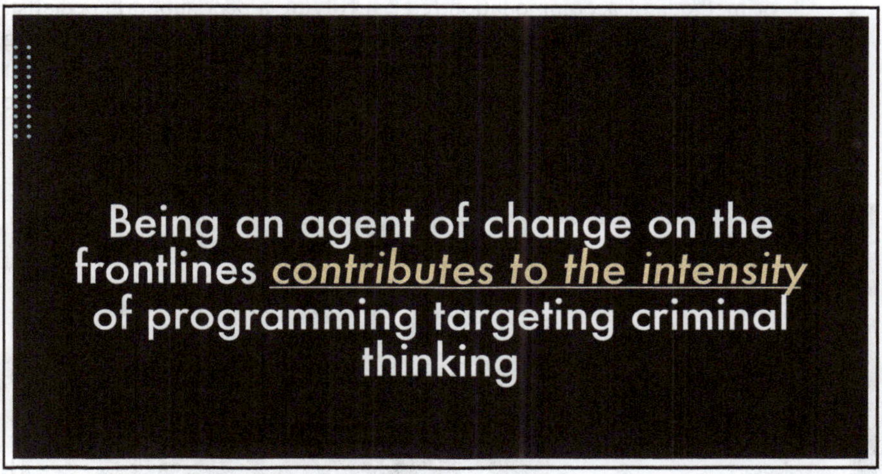

Slide 45 This slide begins the discussion of the Responsivity principle.

Slide 46 This slide provides a basic definition of the responsivity principle and lists several responsivity considerations. Ask trainees to think about examples in which they've observed these factors play out in intervention activities such as educational classes, anger management groups, art therapy, etc. They could discuss how these factors were a barrier and/or methods of accommodation (e.g., involving a peer support specialist, getting someone stabilized on psychiatric medication before enrolling them in a treatment group). Prompt trainees to think of other factors that could impact responsivity. Finally, before moving to the next slide, gauge the audience's initial impressions about the importance of this principle.

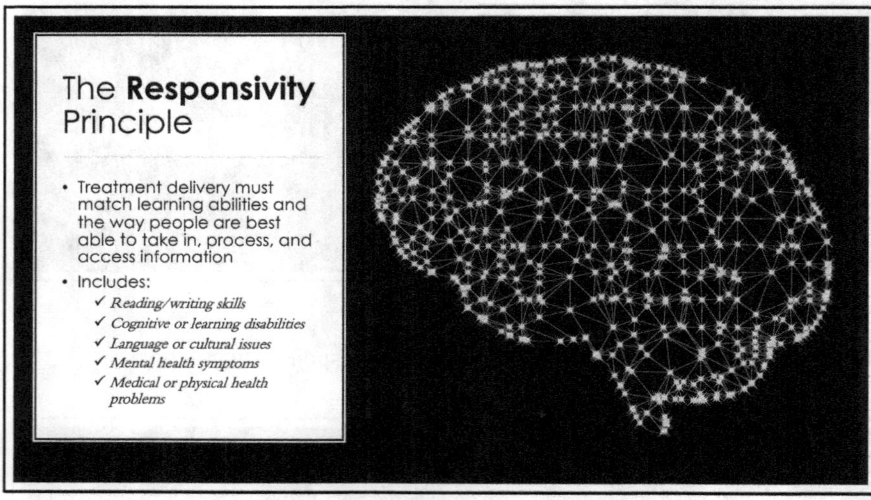

Slide 47 This slide reveals the answer to the question "why is this principle important?" Essentially, interventions won't work if responsivity factors aren't considered because the content and material won't "stick." It could be argued this is the most important of the three principles.

Slide 48 If it wasn't mentioned in your discussion on Slide 46, staff can be a responsivity consideration, too! If your trainees were able to identify themselves as a consideration during that discussion, a hypothetical pat on the back is in order. Most staff will not recognize themselves as part of the equation. To reinforce this point, ask trainees to consider how negative interactions with others have impacted their behavior or ability to grow and change. Two examples are provided in the slides, but you could think of other scenarios or encourage people to share their own.

Slide 49 This slide transitions into some of the scientific research on the RNR model. Don't worry, we won't get too technical. Just enough to establish confidence in the model as a good approach to correctional case planning and treatment.

Slide 50 This looks like a more complicated slide than it is, and you'll have the script within the slide to guide you in explaining the results. The bar graph is recreated from the Romani et al. (2012) article. There is one animation (using a mouse or keyboard click) on this slide that reveals interpretations of the bars within the graph. Once you review the graph, ask trainees to describe the outcome in their own words. The main takeaway is that, if the department is spending money on rehabilitation, there will be a "bigger bang for the buck" if programs follow the principles of RNR.

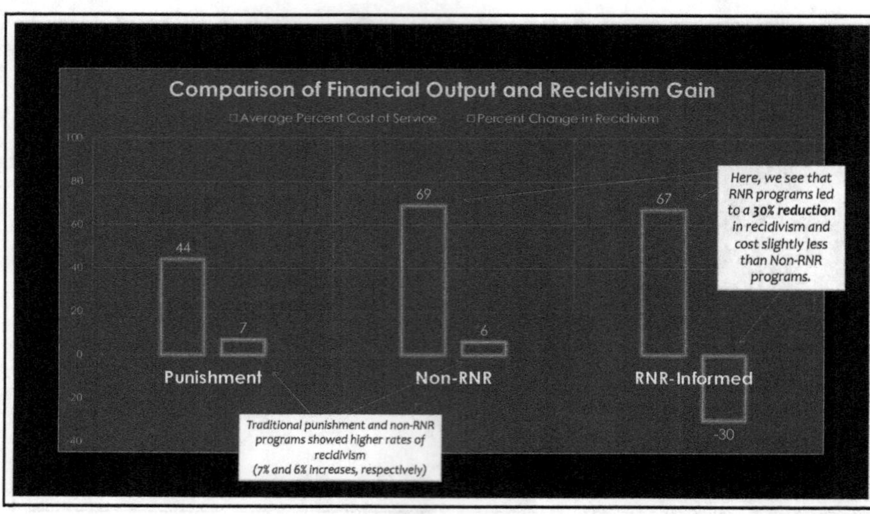

Slide 51 This slide displays the title, authors, and abstract from the Romani et al. (2012) article. The full reference for this paper is in the reference list of this workbook.

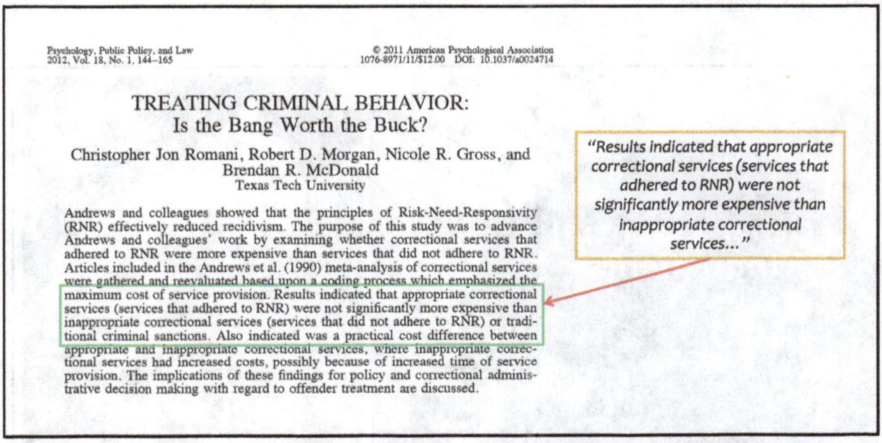

Psychology, Public Policy, and Law
2012, Vol. 18, No. 1, 144–165

© 2011 American Psychological Association
1076-8971/11/$12.00 DOI: 10.1037/a0024714

TREATING CRIMINAL BEHAVIOR:
Is the Bang Worth the Buck?

Christopher Jon Romani, Robert D. Morgan, Nicole R. Gross, and Brendan R. McDonald
Texas Tech University

Andrews and colleagues showed that the principles of Risk-Need-Responsivity (RNR) effectively reduced recidivism. The purpose of this study was to advance Andrews and colleagues' work by examining whether correctional services that adhered to RNR were more expensive than services that did not adhere to RNR. Articles included in the Andrews et al. (1990) meta-analysis of correctional services were gathered and reevaluated based upon a coding process which emphasized the maximum cost of service provision. Results indicated that appropriate correctional services (services that adhered to RNR) were not significantly more expensive than inappropriate correctional services (services that did not adhere to RNR) or traditional criminal sanctions. Also indicated was a practical cost difference between appropriate and inappropriate correctional services, where inappropriate correctional services had increased costs, possibly because of increased time of service provision. The implications of these findings for policy and correctional administrative decision making with regard to offender treatment are discussed.

Slide 52 This slide circles back to the question of whether there is support for the RNR model. Click the mouse or keyboard to display the "YES" text box. If trainees raise concern that this statement is being made on the basis of one study, commend them for this observation. However, you can assure trainees there is a whole body of scientific literature on the RNR model but reviewing it in detail is beyond the scope of this training.

Slide 53 In this slide, other active components of effective interventions are acknowledged. All of these components can work alongside the RNR principles to enhance the potency of our intervention efforts. You'll also have a script in the slide to briefly describe the last two components, as these may be less familiar therapeutic concepts to trainees.

Slide 54 This slide transitions into a brief historical overview of criminal thinking and its subcomponents. Trainees will be exposed to more examples of criminal thinking over the next few slides and be asked to consider ways they personally engaged in criminal thinking patterns.

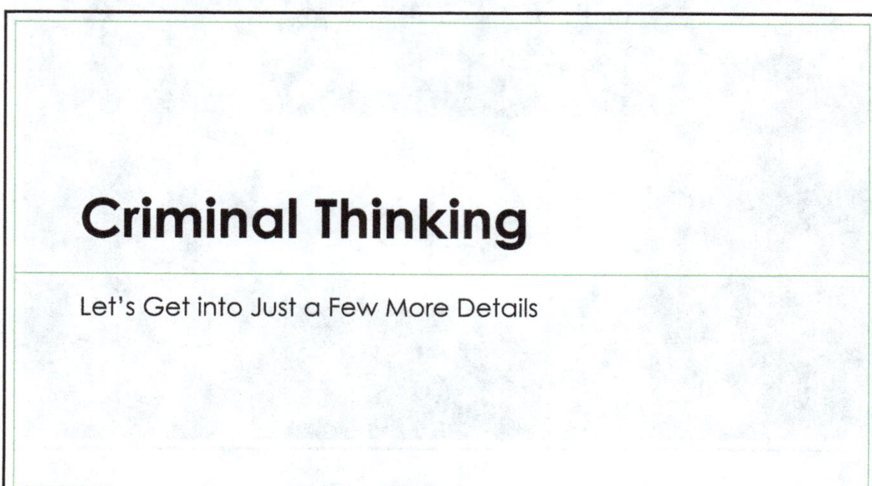

Slide 55 The idea of criminal thinking began in the 1970s with the work of Yochelson and Samenow (1976). They proposed a lot of different styles of criminal thinking! Glenn Walters, a research psychologist, later consolidated these styles and is currently the leading voice for how criminal thinking is conceptualized, studied, and integrated into treatment (see Walters, 1995a; Walters, 1995b).

Slide 56 This slide shows more specific categories of criminal thinking and how each one may present in the real world. As you walk through the examples, ask trainees if they can relate to or provide their own examples.

Thinking Error	Example
Rationalizing or minimizing behavior by blaming others or the situation	"If staff would just get off my ass, I wouldn't have to break the rules."
Thinking on impulse	"This isn't worth my time," or "Fuck this!"
Sense of ownership, privilege, and uniqueness is used to avoid taking responsibility (entitlement)	"If I want something that belongs to someone else, I'm going to take it. If he's not man enough to stop me, then he didn't deserve it in the first place."
Craving power or control (usually to boost one's own self-esteem)	"The homework wasn't that hard anyway. Anyone idiot could have done a good job."
Believing that doing something good or nice overrides a bad behavior	"If I'm nice to my girlfriend and buy her flowers, she'll forgive me for hitting her and everything will go back to normal."
Believing you can avoid or get away with negative outcomes	"The cops are too dumb, I'll never get caught."
Thinking that taking shortcuts is ok (taking the easy way out).	"I didn't sleep well last night, so I'm going to skip work crew. I wouldn't be able to focus anyway."

Slide 57 It's important for trainees to understand that criminal thinking falls along a continuum based on frequency and severity. Usually, frequency and severity go together such that someone who uses criminal thinking often usually ends up with more serious consequences. Criminal thinking is also not absolute, meaning that even people who engage in criminal thinking with high frequency are capable of using other, more helpful ways of thinking. And, you don't need to be a criminal to fall into the trap of criminal thinking. Conceptualizing criminal thinking in this manner helps normalize the experience and shows trainees they aren't immune to these types of thoughts (or their behavioral consequences) either. We have all done it!

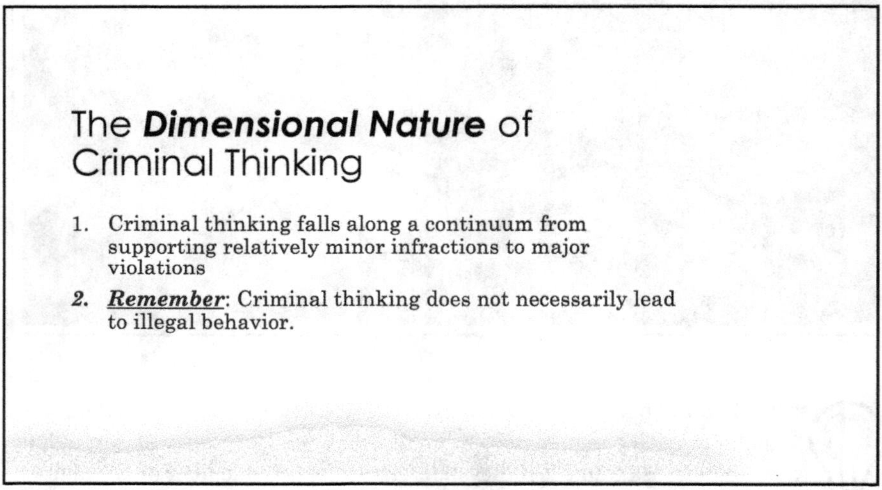

Slide 58 This slide illustrates what this criminal thinking continuum might look like. When the slide first appears, only the bi-directional arrow will be displayed. First ask trainees to think of a few examples of criminal thinking that might fall toward the less serious vs. more serious side of the scale. Click the mouse or keyboard to reveal additional examples. Note, these examples are somewhat arbitrarily placed on the scale but generally move from less serious (and legal) behaviors that are supported by criminal thinking to more serious (and illegal) behaviors. Click the mouse or keyboard again to emphasize that more serious offenses are more likely to result in legal repercussions.

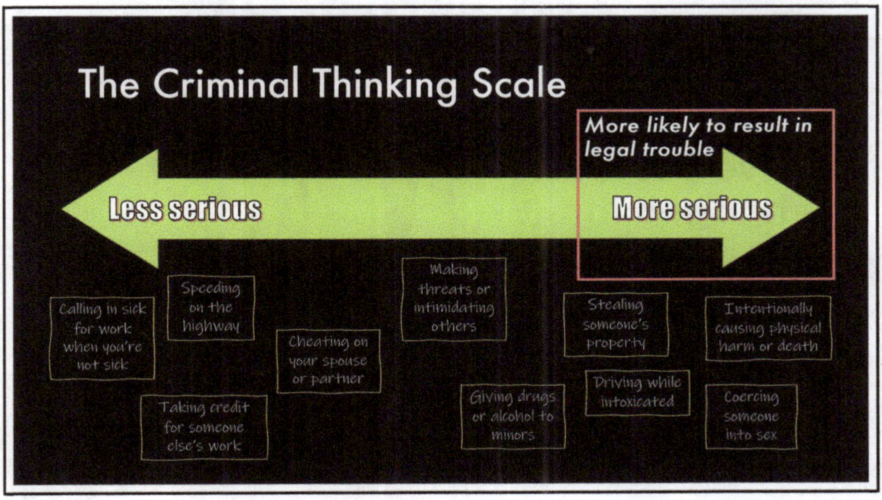

Slide 59 This slide is for the brave souls willing to share a personal example of criminal thinking! In truth, this should be a relatively benign, and potentially humorous, exercise. Trainees, of course, do not need to share illegal activity (or at least not serious illegal activity). There are plenty of low-stakes examples. If trainees are stuck or hesitant, encourage them to share a brief story similar to the examples displayed on the slide (e.g., a time they took credit for someone else's work). In fairness, you should have an example of your own ready-to-share; it may be helpful to kick-start the conversation. This slide is intended to reinforce an empathic understanding of the way people in prison think about their world and the processes that often drive their choices.

Slide 60 While we all engage in criminal thinking, most of us do not primarily rely on these processes to navigate our environment. This is not the case with people who become involved in the correctional system. Their criminal thinking is more engrained, meaning it is more habitual. Engrained ways of thinking and behaving are hard, but not impossible, to change.

Slide 61 As most of the training is focused on techniques that are helpful in addressing criminal thinking, it's important to pause for a moment and quickly review interventions that are not helpful; approaches that are likely to make the situation worse and even put officers/staff in danger. Walk trainees through each of the three ineffective strategies. You may get some resistance about the idea that write-ups or solitary/segregation are unhelpful. Be clear you are not advocating to eliminate these practices entirely; they serve a purpose. As you likely know, punishment is often necessary when the person's behaviors are extreme, dangerous, or they have been persistently resistant to other strategies. Even when addressing criminal thinking with incarcerated persons, a write-up or the use of administrative segregation may be warranted per institutional policies. The point is that we want to reduce the reliance on punishment and continue to have a rehabilitative focus even if punishment is applied. If there's time, ask trainees for additional examples (either hypothetical or from their experience).

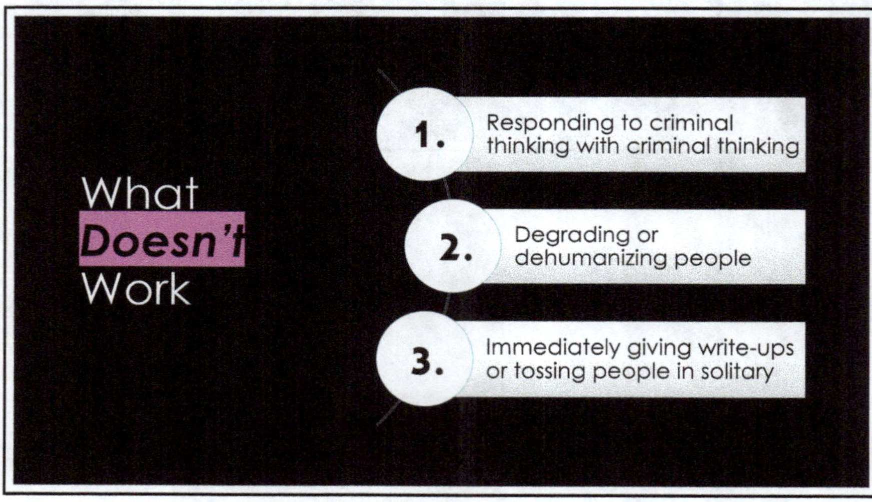

Slide 62 Give trainees about a 10-min stretch break. Encourage the group not to stray too far from the training room.

References

Romani, C. J., Morgan, R. D., Gross, N. R., & McDonald, B. R. (2012). Treating criminal behavior: Is the bang worth the buck? *Psychology, Public Policy, and Law, 18*(1), 144–165. https://doi.org/10.1037/a0024714

Walters, G. D. (1995a). The Psychological Inventory of Criminal Thinking Styles: I. Reliability and preliminary validity. *Criminal Justice and Behavior, 22*(3), 307–325. https://doi.org/10.1177/0093854895022003008

Walters, G. D. (1995b). The Psychological Inventory of Criminal Thinking Styles: II. Identifying simulated response sets. *Criminal Justice and Behavior, 22*(4), 437–445. https://doi.org/10.1177/0093854895022004007

Yochelson, S. & Samenow, S. E. (1976). *The Criminal Personality: The Change Process*.-1985-Xvi, 578 S. Aronson.

Chapter 4
Module 3 Guide

Module 3. Addressing Criminal Thinking

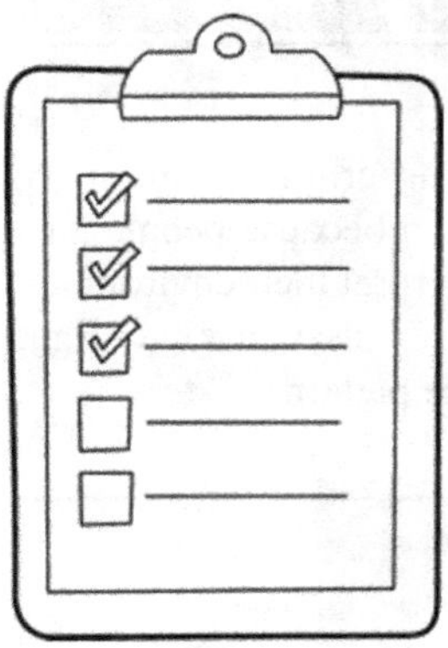

Materials Needed:

1. *PowerPoint Slides 63-93*
2. *Whiteboard or large writing pad*
3. *Blank piece of paper for each trainee*
4. ***Optional:*** *Movie Clip Practice Guide (Appendix or e-Resource 4.1)*
5. *3-Step Desktop Reference (Appendix or e-Resource 4.2)*
6. *Criminal Thinking Rewind (Appendix or e-Resource 4.3)*
7. *Staff Intervention Log (Appendix or e-Resource 4.4)*

The annotations below are intended to help you prepare for the content and discussions related to each slide. Remember, there are also presenter notes within the PowerPoint slide deck to help you along in real time.

Supplementary Information The online version contains supplementary material available at https://doi.org/10.1007/978-3-031-88404-7_4.

© The Author(s), under exclusive license to Springer Nature Switzerland AG 2025

A. B. Batastini et al., *Training Correctional Staff to Recognize Criminal Thinking*, https://doi.org/10.1007/978-3-031-88404-7_4

Slide 63 This is a transitional slide to start Module 3.

Slide 64 This slide helps set the expectation that changing criminal thinking is going to be difficult and likely requires significant repetition because people have been relying on criminal thinking to make decisions and interpret their environment for a long time (perhaps even decades). It isn't going to simply disappear overnight. Your trainees can play a meaningful role in unlearning these patterns.

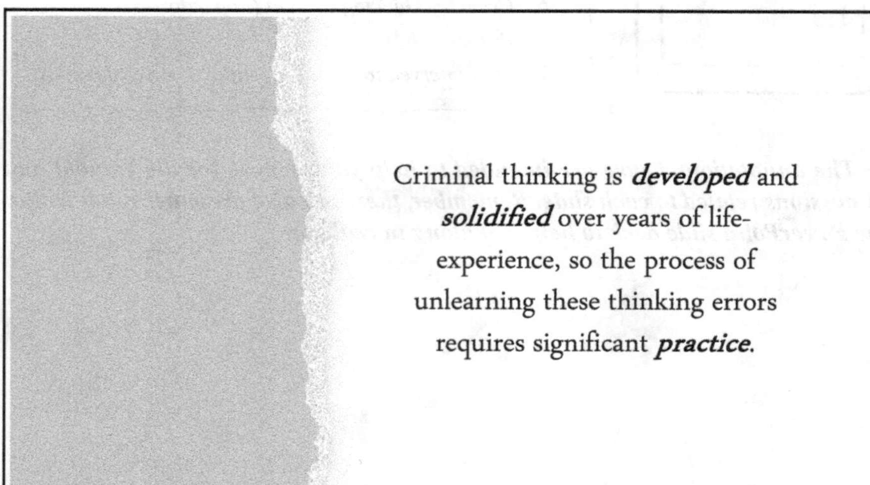

Slide 65 Here, we're acknowledging that criminal thinking has causes or roots that are often not the person's fault. For example, they may have a biological predisposition toward impulsivity, emotional dysregulation, or poorer decision-making skills. Or, they may have learned that criminal thinking errors were acceptable because people in their family, community, or friend groups were relying on these thought patterns. Criminal thinking can also be formed as a response to trauma or a way to survive an environment that is difficult or unfair to navigate. It can also be reinforced when there are little to no consequences for the behavioral outputs associated with criminal thinking. Of course, these causes frequently overlap and it's likely a combination of these causes that substantiates criminal thinking as an engrained pattern. This slide helps humanize the people in our custody by showing that the formation of criminal thinking comes from somewhere; most people aren't inherently bad. We do, however, hold people accountable for the harms they've caused and for making necessary changes.

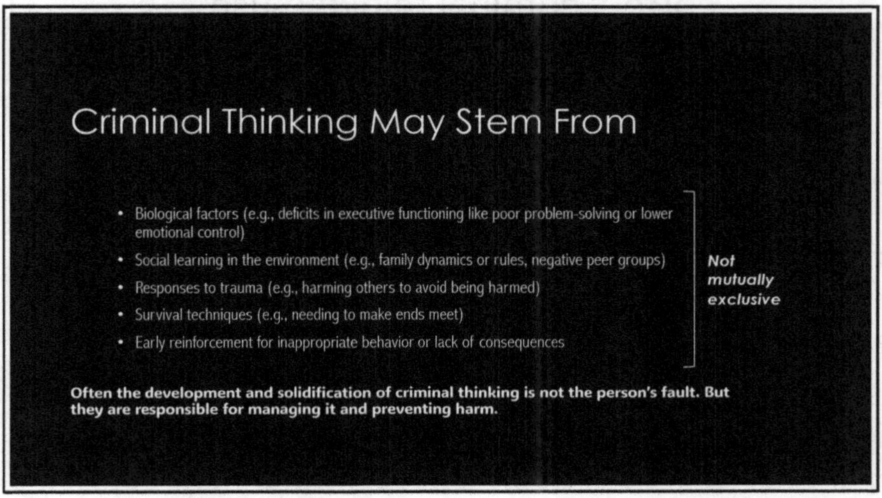

Slide 66 Although there are other theoretical frameworks that can be used to address unhelpful thoughts and behaviors, cognitive behavioral therapy (CBT) strategies are the most effective for clients in correctional settings in reducing recidivism and misconduct (Lipsey et al., 2007). It also makes sense given how criminal thinking is conceptualized (i.e., as a direct connection between cognitive processes and behavioral choices that are often in violation of rules or the rights and well-being of others). Pages 13–15 in this workbook are worth reviewing.

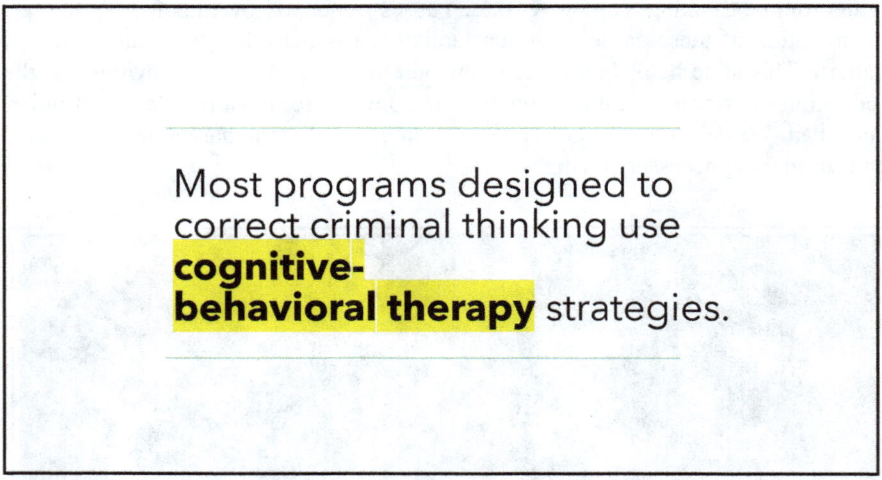

Slide 67 Here, the basic thought-behavior connection is illustrated. It's important to emphasize we sometimes act so quickly that the thoughts preceding our behavior may not be obvious until we spend some time later reflecting on what we must have been thinking at the time. For the people in your custody, we're trying to help them (a) become aware of this connection and (b) slow down the process so they can learn to change their thoughts before they act. If time allows, ask trainees about a time when they had to reevaluate the thoughts that drove them to act a certain way.

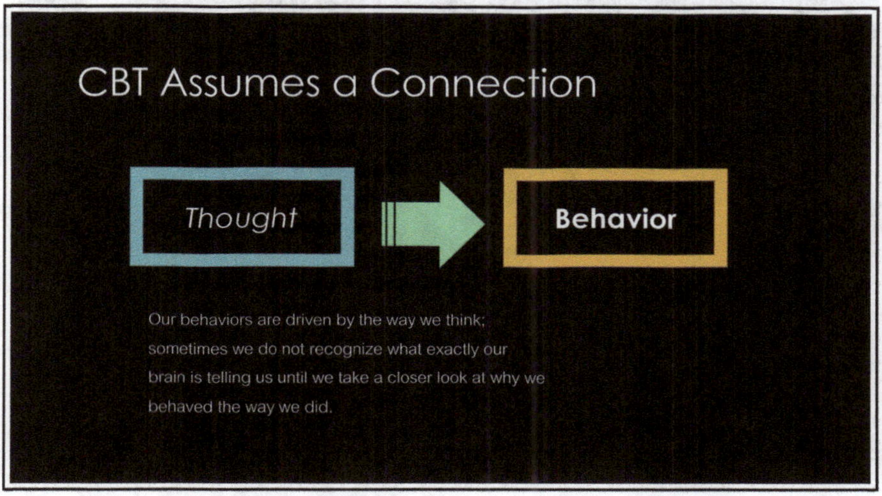

Slide 68 This slide shows an example of how criminal thinking fits into the thought-behavior connection. Again, this is an oversimplified example to get the point across. In a way, criminal thinking functions similarly to other types of maladaptive or unhelpful thought process like depression or anxiety. However, criminal thinking often leads to more significant harm, especially for people living and working in correctional facilities. It may need to be emphasized here that we are not using this model to excuse criminal thinking or its negative consequences; rather, it helps explain the basis of antisocial behavior so we can help prevent and correct it.

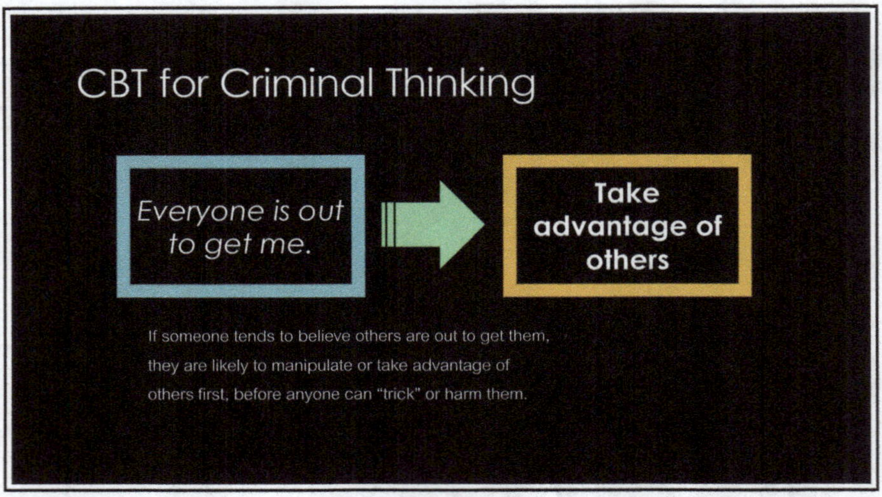

Slide 69 Trainees have so far only seen one segment of the CBT model. However, the thought-behavior connection can turn into a vicious cycle that becomes difficult to break. This slide shows how criminal thinking can be maintained by desirable outcomes or the perception that an outcome was desirable. In other words, people sometimes interpret criminal thinking as beneficial and rely on it more. The example here is an extension of the example that was started on the previous slide.

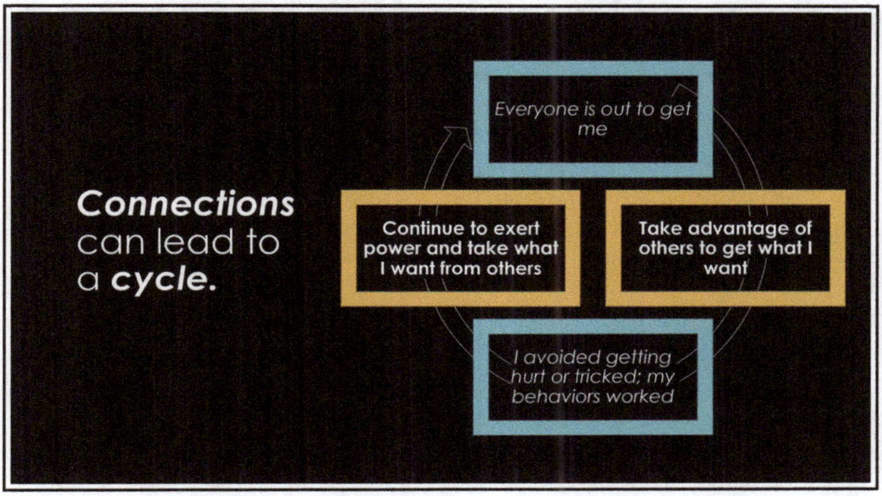

Slide 70 Again, the thought-behavior connection can happen quickly, making it hard to intervene before something bad happens. When thoughts trigger behaviors so quickly that they don't make it into our conscious awareness, they're called "automatic thoughts." Most instances of criminal thinking can be thought of as a type of automatic thought. However, it is important to note that some forms of criminal thinking are calculated and well-thought out. Nonetheless, because the automatic styles happen more frequently and create the most problems in everyday staff interactions, we'll spend some time talking about how these thoughts are addressed in treatment.

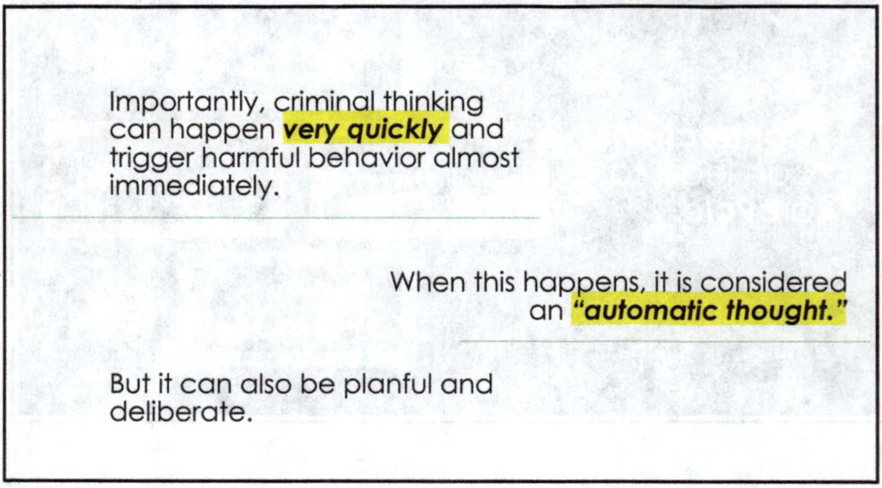

Slide 71 This slide gives more detailed criteria for automatic thinking patterns, which can include criminal thinking. These criteria show how automatic thoughts can develop and how wide-ranging their impact can be. Draw each point back to the examples that were already reviewed for additional reinforcement or ask trainees to help elaborate and offer examples. For example, if we expect others will treat us poorly because we've been treated poorly before (reflecting a core value of "people have bad intentions"), we may be more likely to make impulsive and premature decisions to keep ourselves out of harm's way even if other people are harmed in the process.

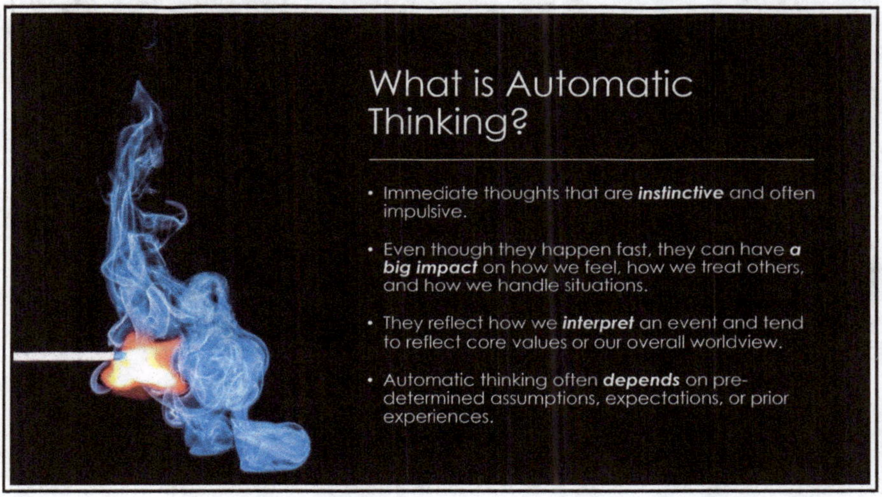

Slide 72 If time permits, provide trainees with a blank piece of paper. If you feel time is tight, simply pose questions to the group for a quick open discussion. You'll first ask trainees to discuss how they'd react, then work backward to process the thoughts associated with the behavior. Working backward will more clearly illustrate the automatic nature of thoughts.

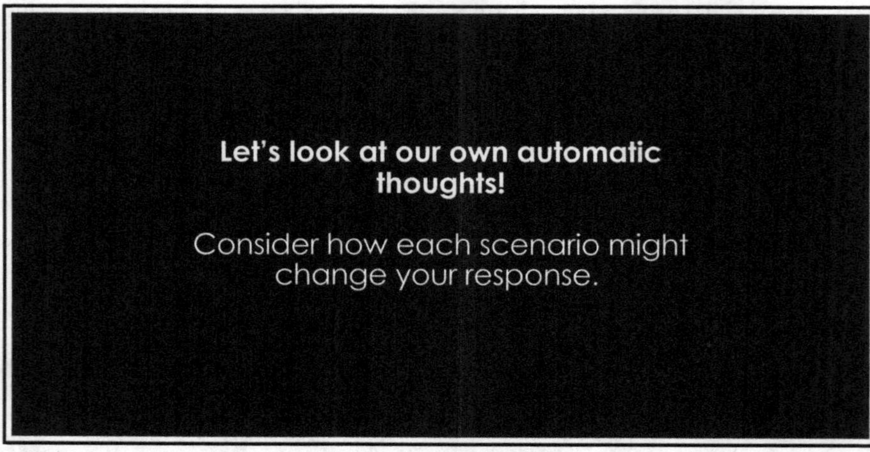

Slides 73 and 74 Slides 73 and 74 are essentially the same scenario except for the context. On slide 73, the individual is another shopper in a grocery store and on slide 74, the individual is an incarcerated person. In most cases, trainees will be more forgiving or more likely to blow off the situation on slide 73 than on slide 74. For example, common responses to slide 73 might include "Maybe give him a look and just walk away" or "I'd say, 'hey, watch where you're going.'" In slide 74, you're likely to get more adversarial or punitive responses such as "I'd write him up" or "I'd grab him and pat him down for contraband." While some of these responses may be appropriate to ensure safety and security, they are nonetheless associated with a different set of automatic thoughts or assumptions, which may or may not be accurate.

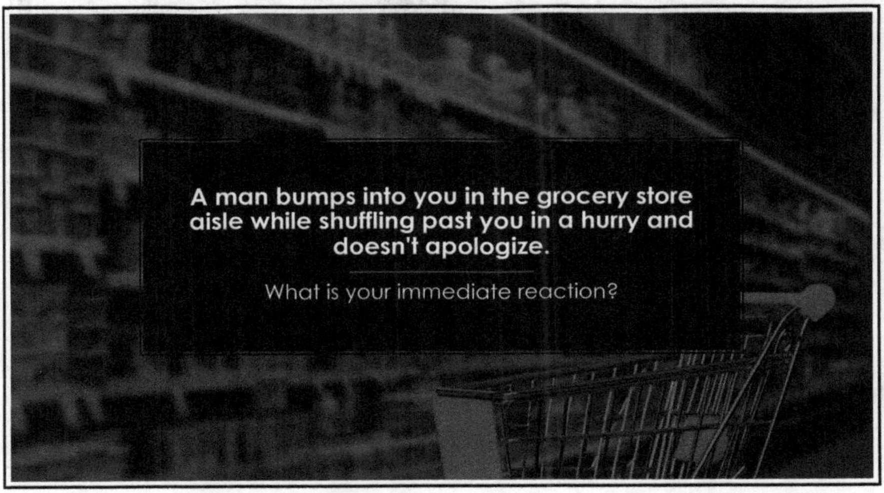

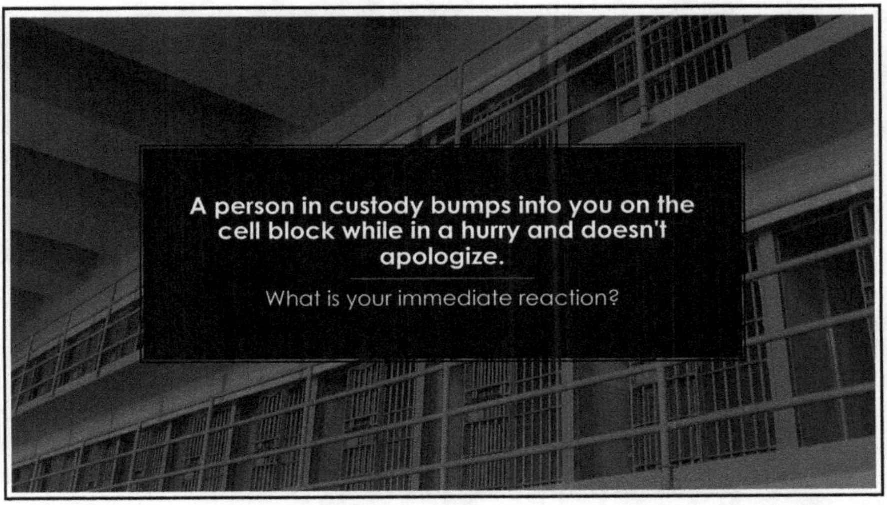

Slide 75 Now, you'll guide the group in a discussion about the differences in automatic thoughts that led to different responses in each scenario. As mentioned in a previous slide, these thoughts are influenced by personal and situational factors. In the first scenario, trainees are likely to make more benign assumptions such as "the person wasn't paying attention," "maybe their kids were waiting in the car," or "they're just rude." In the second scenario, trainees are more likely to talk about explicit bad intentions (e.g., "he was probably just trying to cause trouble") or a deeply engrained character flaw (e.g., "because inmates just don't give a shit about anyone").

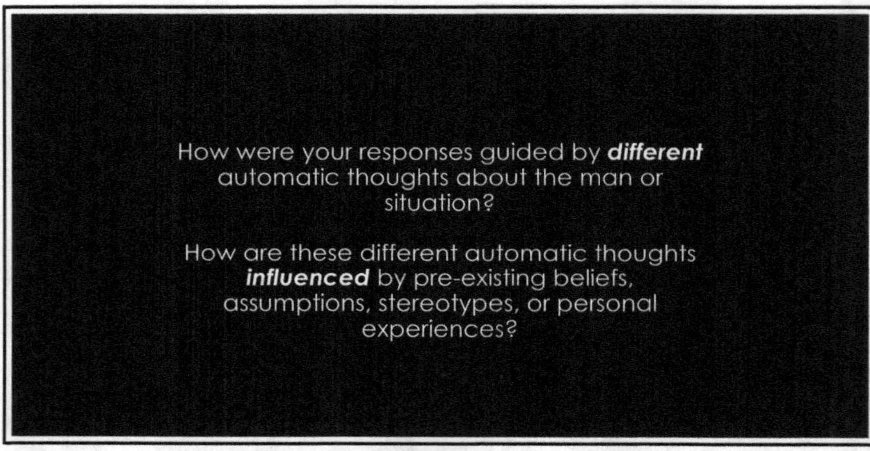

Slide 76 Automatic thoughts are part of a larger process between an event and an outcome. Ask trainees to give an example of a triggering event they might experience on their unit and have them discuss how their own reliance on criminal thinking might lead to a poor outcome. If you have time, you might ask the group to consider how a more positive or helpful thought process could change how the situation evolves.

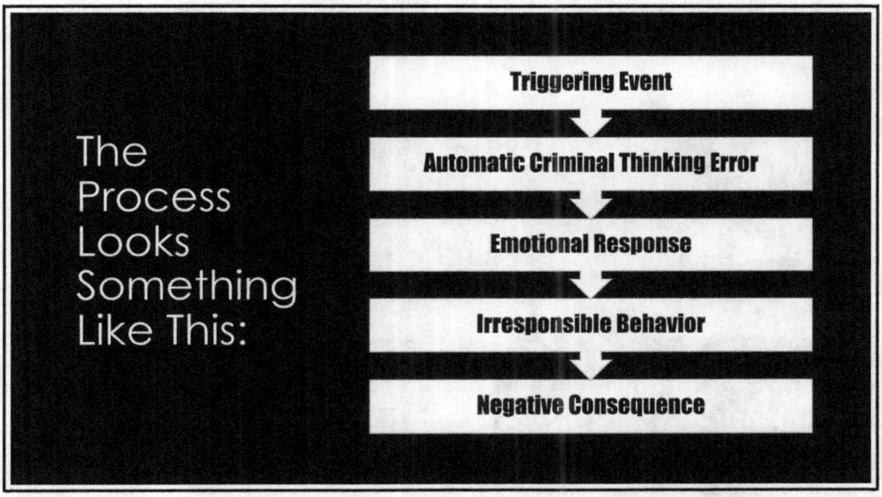

Slide 77 This slide shows several examples of existing manualized programs that address criminal thinking from a CBT framework. This is not an exhaustive collection but will give trainees some understanding of how common this concept is in treatment. This would be a good place to discuss specific intervention programs available in your institution. If you don't know what programs are offered, ask someone in your mental health department or whoever provides these services if they use any CBT-focused programs targeting criminal thinking. You could also invite mental health staff to stop by the training during this portion and summarize programming for criminal thinking and/or prepare a handout you could distribute to trainees.

Slide 78 Here, trainees see the same progression from triggering event to negative consequences as illustrated on slide 76. Trainees can see how commonly available programs work to interrupt this process. You can also revisit the grocery store example to show how a corrected thought process can change the course of a situation. It is important to emphasize that early intervention takes a lot of practice and when clients fail to address their criminal thinking before experiencing a negative outcome, it is an opportunity to critically evaluate what happened and what the person needs to do better in the future to ensure they're using their skills.

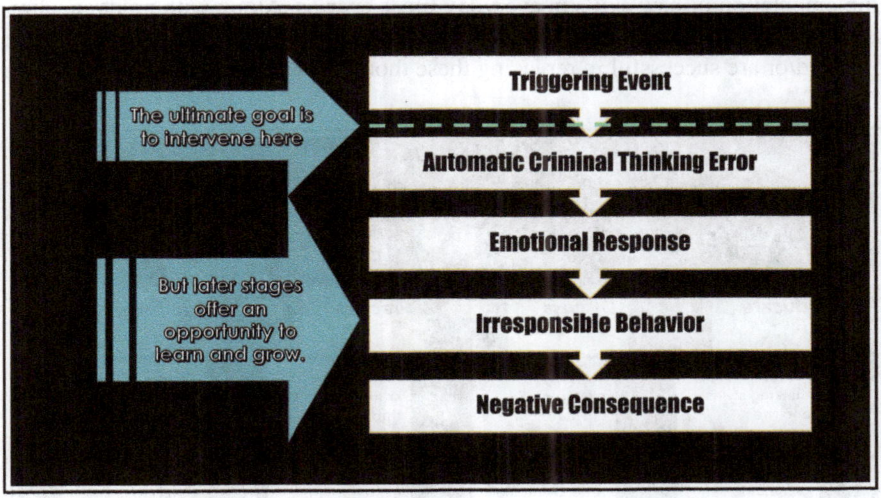

Slide 79 The diagram in this slide shows the typical process of addressing criminal thinking that is used in some form or another by CBT-based programs. Regardless of the name-brand, most programs begin with some basic education about criminal thinking and its role in fueling unhelpful feelings and behaviors that can lead to crime or rule violations. These programs then engage clients in a discussion about their own use of criminal thinking, often using personal examples from clients' lives, and how these thought processes have led to negative consequences. Throughout treatment, clients practice identifying and correcting criminal thinking through out-of-group homework exercises, in-group activities (e.g., role-plays), and implementation of new skills in everyday life scenarios. Along with practice, clinicians continually reinforce clients when they recognize criminal thinking on their own and/or are successful in replacing these thoughts with more productive ones.

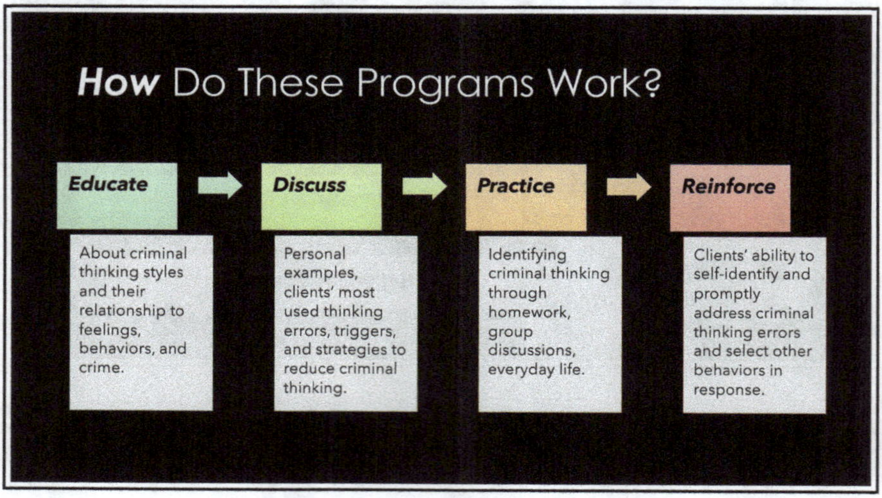

Slide 80 The diagram from slide 79 is depicted again to show trainees how they fit into the primary stages of treatment. By encouraging and guiding on-the-unit practice and providing more immediate reinforcement, officers and other staff can create greater continuity between the CBT skills taught in therapeutic settings and the application of these skills to de-escalate everyday events. Further, all staff are supporting the work of their mental health colleagues rather than responding in ways that may be counterproductive. You may need to restate that officers or other non-mental health staff are not expected to do the work of mental health staff: only to serve in a supporting role. If trainees are wondering "how" exactly they will do this, let them know this will be the focus of Modules 4 and 5.

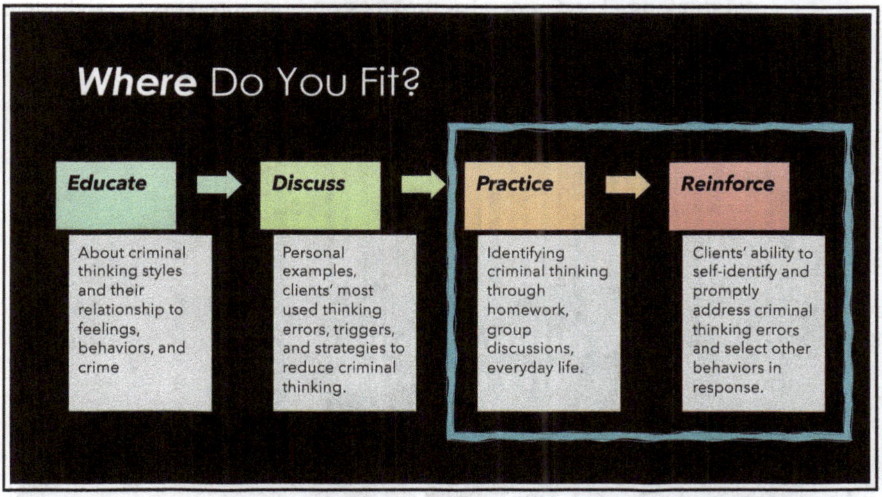

Slide 81 If time allows and the training site has Internet access, you can use the Module 3 Movie Clip Practice Guide to walk trainees through examples of criminal thinking by characters in popular movies. The Guide is primarily for trainer use, but copies could be distributed to trainees for reference. At least one or two of the suggested movie clips, which can be easily found on YouTube or other web-based video applications, is recommended to illustrate how criminal thinking can "pop up" in everyday interactions, even if it's not directly tied to a crime. Alternatively, you can think of your own clips. Or, if the training site does not have an Internet connection, you could describe scenes from these movies or any other films/shows of your choice that depict criminal thinking. The Guide also provides question prompts to facilitate a group analysis of each clip. You may also remove this slide if time is short, or you do not have the means to show video.

Slide 82 Following the movie clips, or instead of the movie clips, have trainees share de-identified examples of behaviors they observed while working in the facility that were likely driven by underlying criminal thinking. Examples could be from incarcerated persons or other officers. Refer to page 15 of this workbook for additional examples if you need help kick-starting the conversation.

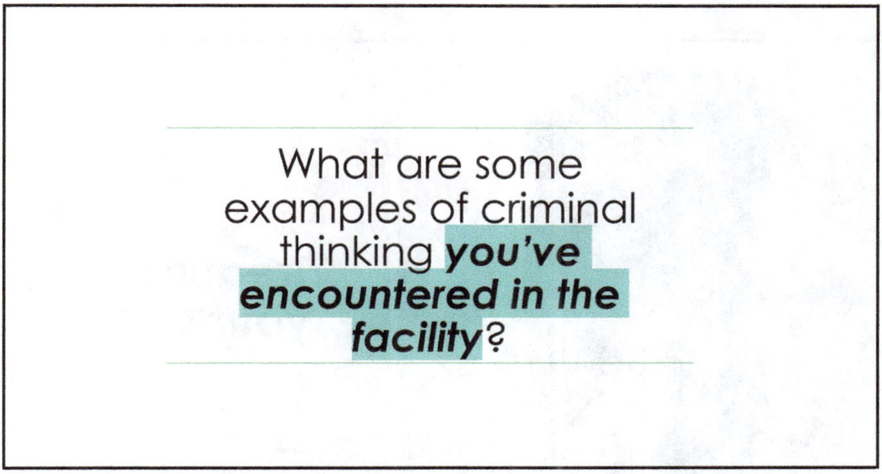

Slide 83 Although criminal thinking is something we all do on occasion, the people who are most vulnerable to these styles of thinking are those who become involved in the criminal legal system. This slide provides examples of the populations for which addressing criminal thinking is likely to be useful. It doesn't matter whether individuals are men, women, high risk, low risk, young, old, mentally ill, or cognitively limited—criminal thinking applies!

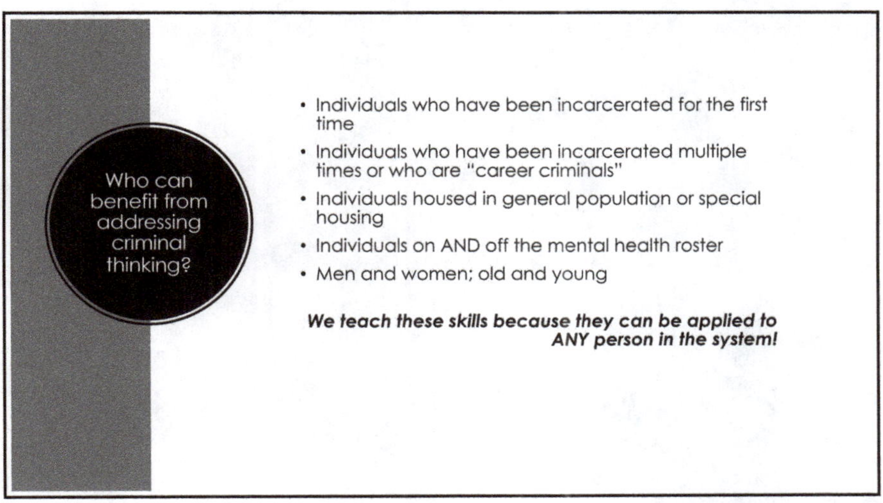

Slide 84 Using a metaphor of treating a common cold, trainees are given a disclaimer that the techniques and strategies they're about to learn and practice may not fit exactly the same way for everyone. Setting this expectation up-front may prevent or at least reduce staff frustrations when a strategy doesn't "land" as smoothly as they hoped. If their efforts don't seem successful with a particular person, they may think back to this metaphor and remind themselves, "Maybe I just need to pick a different medicine or add another type of remedy."

Slide 85 Here, you'll introduce trainees to the basic three-step model for intervening. Refer to page 16 of this workbook for an overview of these steps. A Desktop Reference is included in e-Resource 5 that could be distributed to trainees at this point in the session. The Desktop Reference summarizes these steps and can be visibly placed in an office or unit control center as a daily reminder. This might also be a good spot in the training to preface the repetition of these three-steps. Just as the repetition of addressing criminal thinking is important to change the behaviors of incarcerated people, trainees also need repetition to build muscle memory for these steps. Even if it gets tiresome on training day, that muscle memory will come in handy when staff need to think on their toes, in the moment a criminal thinking error occurs.

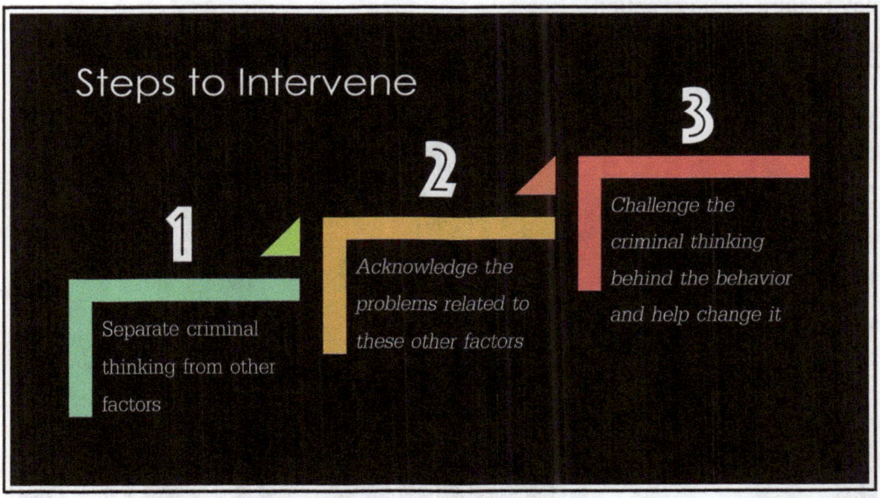

Slide 86 Step 1 differs from the other two in that it takes place before any contact is made with the individual. Staff must first do a mental analysis of the situation and make an educated guess about (1) how the individual is using criminal thinking to justify their inappropriate behavior and (2) what other justifiable factors are contributing to the situation. A reliance on criminal thinking doesn't take away the fact that the person may have a real concern, issue, or impairment. Our job is to help them find more helpful ways to express their needs, which starts by reframing the way they think about themselves, others, and the situation. Step 1 also involves some initial brainstorming about what feasible solutions can be discussed or offered. It's worth emphasizing again (because you may get pushback from trainees) that a solution doesn't mean appeasing the person or giving in; a solution is something that mitigates the current stressor enough to avoid escalation and encourage self-reflection. However, in more extreme cases of violence or aggression, a solution may require punitive action.

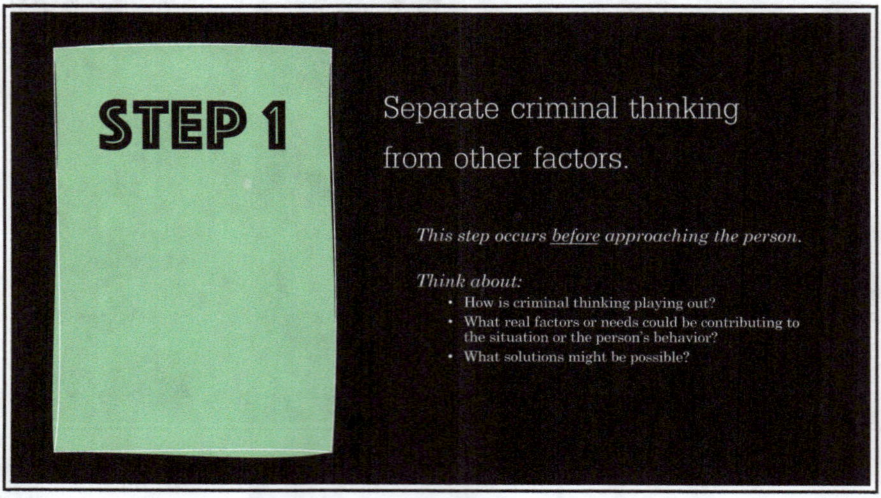

Slide 87 Step 2 is primarily about expressing empathy and concern for the underlying needs of the person, even if their attempt to meet this need is downright disrespectful or nasty (you'll get to addressing that part in Step 3). It may be helpful to acknowledge it is often extremely difficult to maintain composure and find compassion for someone who is acting like a jerk or worse. To improve the chances of having their message heard and being an agent of change, staff must avoid the trap of mirroring the person's attitude, tone, or behaviors. Taking this approach isn't "being soft" or "therapizing" the person, it's merely creating a calmer set of conditions to intervene on the problematic thinking and behavior, and eventually see longer term changes. You might even frame Step 2 as a de-escalation tactic (kind of like a hostage negotiator!).

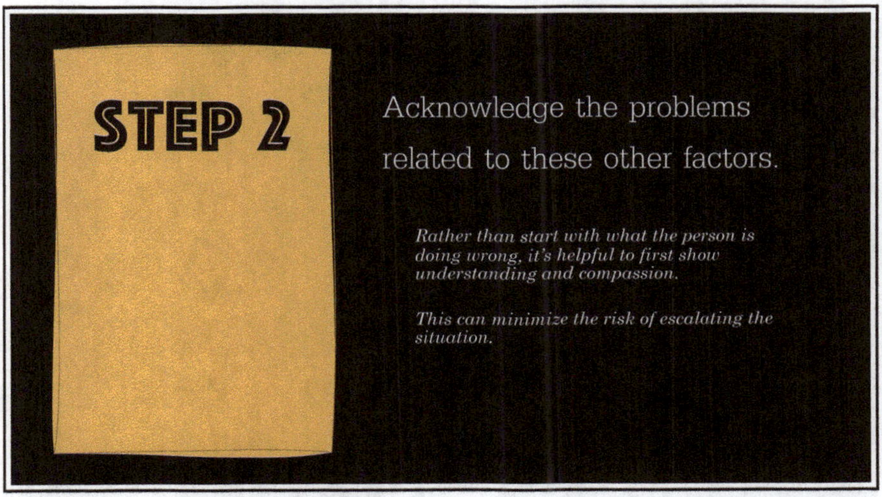

Slide 88 In this final step, individuals are calmly and directly "called out" for their criminal thinking, and attention is drawn to their use of criminal thinking to justify an action that violates the rights or well-being of others. Remind trainees to maintain a calm but firm and direct tone of voice. This step is unlikely to end well if the officer changes from an understanding demeanor to one of anger or disdain. However, this doesn't mean they can't express disappointment, frustration, or hurt. These feelings or reactions may be a natural consequence of the individual's behavior, and they should know that. Step 3 is also where trainees will propose some of the solutions they thought about in Step 1. Finally, emphasize the importance of reinforcement to positive behavior change. Just as you reviewed on slides 79 and 80, reinforcement is part of this process. Reinforcement can be as simple as a "good work today" or "I'm going to let your counselor know how well you used these skills."

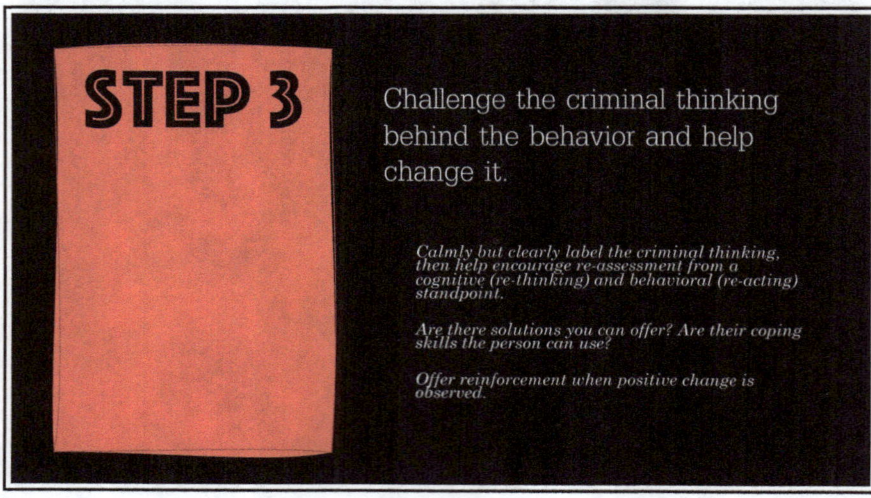

Slide 89 In e-Resource 6, you'll find a copy of a thought log called "Criminal Thinking Rewind." This would be a good time to distribute a copy to your trainees if you haven't already. Or, you may choose to modify this slide so it depicts a thought log used by mental health staff in the institution and provide trainees with a copy of that version. Most CBT-based thought logs are similar in structure and purpose, and it may be more helpful for purposes of continuity to use the same one the person in custody might already be accustomed to. But, it can't hurt to have more options! If staff feel stuck on what solutions to offer, they can have this thought log handy. Depending on their time or comfort level, staff can walk individuals through each step of the log or encourage the person to complete it on their own. Maybe a deal is made whereby the individual can reapproach the staff person or the situation only after they've worked through the log. Remind trainees that individuals should focus specifically on how their criminal thinking got in the way.

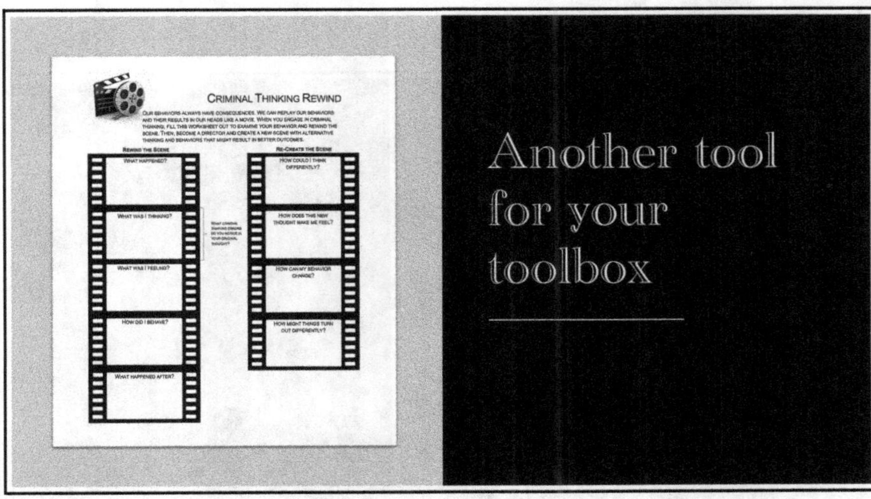

Slide 90 Alright, time to get our heads out of the clouds! You know more than anyone that working with incarcerated people is hard and sometimes we never end up seeing much change no matter how much effort we put in. Often the investment doesn't feel worth the return. You may already be dealing with resistance from trainees by the time you get to this slide, but here's where you can get real and set clear expectations. Intervention techniques aren't foolproof, nor do they work every time. All we can do is our best and hope we reach at least a few people. This slide normalizes feelings of frustration but reiterates the importance of pushing forward. Conclude with a discussion about how trainees cope with work-related stress. Be sure to reinforce healthier coping such as exercise, relaxation, talking it out with a colleague, or stopping for their favorite french fries on the way home. If trainees offer more destructive outlets such as getting drunk or extended periods of isolation (some me-time is okay), ask if those coping skills ever lead to negative consequences and, if so, prompt them to think of other methods that might be less harmful.

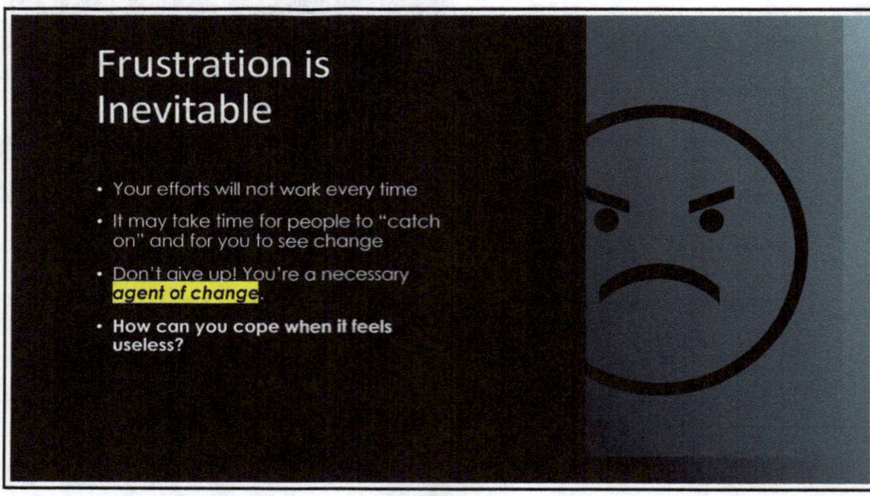

Slide 91 Of course, one way for trainees to cope is to apply CBT principles to themselves! They, too, can work on restructuring their thoughts about the situation to avoid more serious impacts on their emotional or mental well-being (which sometimes translate to physical well-being such as fatigue or muscle aches). This slide shows a few examples of go-to cognitive reframes. Ask trainees to shout out their own examples.

Slide 92 To close out Module 3, this slide and the next highlight the importance of maintaining good and frequent communication with mental health staff about individuals' progress on the unit. This is the mechanism by which the overarching goals of this training can be achieved: to create a more unified responsibility across the institution to facilitate change and greater continuity between everyday staff interactions and mental health programs that teach about criminal thinking. Trainees need to understand this isn't about throwing someone under the bus or being a snitch; it's about upholding a team-based approach to promoting accountability and engendering change. In fact, knowing the situation may be reported to their counselor could be a source of motivation for the person to do better (generally, clients like to make their counselor "proud").

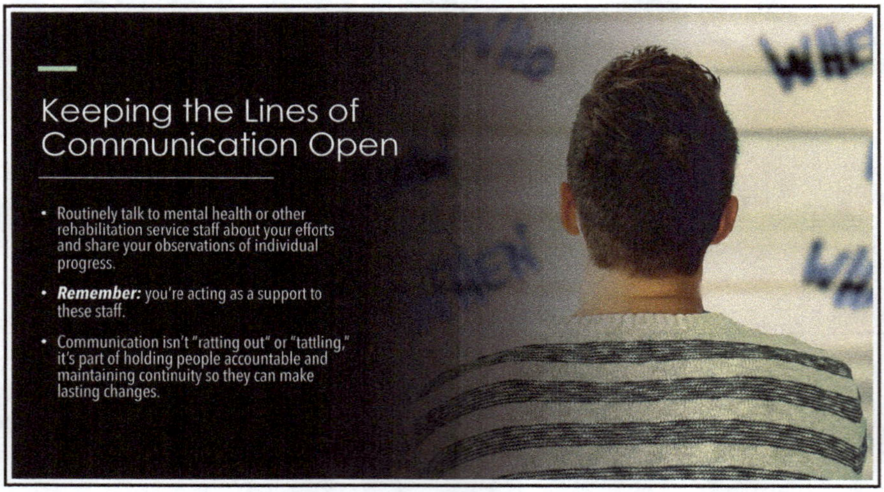

Slide 93 Here, trainees can see an example of how they might log their attempts to address criminal thinking on a daily basis. This log is provided in e-Resource 7. You may wish to distribute a copy of this log to trainees if they weren't already provided copies of training materials at the beginning of the day. You or your facility may also choose to develop your own tracking system. Just remember it should be something simple that doesn't add too much additional strain to daily operations.

CRIMINAL THINKING STAFF INTERVENTION LOG

WHEN YOU CHALLENGE SOMEONE'S CRIMINAL BEHAVIOR, USE THIS QUICK LOG TO TRACK THEIR RESPONSE TO YOUR INTERVENTION.

Date of Incident	Individual's Name	Intervening Staff Person	Summary of criminal thought/behavior	Was there improvement after receiving feedback?	Additional Notes
4/21/2023	Jermaine Johnson (Block C)	Shift Sgt. Miller	Thinking it's ok to raise his voice and step toward staff.	Yes	Mr. Johnson used deep breathing to calm down and completed a thought log.

Slide 94 Time to take a lunch break! This slide let's trainees know it's time for lunch.

Appendices

Appendix 4.1: In the Act Movie Clip Practice Guide

General Instructions While watching each clip, look for instances of criminal thinking or negative automatic thoughts.

Post-clip Analysis Questions

1. How are the characters engaging in criminal thinking? In what ways are they violating the rights or well-being of other people?
2. Did they get what they wanted in the moment?
3. What are the consequences or possible consequences of the character's thought processes in the long run?
4. Could the character(s) have taken a different approach that was less harmful?

Clip 1: Clueless (1995) "Ride Home"

In this scene, Cher, Tai, Elton, and Summer are high school students leaving a holiday party. Based on where everyone lives, the four of them try to decide whether Elton or Summer should take Tai or Cher home.

Behavioral examples of criminal thinking:

- Summer stealing the snowman decoration from the party host's lawn
- Cher forcing her wishes on Elton and Tai
- Elton grabbing Cher to his car when she doesn't want to ride with him
- Elton pulling over the car instead of driving Cher home as she's expecting
- Making several moves on Cher then kissing without her consent and after her clear attempts to push him off

Clip 2: American Psycho (2000) "Break Up Scene"

Scene in which Patrick breaks up with his girlfriend, Evelyn, at a crowded restaurant.

Behavioral examples of criminal thinking:

- Patrick drawing on the restaurant's tablecloth
- Evelyn seemingly caring only about the wedding and not wanting to listen to Patrick
- Patrick bluntly breaking up with Evelyn in a public space without much regard for her feelings
- Patrick wanting to break up to focus more on fulfilling his "homicidal tendencies"
- Patrick aggressively grabbing and pulling Evelyn's hand away when she goes to touch his face
- Patrick leaving Evelyn alone at the table, and possibly to pick up the bill

Clip 3: Bridesmaids (2011) "Reckless Driving"

In this scene, Annie attempts to get the attention of Rhodes (a cop she's been dating but is currently upset with her) while a fellow bridesmaid is in the passenger's seat.

Behavioral examples of criminal thinking:

- Basically, all of Annie's driving behaviors! Speeding, throwing trash out of the window, burning circles, texting while driving, public indecency, bumping her car into Rhode's cop car
- Rhodes ignoring her behavior until she hits his back bumper

Clip 4: Mean Girls (2011) "Sweatpants on Monday"

This scene shows Regina and Cady sitting at the lunch table as Gretchen and Karen walk over with their lunch trays.

Behavioral examples of criminal thinking:

- Cady falsely telling Regina butter is a carb (for those unfamiliar with the premise, Cady is plotting with her nerdy friends to make Regina fat)
- Gretchen criticizing Regina for wearing sweatpants because of how she makes the group "look"
- Regina gaslighting Gretchen and Karen into thinking the "rules" she established don't apply to her
- Regina putting down Karen by calling her skirt "disgusting"
- Gretchen forcing Regina to leave and eat by herself

Based on these examples or others provided by the group after viewing each clip, prompt trainees to consider the post-clip analysis questions above.

Appendix 4.2: Three-Step Model to Challenging Criminal Thinking

A Desktop Reference for Officers and Unit Staff

1

SEPARATE criminal thinking from other factors (such as mental illness, trauma, cognitive ability, maturity)

Think: *"What part(s) of the person's behaviors are rooted in genuine struggles or impairment? What part(s) shows criminal thinking?"*

2

ACKNOWLEDGE their problems or frustrations related to these other factors.

For example, say: "*I know ________ makes this worse and that can be hard."*
Or "I realize you have gone through something really difficult."

3

CHALLENGE the criminal thinking behind the behavior and **HELP** change it.

For example, say: *"The way you are behaving right now is an example of criminal thinking because ________. I don't think it's helping you in the end, so how else can you approach this situation?"*

Appendix 4.3: Criminal Thinking Rewind

Our behaviors always have consequences. We can replay our behaviors and their results in our heads like a movie. When you engage in criminal thinking, fill this worksheet out to examine your behavior and rewind the scene. Then, become a director and create a new scene with alternative thinking and behaviors that might result in better outcomes.

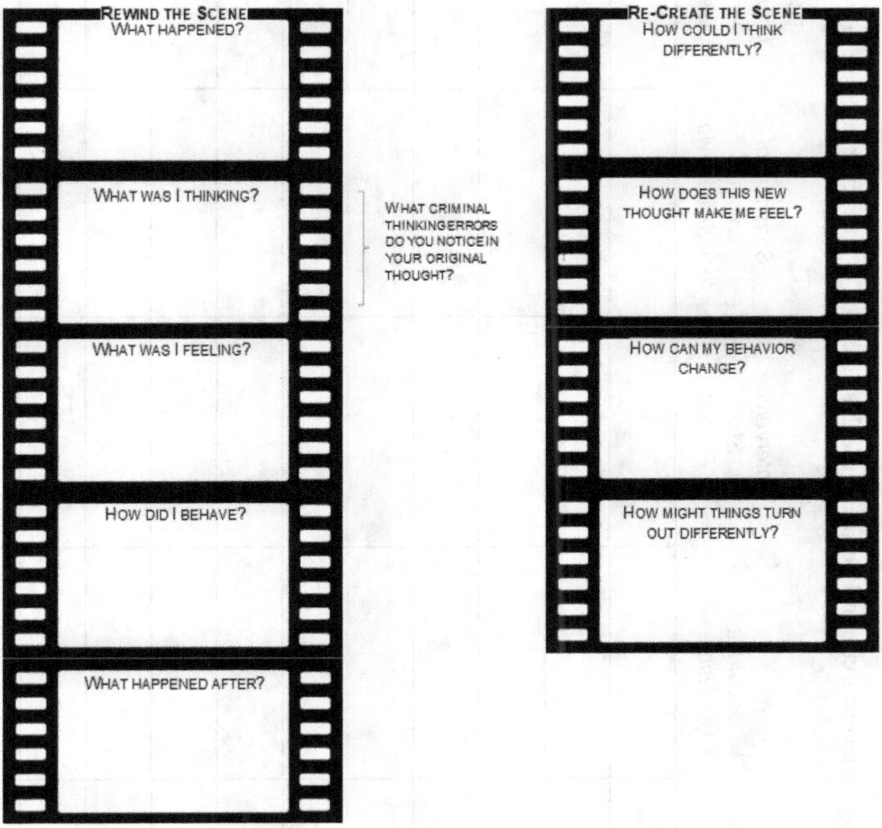

Appendix 4.4: Criminal Thinking Staff Intervention Log

When you challenge someone's criminal behavior, use this quick log to track their response to your intervention.

Date of Incident	*Individual's Name*	*Intervening Staff Person*	*Summary of criminal thought/behavior*	*Was there improvement after receiving feedback?*	*Additional Notes*

References

Lipsey, M. W., Landenberger, N. A., & Wilson, S. J. (2007). Effects of cognitive-behavioral programs for criminal offenders. *Campbell Systematic Reviews, 6*. https://doi.org/10.4073/csf.2007.6

Chapter 5
Module 4 Guide

Module 4. Specific Populations

Materials:

1. *PowerPoint Slides 95-162*
2. *Whiteboard, writing pad, or chalk board*
3. *Blank piece of paper for each trainee*

The annotations below are intended to help you prepare for the content and discussions related to each slide. Remember, there are also presenter notes within the PowerPoint slide deck to help you along in real time.

Supplementary Information The online version contains supplementary material available at https://doi.org/10.1007/978-3-031-88404-7_5.

© The Author(s), under exclusive license to Springer Nature Switzerland AG 2025

A. B. Batastini et al., *Training Correctional Staff to Recognize Criminal Thinking*, https://doi.org/10.1007/978-3-031-88404-7_5

Slide 95 This is the transitional slide to begin Module 4.

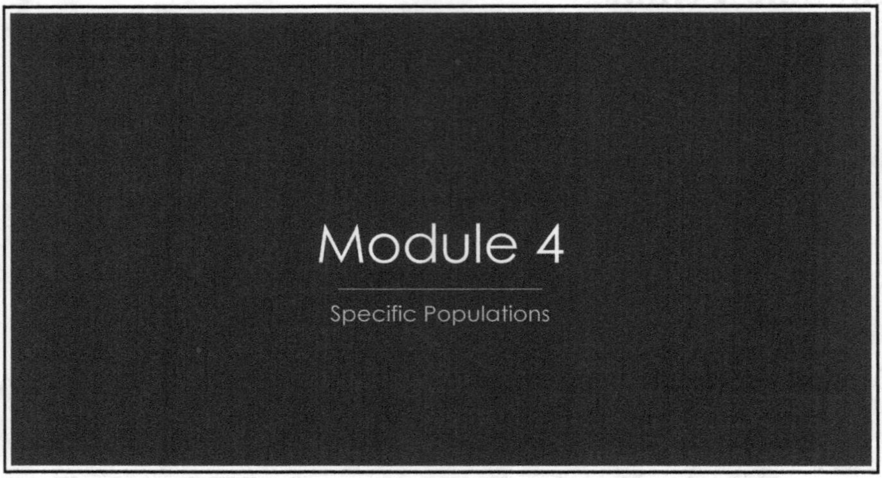

Slide 96 This slide outlines the four unique populations that are subsections within this module. It may be worth emphasizing that, although you will be discussing these groups broadly, there will still be individual differences. For example, not all people with serious mental illnesses present the same way.

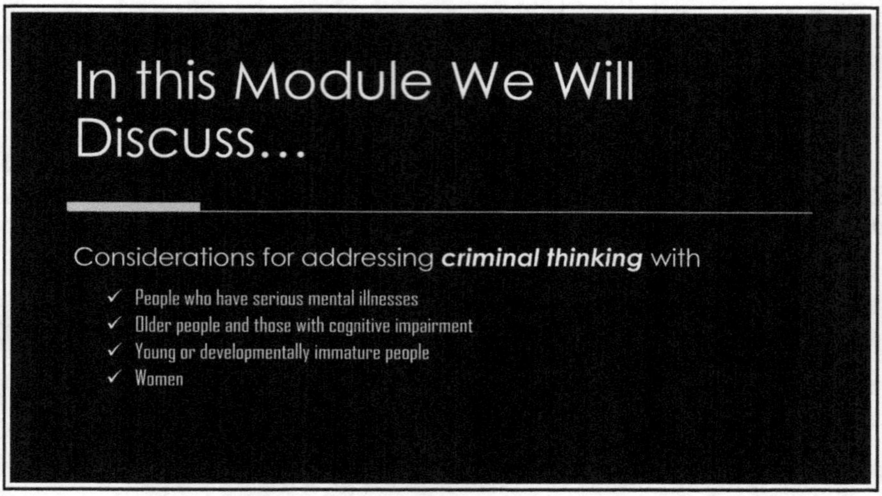

Slide 97 Here we see the general three-step model again as a refresher after the lunch break. Briefly review each step. With some slight tailoring, these same steps will serve as the framework for addressing criminal thinking by each specific population discussed in this portion of the training.

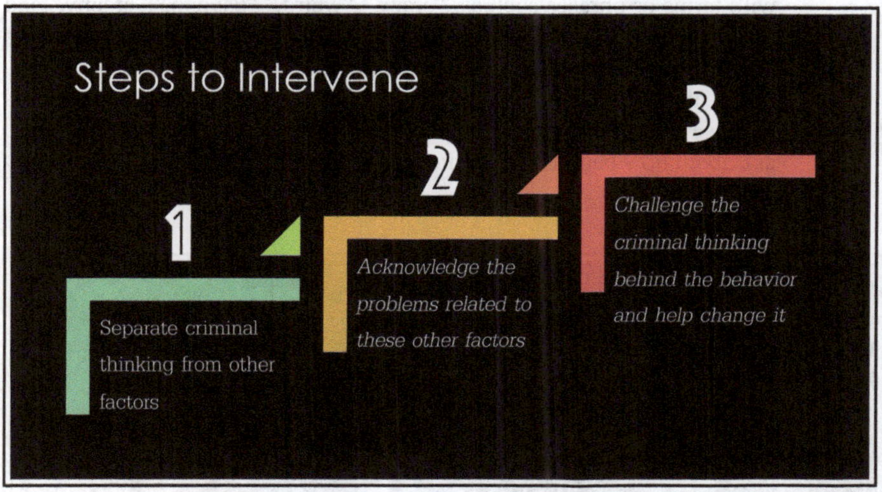

Slide 98 This slide begins the first of the four population-specific subsections. Several initial slides focus on myth-busting to help trainees better understand and recognize serious mental illness (SMI). Especially in correctional environments, signs and symptoms of SMI are often misunderstood and mistakenly treated as intentional acts of non-compliance.

Slide 99 To get a sense of how your group of trainees view people with mental illness and, as a result, how knowledgeable they are about mental illness, prompt trainees to provide candid responses to the question posed on this slide. If trainees have a more superficial or stereotypical understanding, their responses will likely reflect fear, rejection, or avoidance with terms or phrases such as, "crazy," "weird," "psycho," "creepy," and "belong locked up in a loony bin." They may also list infamous criminals like Charles Manson, Ted Bundy, Jeffrey Dahmer, or recent mass shooters in the media. If trainees seem hesitant to offer candid responses because of how they might be perceived, you can modify the question to ask about how people with serious mental illness are typically viewed by society.

Slide 100 The questions from this slide were taken from an actual measure of stigmatizing attitudes toward people with serious mental illness (Link et al., 1999). How trainees respond to these questions will give you additional information about whether they ascribe to some of these attitudes. To show trainees they aren't alone in their beliefs, it is recommended they respond by raising their hand after each statement is read aloud; however, if you think trainees will not answer honestly, you could have them write down their answers on a blank piece of paper. Trainees should say "agree" if they mostly or always agree (i.e., do they agree more than they disagree?). Some trainees may push back after you inform them these statements reflect stigmatizing attitudes, instead arguing they are true for people in prison. You can affirm the need to be safety-conscious while working with people who have SMI and not assume they are necessarily any more dangerous than someone without SMI. Mental illness is usually not the sole reason someone is acting out or is a danger.

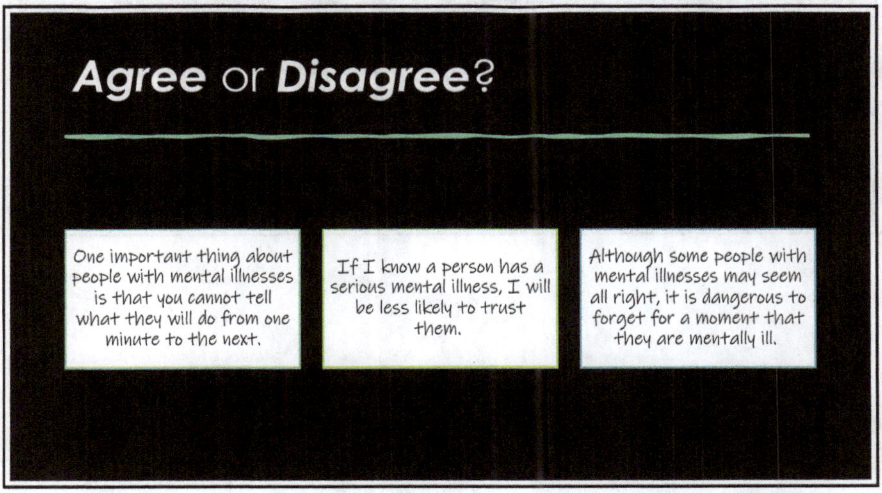

Slide 101 This slide provides the National Institute of Mental Health's definition of "serious mental illness." The important point here is to emphasize that SMI is not just everyday anxiety, mood fluctuations, or a normal response to stress. It is a set of symptoms that leads to significant impairment for the person, meaning their ability to complete tasks, engage with others, and/or perform basic functions (e.g., bathing, following simple instructions) may be seriously disrupted.

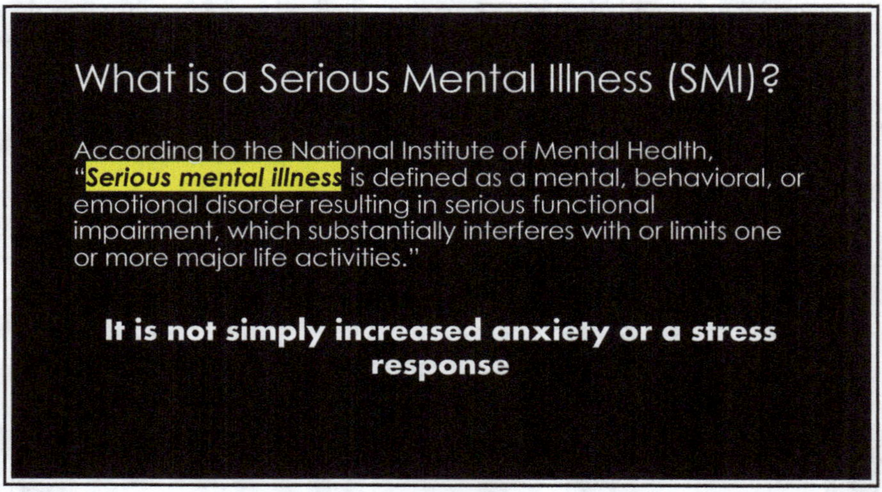

Slide 102 There are many different types and categories of SMI. In correctional settings, the most common disorders tend to be mood-related disorders such as depression or bipolar disorder, post-traumatic stress disorder (PTSD), or psychotic disorders that may include delusions (i.e., odd or unusual beliefs that may have themes of paranoia or grandiosity) or hallucinations (i.e., sensations that are not reality-based like hearing voices). Although in a slightly different diagnostic category, borderline personality disorder (BPD) is also worth mentioning here due to its prevalence among incarcerated populations, particularly women. BPD is also frequently confused with bipolar. Let trainees know you will only be briefly reviewing these categories to improve their awareness; this slide is not a crash course in mental health diagnosis. If time allows, ask trainees for examples of symptoms they've encountered while working with people who have SMI.

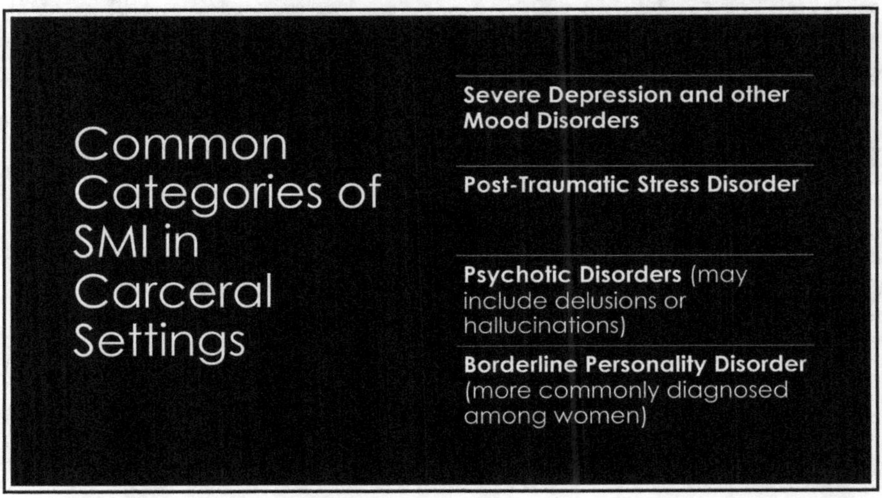

Slide 103 Slides 104 through 106 show trainees several statements about the relationship between mental illness and crime or criminal thinking. These slides are intended to be a group activity with trainees shouting out whether they think the statement is a myth or a fact.

Slides 104–106 For each of these slides, you'll first show and read the statement out loud, pause for audience participation, then click the mouse or keyboard to reveal the answer. All answers are supported by scientific research that has examined the link between mental illness, criminal justice involvement, and/or criminal thinking patterns (Morgan et al., 2010, 2012, 2013; Lamb & Bachrach, 2001). A script is included in the notes section of each PowerPoint slide to help explain the rationale for each answer. Be careful—slide 106 is a bit tricky!

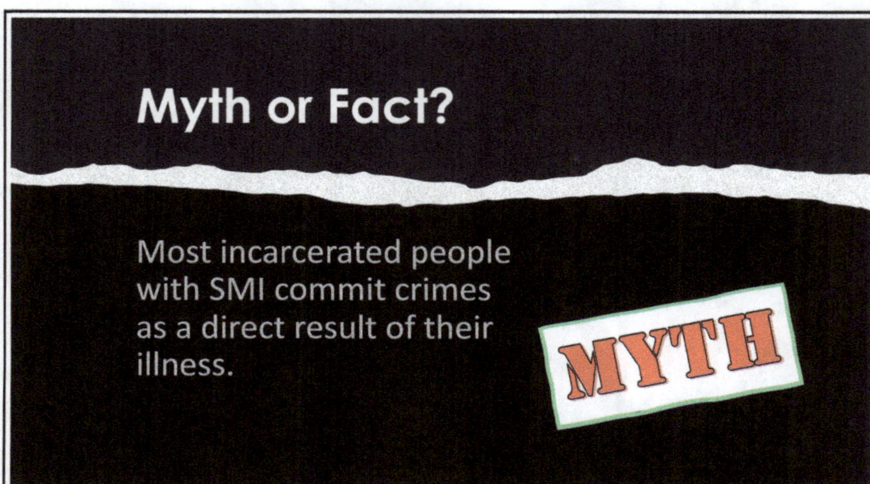

Myth or Fact?
Incarcerated people with SMI can express criminal thinking just like incarcerated people without SMI.
FACT

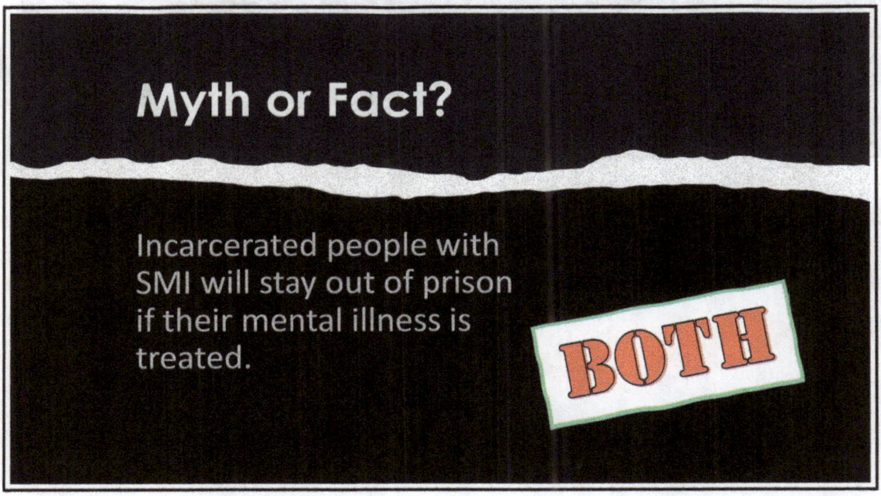
Myth or Fact?
Incarcerated people with SMI will stay out of prison if their mental illness is treated.
BOTH

Slide 107 Criminal thinking may present itself differently among people with SMI than people without SMI. As a result, it may be harder to spot. Addressing criminal thinking with this group must also be approached delicately because we don't want to misclassify genuine issues associated with SMI as criminal thinking; on the other hand, we don't want to excuse criminal thinking just because the person has SMI. The slides that follow give more guidance about how to strike this balance.

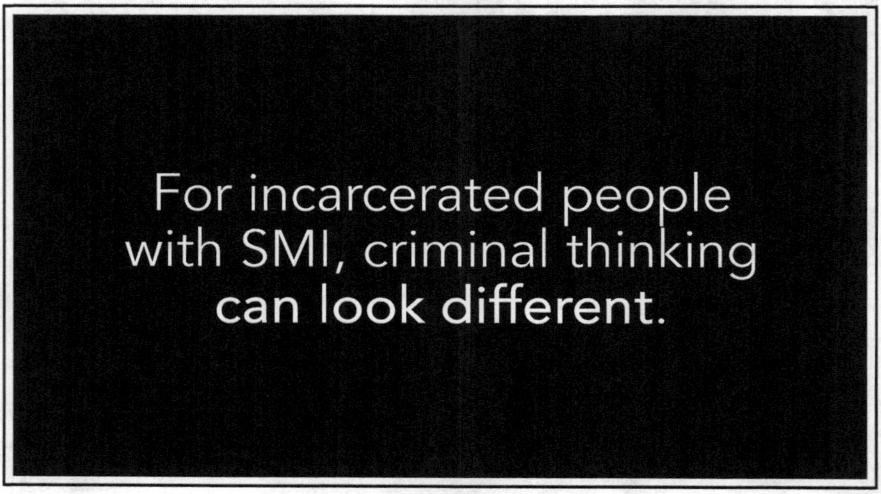

Slide 108 These are just a few examples of how criminal thinking may present in the context of mental illness or symptom management. Have trainees discuss how each example reflects criminal thinking. Remind them to consider how these behaviors show irresponsibility and/or violate the rights or well-being of other people. For example, when people blame others for their illness, they give themselves permission to ignore aspects of their illness they can control while expecting other people to take on their resentment or deal with other consequences of their untreated illness. It's less work to feel angry toward another person than to change our own mindset or behaviors! Even if someone else contributed to the onset of a mental illness, which is often the case with PTSD, people can choose to process what happened to them and cope. We can help people modify their thought processes from, "I can't help that I have a mental illness so why should I have to waste my time in treatment?" to "I know it's not my fault I have these problems, but I don't deserve to keep suffering."

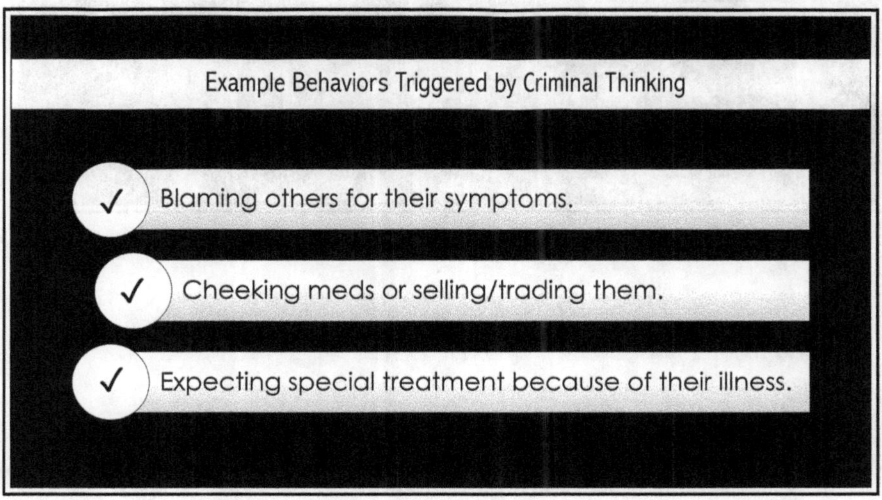

Slide 109 As depicted here, the three-step model is applied specifically to individuals with serious mental illness. In fact, any time you see these three-steps in Module 4, the steps will be essentially the same except that we're interchanging the specific problem or circumstance that needs to be separated from the person's criminal thinking. For those with mental illness, trainees will learn to separate genuine needs related to their illness or symptoms from their approach to addressing these needs rooted in criminal thinking.

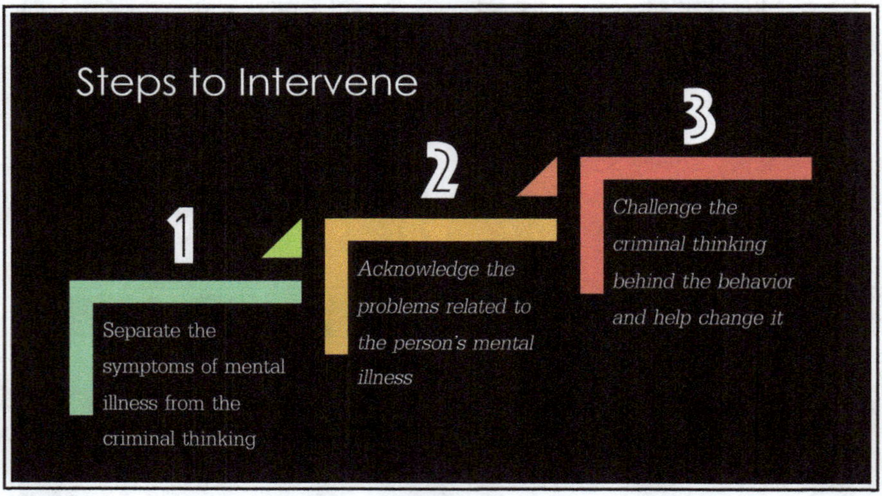

Slide 110 For Step 1, staff are simply attempting to differentiate between the genuine mental health need and the criminal thinking error. Remember, a reliance on criminal thinking doesn't necessarily mean the person doesn't have a real problem or challenge. For example, someone who checks their medications may be doing so, in part, because they find their side effects intolerable. However, instead of requesting to see their prescribing doctor to adjust their meds, they choose to stop taking them altogether and sell them for commissary money. They're not only putting themselves at risk but are also introducing contraband onto the unit. By understanding both can occur at the same time, staff can address the irresponsibility while not dismissing the person's problems. Recall that Step 1 takes place before the staff member engages with the individual.

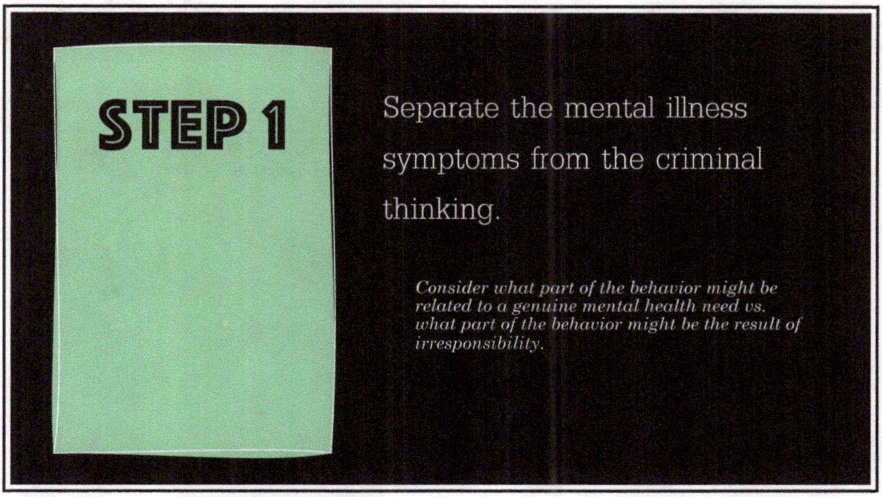

Slide 111 This story of Damon will facilitate a discussion about how to separate real needs from criminal thinking. Have someone first read the scenario to the group or you may choose to read it aloud. You'll then engage trainees in an open dialogue about which aspects of the story highlight an actual need related to Damon's mental illness and which aspects highlight his criminal thinking. Damon seems to have a genuine need to talk with a mental health provider given his change in mood. However, even though he properly asked to see someone, he grows impatient and starts threatening to flood his cell thinking this might speed up his request. He fails to consider the direct health risks to the officers, not to mention the fact that his behavior is likely to prolong his ability to see someone even further. To further put this step into practice, you could ask trainees if they ever encountered a similar situation and how they would have separated the mental health need from the criminal thinking in that case.

Slide 112 Now that we've identified the issues associated with the person's mental illness and separated them from their criminal thinking, we can acknowledge these distinctions when engaging with the individual. In Step 2, we're focused on acknowledging the needs or barriers related to mental illness. Doing this first (before addressing criminal thinking) will reduce the likelihood of an adversarial outcome, as it communicates a sense of understanding about their personal experience rather than jumping immediately to what they did wrong.

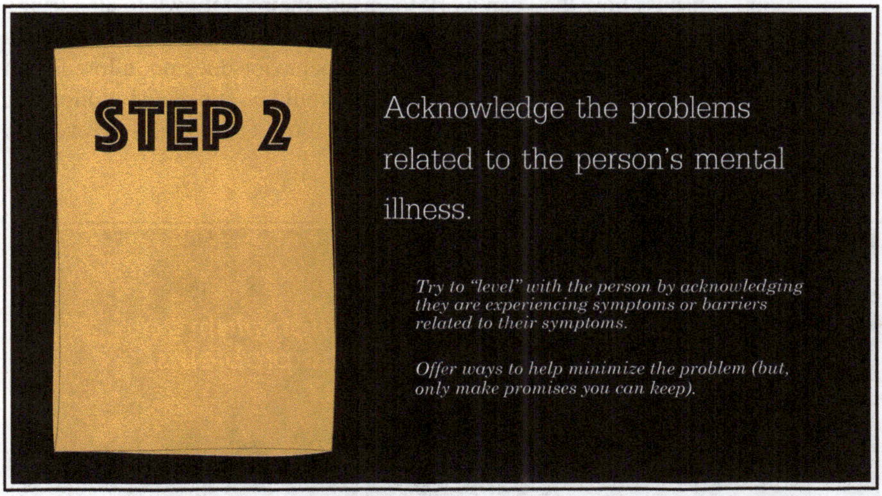

Slide 113 Returning to the story of Damon, help trainees come up with potential responses that acknowledge Damon's concerns associated with his mental illness and the understandable frustrations he's feeling about not being seen after multiple requests. Prompt trainees to first offer their own responses. How can they not only recognize Damon's struggles but also offer assistance within their authority? Given that Damon is threatening to flood his cell in his effort to increase the urgency of his request, trainees may default to more punitive options or be resistant to "talking it out." Discuss how they can work to ensure their safety while also trying a more conflict-resolution-oriented approach first. Why risk escalating a situation further? Of course, if Damon's behavior does not allow for an officer to approach him safely, the officer would be expected to follow the protocol of the institution. Then click the mouse or keyboard to reveal an example response.

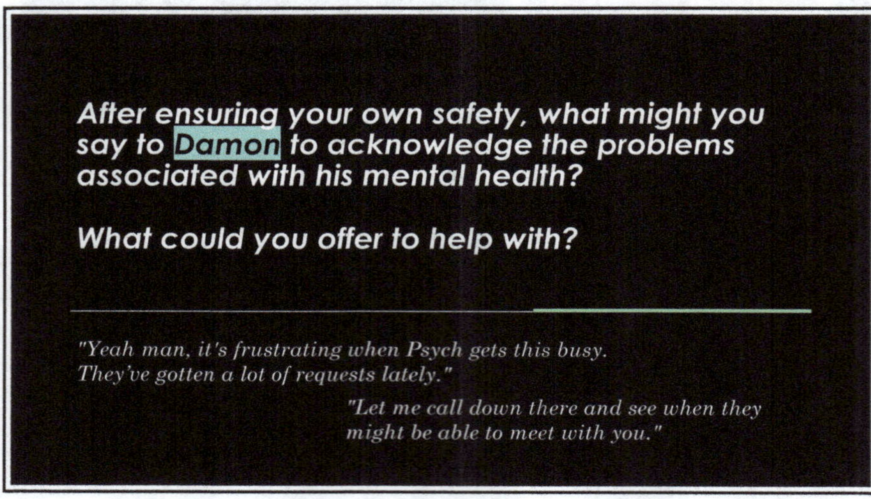

Slide 114 Trainees may get "stuck" in the moment when trying to think of what to say during Step 2. This slide provides some templates to keep in mind. Once you read the template, you'll click the mouse or keyboard to reveal an example statement. If you want, you can ask trainees to develop their own go-to template. This would be a good place to remind trainees about the Desktop Reference they can also use when they're unsure how to respond.

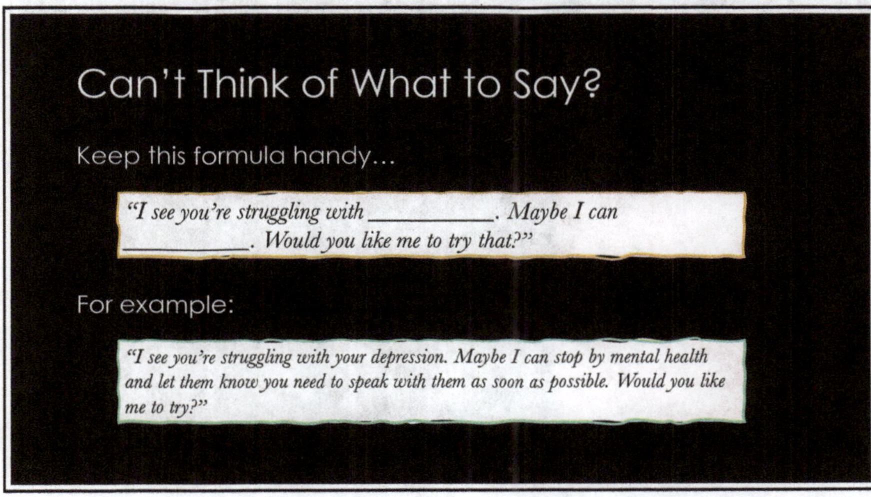

Slide 115 As before, Step 3 is where we'll directly, but therapeutically, challenge the criminal thinking driving the person's poor behavioral choices, even if those behaviors may be related to the person's mental illness; for example, someone with Attention Deficit-Hyperactivity Disorder (ADHD) has more difficulty with impulse control. Mental illness does not excuse criminal thinking or the behaviors that result from it.

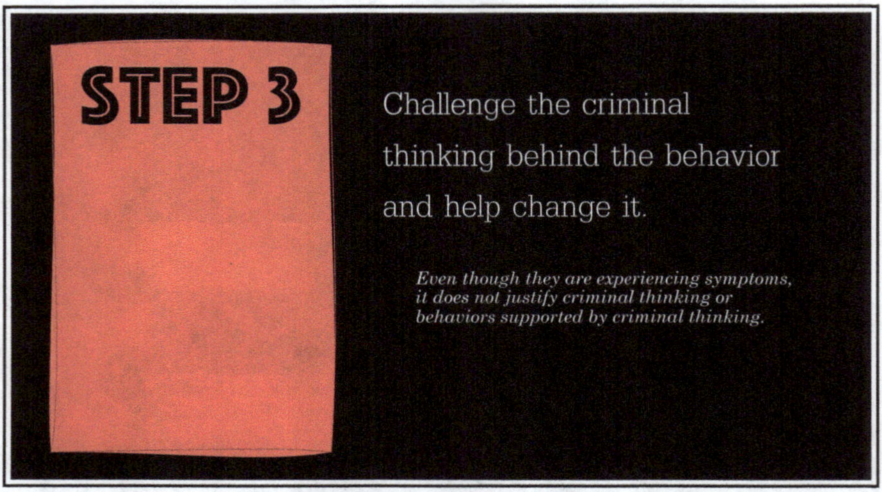

Slide 116 This slide includes a few examples of how to show empathy for the person's mental illness while calling out behaviors reflective of criminal thinking. Once you review these examples, ask trainees to provide real-world examples from their work on the unit and have them talk through ways they might have applied Step 3. Taking each example a step further, you could also prompt trainees to think about how they would encourage the person to reframe their thoughts and choose a different behavioral response.

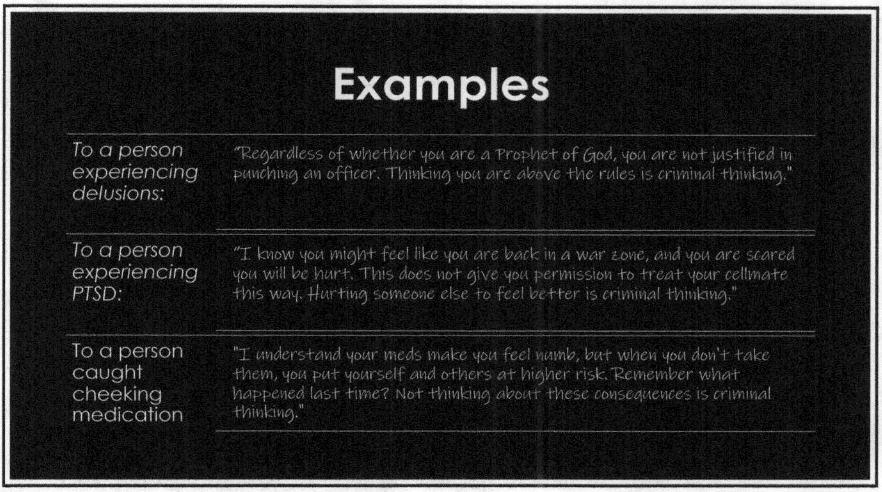

Slide 117 The amount of time you spend on this slide will depend on how much time you can spare. If you're falling behind schedule or right on schedule, this slide may be more transitional with the purpose of reorienting trainees to the Damon story. If you have more time, you could engage trainees in a group discussion, break trainees up into pairs or smaller groups to brainstorm ideas or facilitate a role-play exercise.

Slide 118 Here's an example of what the three-steps might look in action for Damon and his situation.

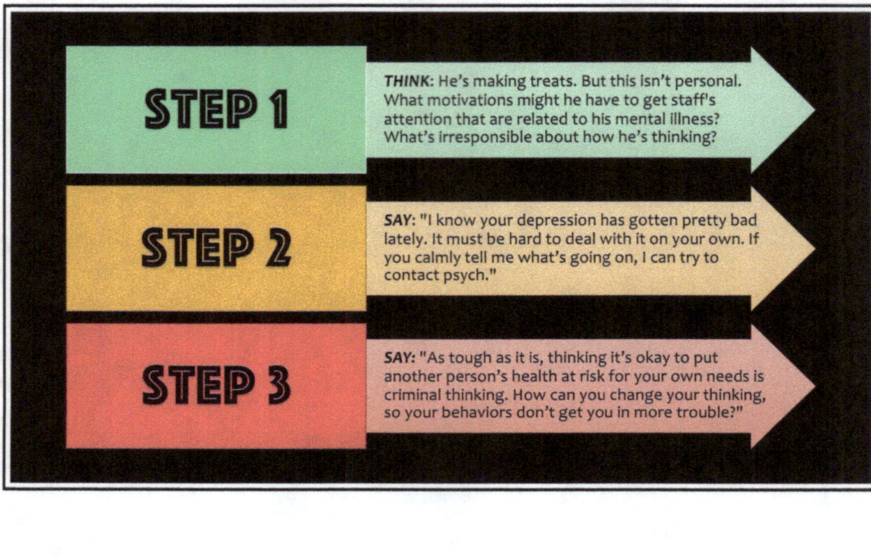

Slide 119 In wrapping up the focus on people with serious mental illness, it is worth warning trainees about the risks of challenging someone on their psychiatric experiences. Especially for people who are not reality-based (e.g., expressing paranoid beliefs or hearing voices), arguing about whether their experiences are real or not will not be productive. That's because these individuals may fully believe their experience is true even when there is compelling evidence to the contrary. Therefore, attempting to correct people on their experiences is likely to create further frustration or agitation rather than effectively solving any problems. Likewise, it's almost never a good idea to tell someone their experiences are over-exaggerated or fake. Even if they aren't being honest about their experiences, being confrontational is likely to escalate the situation. Mental health staff can often use assessment or testing tools to determine the veracity of someone's mental health symptoms. So, a referral for further evaluation might be a better option than challenging the person in the moment.

Slide 120 This is a transition slide to introduce the next unique population: older individuals and those with cognitive impairment.

Slide 121 To better conceptualize what is meant by "cognitive impairment," this slide provides the definition used by the Center for Disease Control (CDC). You may want to visit the CDC's website to ensure this definition is up to date. Remind trainees that, while cognitive impairment is common in older adults, younger people can have serious impairments as well (e.g., if they have an intellectual/developmental disorder or endured a traumatic injury to the head) and many older adults do not show signs of cognitive impairment. Natural cognitive decline due to aging, such as increased forgetfulness, is not necessarily the same as cognitive impairment.

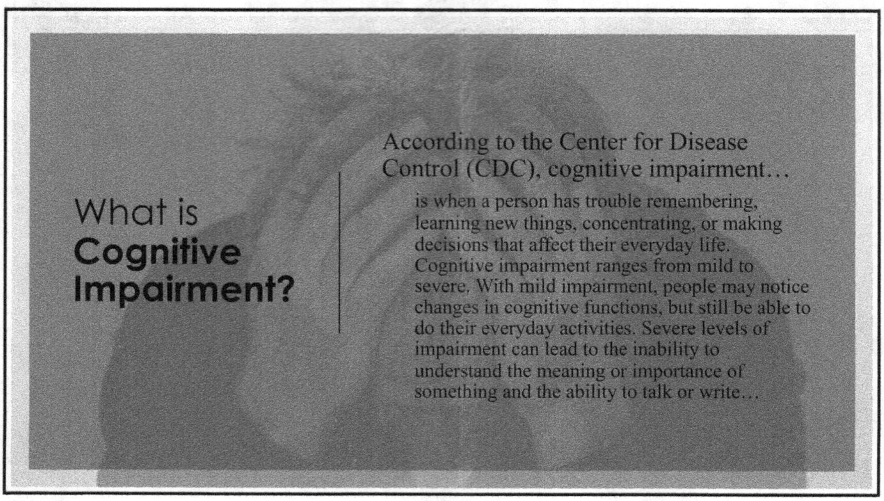

Slide 122 Serious impairments in cognitive functioning can stem from many different neurological conditions including intellectual or developmental disorders, learning disorders, dementia (including Alzheimer's), and traumatic brain injuries. Sometimes these conditions occur because of organic changes to the brain or external factors. This is not an exhaustive list and many other mental health conditions can produce difficulties with cognitive functioning such as ADHD, major depression, substance use disorders, or psychotic spectrum disorders. Briefly ask trainees about any personal experiences they are willing to share related to these conditions. You may prompt trainees to discuss any difficulties interacting with persons who have significant cognitive impairment and/or how they cope.

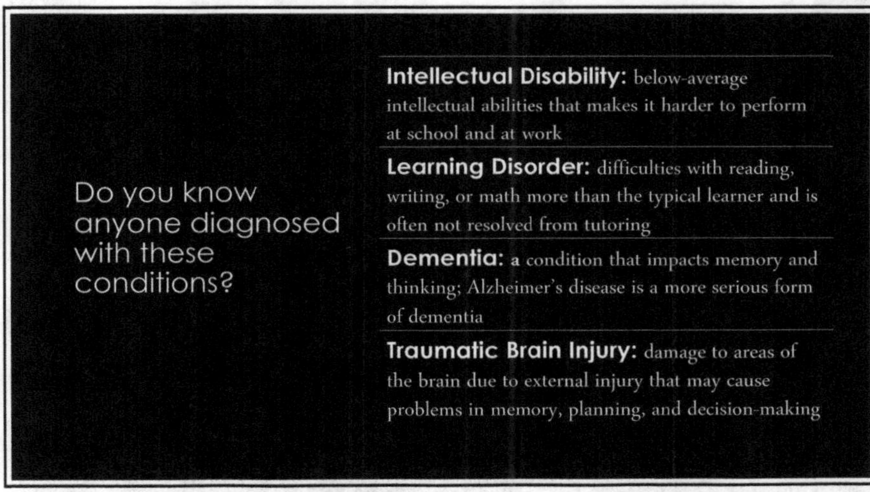

Slide 123 This slide provides several behavioral examples that reflect some degree of criminal thinking. Have trainees consider how these behaviors violate the rights or well-being of others and/or avoid responsibility-taking, and what thoughts may have preceded the behavior. If time allows, prompt trainees to share a few examples of their own.

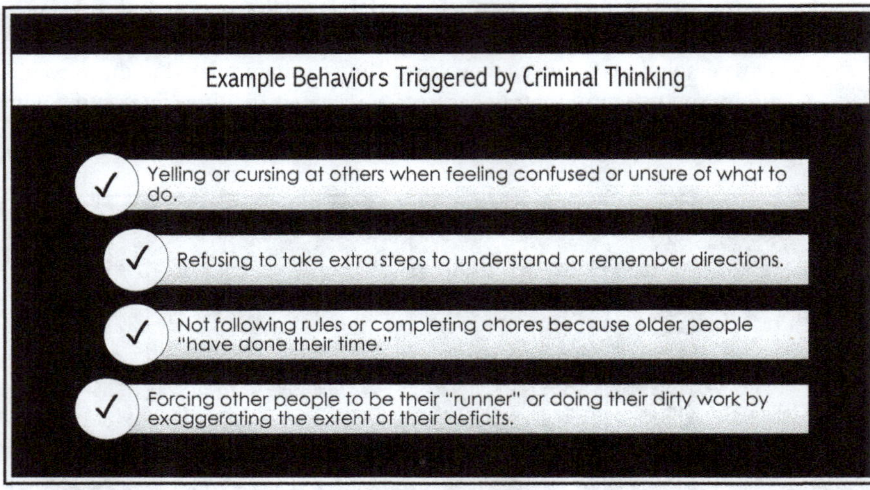

Slide 124 The three-step model is shown here with a minor change: "mental illness" has been replaced with "cognitive impairment."

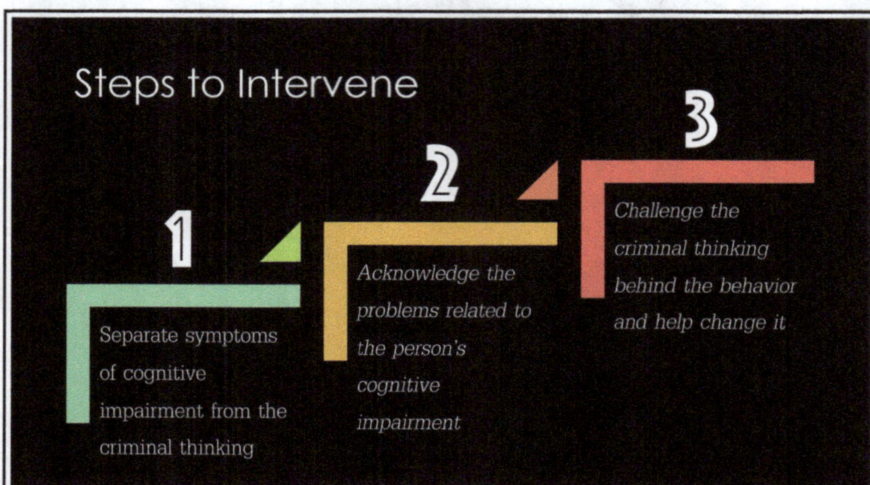

Slide 125 Separating genuine cognitive deficits from criminal thinking can be inherently challenging. Remind trainees they may not always be able to clearly tease these issues apart, but they are likely to achieve more productive outcomes if they at least pause to consider how cognitive issues may be directly impacting a person's ability to make good decisions or control their behavior. However, cognitive impairment doesn't mean a person is completely helpless or unable to perform certain tasks. For example, most people benefit from daily routine and structure. To aid in differentiating impairment from criminal thinking, it may help to reflect on what the person is typically able to do and/or whether their current behavior "fits" how they'd be expected to behave given what is known about their condition and common symptoms.

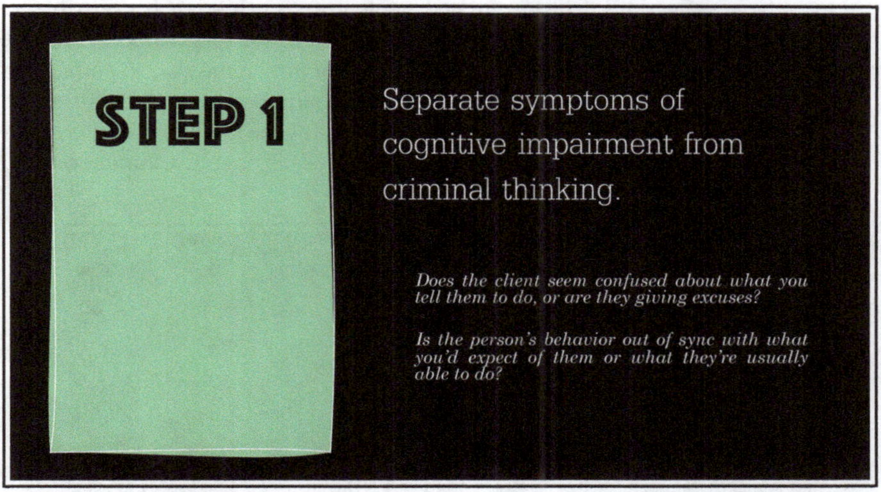

Slide 126 This slide introduces the story of Aiden. Like Damon in the section on mental illness, Aiden's story will be recurrent as you walk trainees through the three-step model. To apply Step 1, trainees should think about what part(s) of Aiden's behaviors might relate to his cognitive limitations and what part(s) might relate to criminal thinking. For example, while he is often forgetful and it's possible his impairment has declined such that he really did mistake his shower time, it's more likely he knew his behavior was wrong given how much exposure he's had to the shower schedule. As someone with more cognitive difficulties, his increased vulnerability on the unit may have also contributed to his desire to shower while others were locked up. Often people with these limitations are aware they can be targets for victimization or bullying. Nonetheless, his decision created a potential security risk. It's possible he leaned into his known impairments as an excuse to get out of trouble. This is something that may have worked for him in the past so perhaps he came to believe he'd get away with it (thinking others are too stupid to catch on). Even if he genuinely forgot the time, he knows he needs to find solutions to help cope with the symptoms of his cognitive limitations.

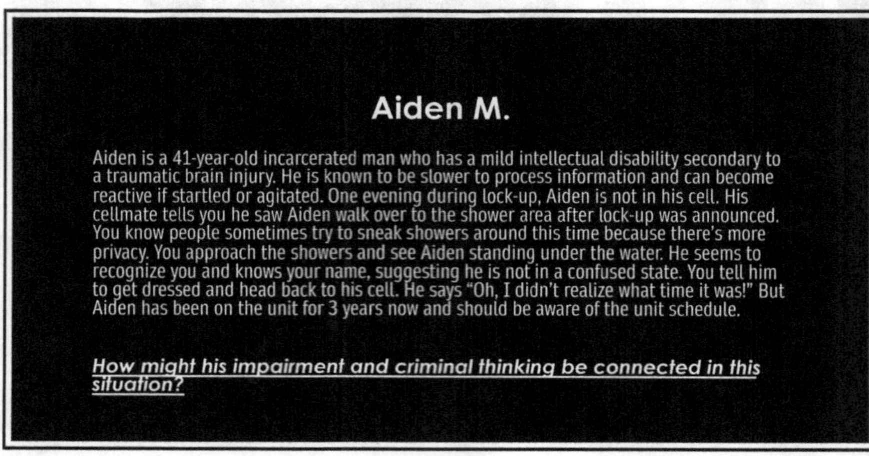

Slide 127 In Step 2, it is especially important for staff to acknowledge the person's cognitive difficulties by using a calm demeanor to avoid heightening fears or feelings of agitation. Staff might be tempted to respond to someone's agitation or confusion with their own frustrations or use punitive sanctions, but this is unlikely to lead to a smooth resolution or help the person learn to modify their behavior. When in the moment with these individuals, it may help to remember that aspects of the person's behavior are not their fault and their inability to effectively problem-solve may be a consequence. You may ask trainees to consider how they would want to be treated in older age as they become less mentally attuned.

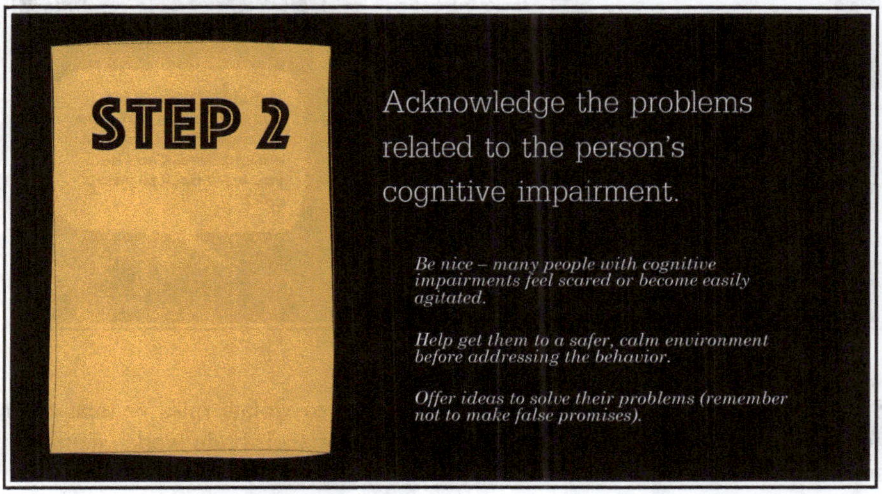

Slide 128 We return to Aiden's story to practice applying Step 2. Two examples of how to acknowledge his cognitive impairment are provided on the slide. Prompt trainees to think of additional examples.

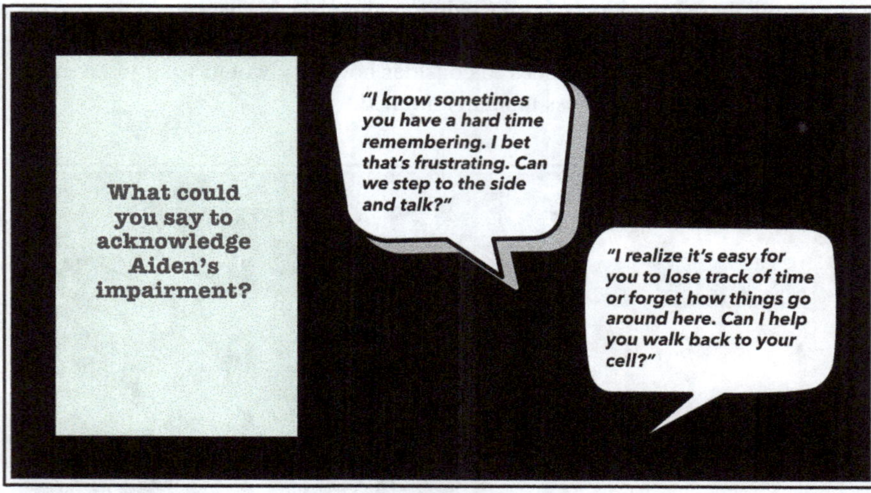

Slide 129 Cognitive impairment is not an excuse to violate rules or treat other people poorly. Just as they are not to blame for how their brain works, neither is anyone else. Remind trainees this is not a time to be confrontational, even if the person is behaving in a confrontational manner. Rather, they should model a calm stance, gently point out the inappropriate behavior, and encourage the person to consider what criminal thinking errors are at play.

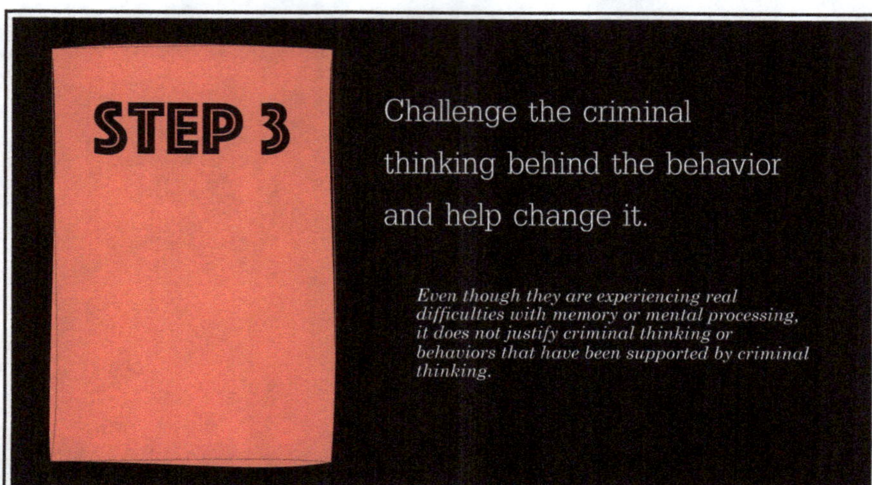

Slide 130 While Aiden's criminal thinking in this scenario was briefly discussed earlier, have trainees identify more specific errors in his thinking (think back to Module 2) they'd want to address with him directly. In preparing to implement Step 3, they may also consider what consequences they want to highlight relative to his thinking and how they would help him reframe his thoughts.

Slide 131 Two examples of how to acknowledge Aiden's criminal thinking are provided on the slide. Prompt trainees to think of additional examples.

Slide 132 In addition to the three-step model for older adults and people with cognitive impairment, trainees can increase the likelihood that their efforts will be successful if they pay particular attention to their style of communication and nonverbal behaviors. This slide includes some of those considerations, such as delivering information more concretely and directly, assessing for comprehension, and giving praise or recognition for understanding and compliance.

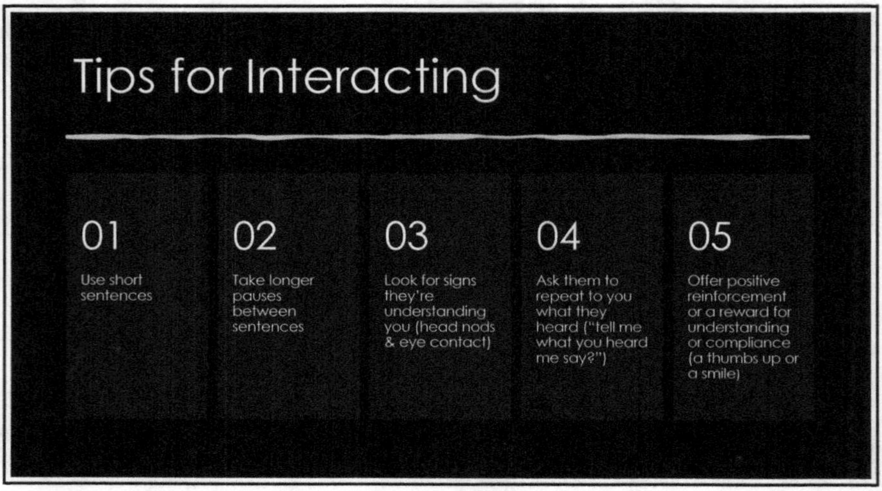

Slide 133 When talking to older adults and people with cognitive impairment, especially those who are also prone to criminal thinking, it's easy to get frustrated by their lack of understanding, stubbornness, deflection of responsibility, or combination thereof. We might be tempted to talk to these individuals like they're stupid or incompetent, which can be reflected in our tone of voice and word choice. Again, normalize the challenges associated with this population, but encourage trainees to be mindful of their own reactions and to evaluate whether they're using a degrading communication style. Treating people with respect even when addressing something they did wrong or inappropriately will likely go further in helping them correct it the next time.

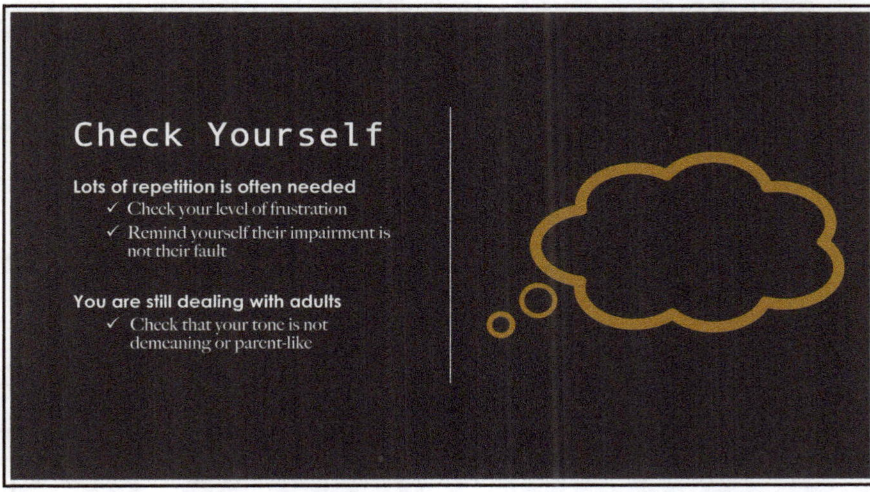

Slide 134 This slide illustrates a poorly executed way of addressing criminal thinking with someone who has an intellectual disorder. After reading the statement, have trainees consider which elements of the hypothetical statement were unhelpful (e.g., name-calling) then discuss an alternate approach using the three-step model as a framework. Here's one alternative: "Hey, can I have a minute to chat with you? I know you feel less stressed when you can follow your regular routine, and it pissed you off when this guy used your normal stall earlier today. Thinking he purposefully slighted you and then retaliating is an example of criminal thinking. He's new to the unit and probably didn't know. However, you also have to understand that you don't rule the roost, and other people can shower where they want when it's their turn. Next time, it might work out better to just talk to him about the importance of your routines."

Take this statement:

"Are you dumb? Just because you've been on this unit forever doesn't mean you can threaten someone else when they mess up your little routine. Knocking over that guy's meal tray as retaliation or whatever was rooted in criminal thinking. And now you caught a violation. That didn't work out so well for you, did it?"

How could you modify this statement so it's more productive?

Slide 135 Now, we'll transition to youth populations. While your facility may not have a juvenile unit, it's likely you house younger or less developmentally mature individuals on the adult side.

Slide 136 People convicted of offenses who are under the age of 18 may be housed in various types of institutions or units, which may or may not be specifically designated for juveniles or younger offenders. In this section, we are primarily talking about any incarcerated person under the age of 18. However, many of the issues discussed in the following slides also apply to people who have a developmental maturity level more consistent with someone under age 18. This slide helps set the stage for understanding why youth require a different approach than adults.

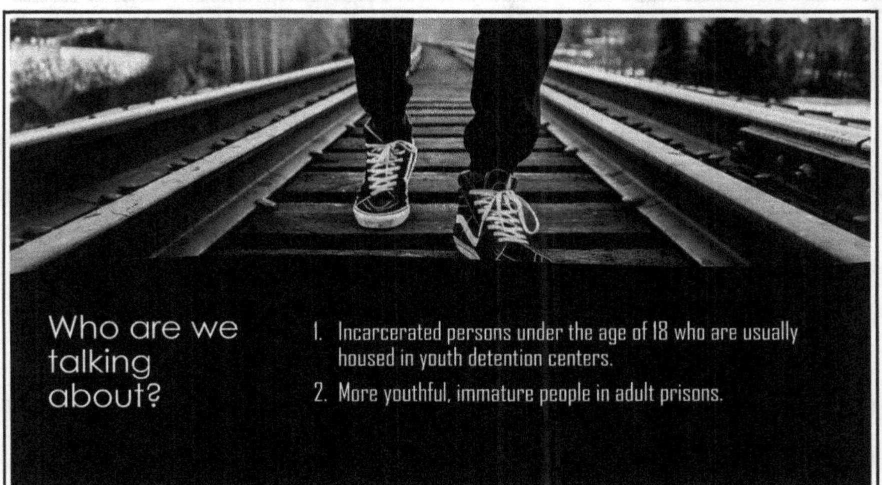

Slide 137 There is a plethora of scientific research showing that youth in general are different from adults across a variety of functions, including decision-making, impulse control, emotional regulation, attention and concentration, and future orientation. Most of these differences are rooted in brain development, as the human brain does not fully mature until our mid- to late-20s. This underdevelopment of the brain, coupled with the survival mentality adopted by many people in prison, is part of what makes youth in our facilities vulnerable and sometimes difficult to manage. The good news is that, because they tend to be less "set in their ways," they are often more successful in making lasting changes with proper intervention. This slide summarizes some of the ways youth differ from adults. Consider asking trainees if they can think of other differences they would add to the list.

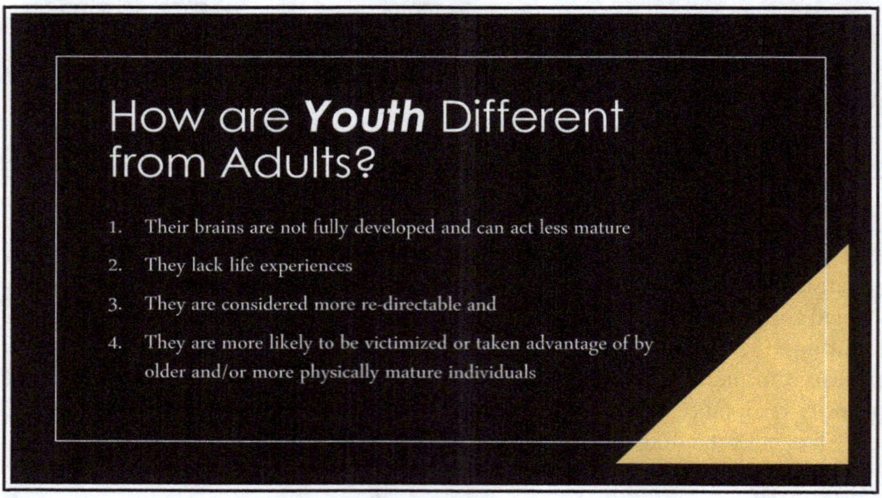

Slide 138 This slide includes behavioral examples that reflect some degree of criminal thinking. As before, have trainees consider how these behaviors violate the rights or well-being of others and/or avoid responsibility-taking, and what thoughts may have preceded the behavior. If time allows, prompt trainees to share a few examples of their own from youth they may have worked with in the past.

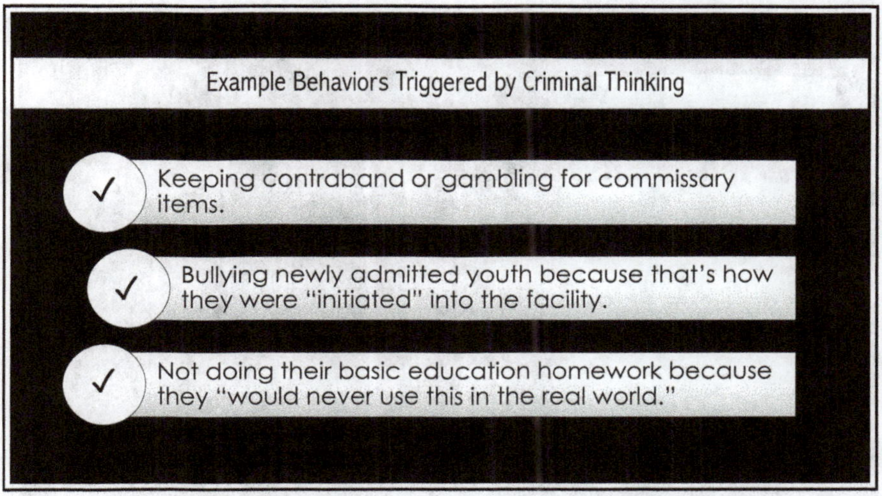

Slide 139 And, we're back to the trusty three-step model! Here, we're separating out and acknowledging issues related to the person's developmental maturity and/or lack of life experiences that are creating problems before addressing the criminal thinking errors underlying their actions.

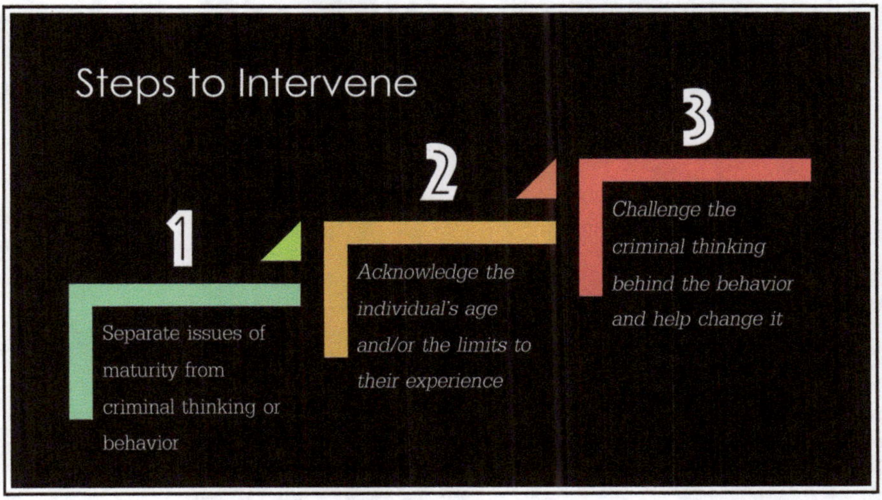

Slide 140 As we know with Step 1, this is the moment where staff need to stop and think about the youth's genuine needs or struggles in a given situation that are related to their maturity level. How is criminal thinking being used as a misguided approach to overcoming these real problems? Maturity-related challenges may involve internal processes (i.e., challenges associated with their mental and physical development) or external circumstances (i.e., challenges associated with their limited time on this planet and/or in the facility).

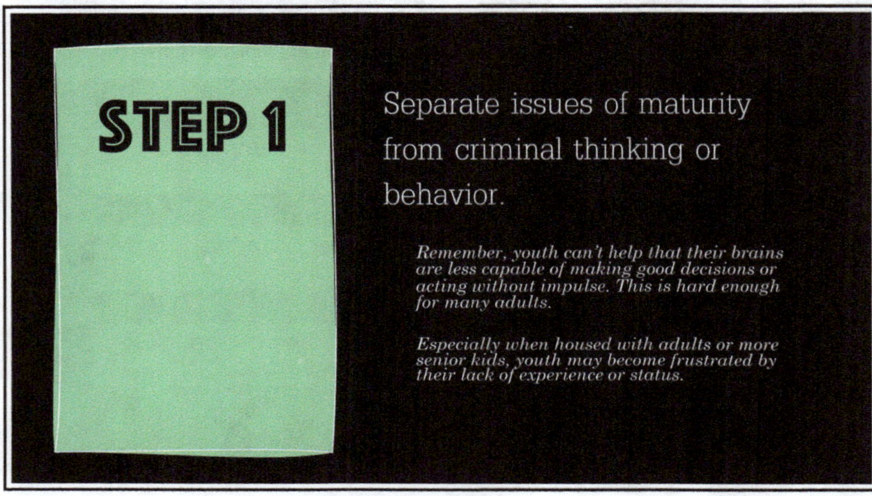

Slide 141 Step 2 reiterates that some aspects of the youth's behavior (which stems from their thoughts and feelings) are normal for any person at their age or with limited life experiences. As with other incarcerated populations, trainees will have a better chance of addressing the criminal thinking if they first show some compassion and understanding. In this case, we're teaching trainees to empathize with the challenges of being a youth, especially when youth are having to navigate an environment intended for adults.

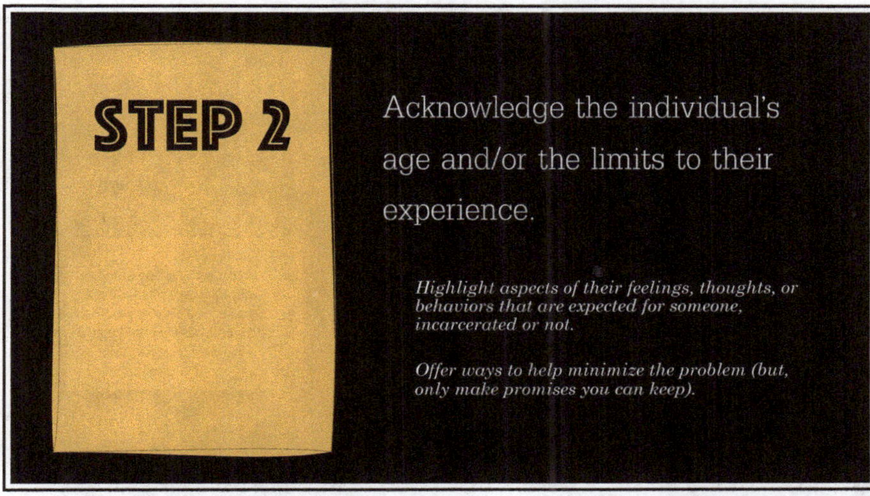

Slide 142 This slide provides examples of statements that normalize youth experiences, even if the youth's decision or behavior is unacceptable, and how help could be offered. Prompt trainees to think of any instances during their time as a correctional officer or staff when they might have been more successful in redirecting a behavior had they acknowledged typical teenage or young adult experiences and helped problem-solve. If they can't think of examples from work, a parenting example would also illustrate the point.

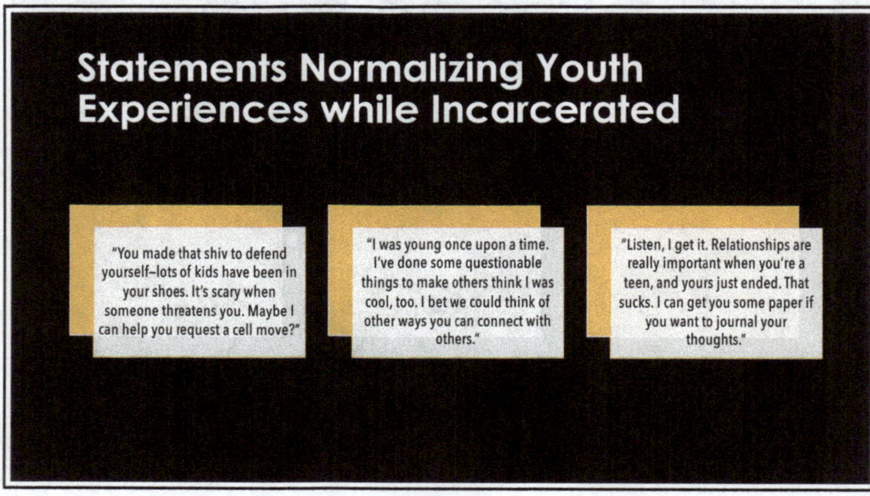

Slide 143 Immaturity is not an excuse for criminal thinking. Youth still have the capacity to make decisions that comply with the rules and avoid harm to other people. Remind trainees about some basic strategies for reframing criminal thinking. At a minimum, they can "play the tape" through and help the youth identify how criminal thinking clouded their judgment.

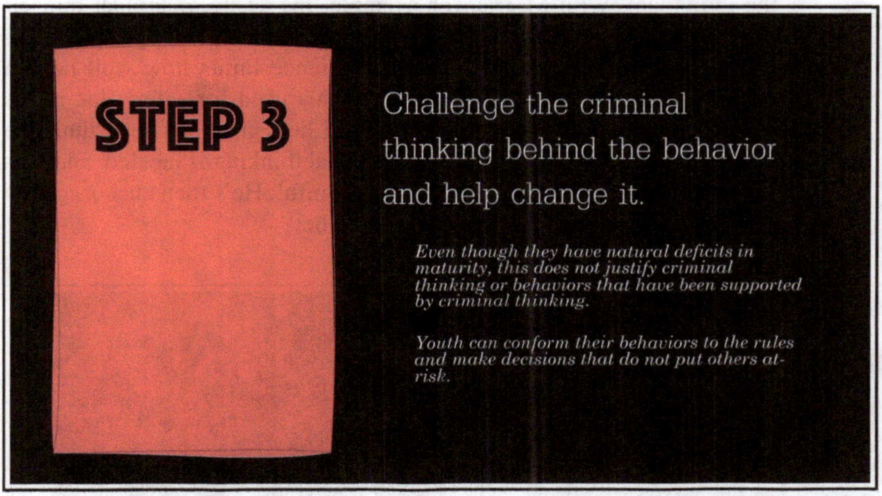

Slide 144 This slide describes two hypothetical scenarios on the left and potential responses on the right that model each of the three-steps. You'll read through the scenarios one at a time and have trainees dissect the response by identifying which components map onto the three-steps. For Step 1, trainees can imagine how the officer may have distinguished between the maturity factors and criminal thinking before approaching the individual. With Morris, for example, his desire to protect himself from older people on the unit is a real need because of his age and physical vulnerabilities, and his lack of experience limits how well he can problem-solve the situation. For Step 2, his need for safety due to his developmental level is acknowledged and he's given an opportunity to discuss alternatives. For Step 3, his criminal thinking is labeled, and he's told why his possession of the razor is harmful. He's then encouraged to think of a better approach to get his need met.

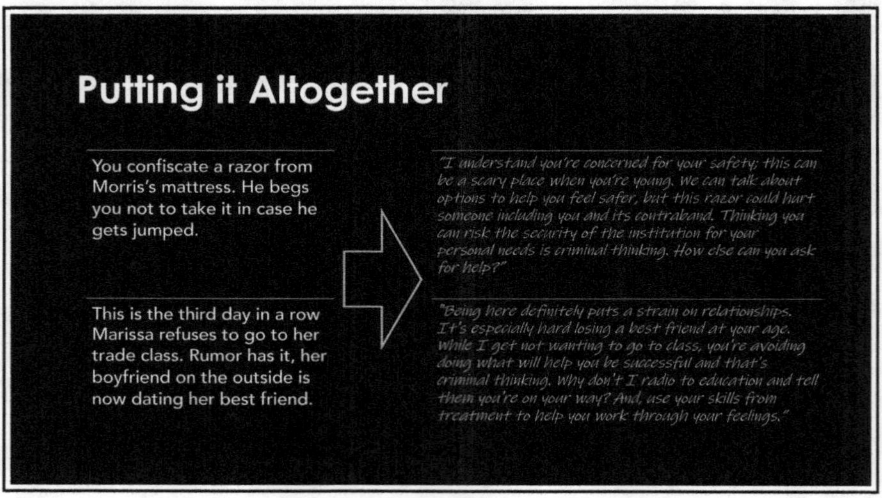

Slide 145 Across the three-steps, several additional strategies are likely to lead to more productive discussions with youth. To minimize frustration and improve their ability to truly empathize, trainees should first remember what they were like as a teenager or young adult. How did they approach their problems and what helped them grow and develop into more mature people? They didn't mature overnight! Similar to interacting with people who have a cognitive impairment, youth typically need simple and direct styles of communication as well as reinforcement when they're correct or doing well. They also tend to learn better when they see appropriate behavior being modeled or demonstrated. So, it's important staff also act in mature ways, which includes taking ownership of mistakes.

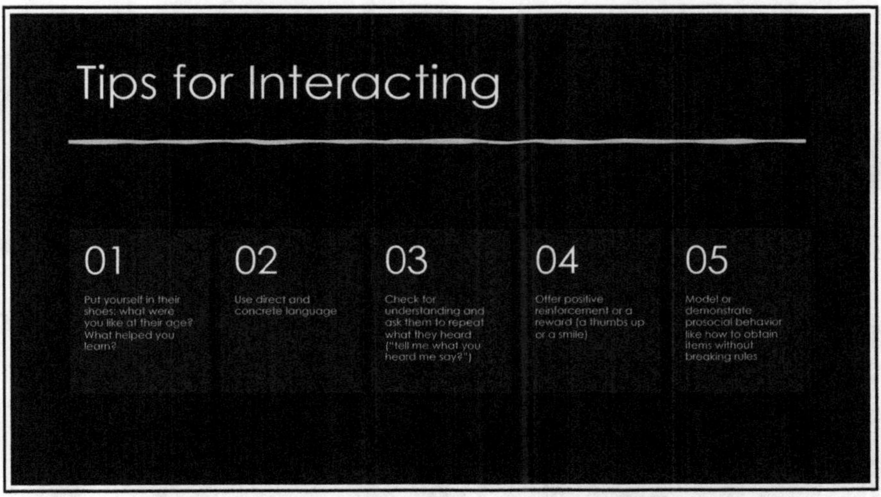

Slide 146 On this slide, have trainees consider the likely role models incarcerated youth are looking to for guidance. These "role models" might not be very good influences and could include gang leaders, friends, or family who commit crime, or rappers or celebrities who are often in legal trouble. Importantly, staff don't need to be role models for every youth they oversee; simply being an approachable and conscientious person can make a lasting impression. Even if staff have to use discipline or punitive approaches in response to behavior, they can still model fair and humane conflict resolution. You'll wrap up the discussion by asking trainees to think of ways they can be a positive influence to any youth on their units.

Slide 147 On to the last section before trainees really get to practice their skills!

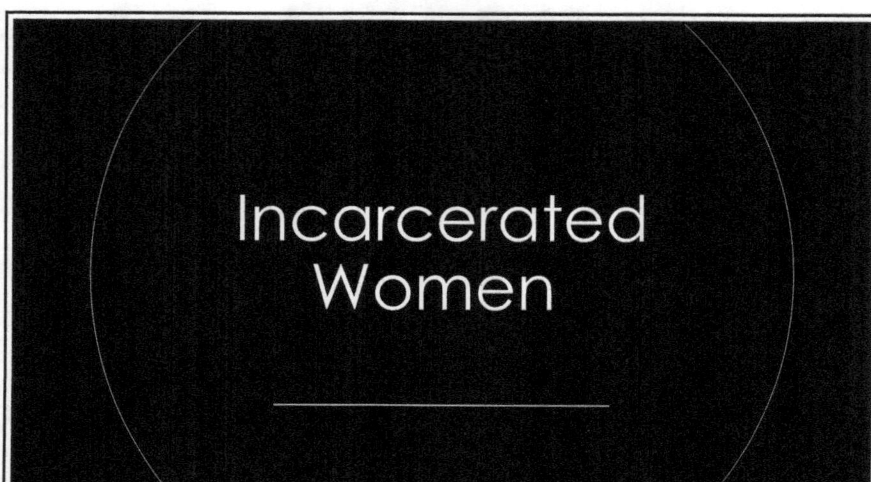

Slide 148 Broadly speaking, women and other minority gender identities can have very different experiences and needs while incarcerated. However, remind trainees we are speaking in generalizations and there's a lot of variability between women. Prompt trainees to discuss ways in which their work with women has been different from and similar to their work with men. Trainees should be encouraged to move away from stereotypes or sexist attitudes about women such that they are more emotional, harder to work with, or "crazy." You can redirect by affirming women can be difficult to engage with for different reasons than men but labeling them in these ways can lead to bias or false assumptions that are ultimately unhelpful.

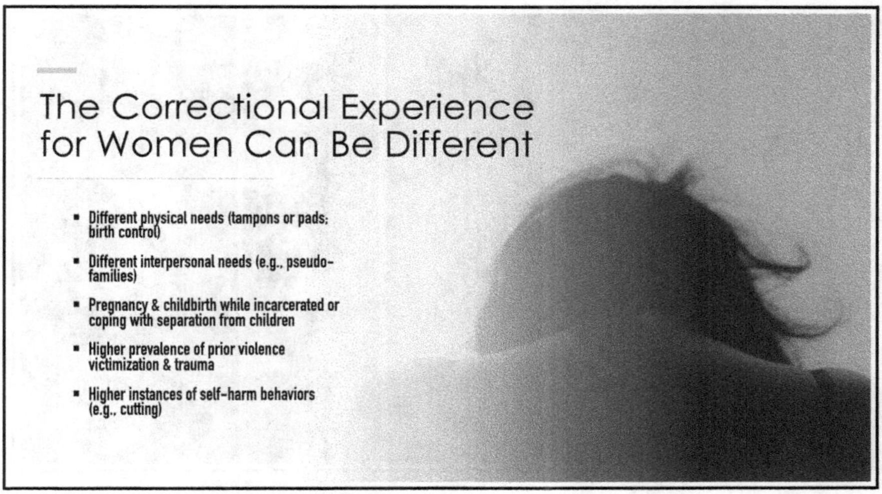

Slide 149 For women, the use of criminal thinking to get what they want, or need may often be associated with survival and safety. This doesn't necessarily mean women are justified in their reliance on criminal thinking, but it may mean they know of few other ways to problem-solve or protect themselves. Although men can also engage in criminal thinking to survive a bad situation, this slide acknowledges that women as a group have more structural obstacles against them because we live in a world that tends to favor the status and security of men. For example, there continue to be gender disparities in salary and leadership positions within corporations, and studies show women's health issues are more likely to be dismissed by medical professionals than men's (Arber et al., 2006; Chapman et al., 2013; Karim et al., 2007; United States Census Bureau, 2019).

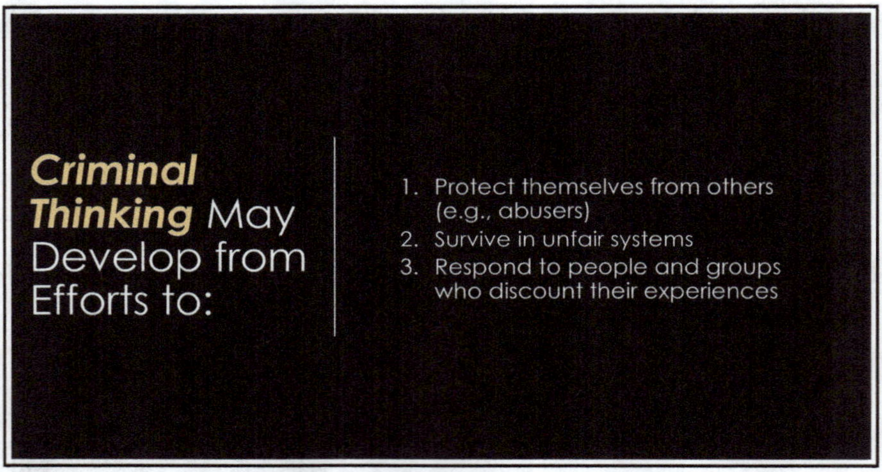

Slide 150 This slide includes behavioral examples that reflect some degree of criminal thinking. As before, have trainees consider how these behaviors violate the rights or well-being of others and/or avoid responsibility-taking, and what thoughts may have preceded the behavior. Prompt trainees to focus on how these behaviors might be rooted in experiences of insecurity, lack of protection, or discrimination. For example, a woman may respond more aggressively to male staff because other men in her life were habitually abusive, and her reaction is intended to prevent additional harm. Flirtation can have a similar cause and effect; she may have learned that being super feminine and "sexy" got her in good graces with men such that she avoided abuse or acquired resources for survival. Remind trainees to never reciprocate flirtation or even seemingly harmless banter. This doesn't mean they can't be friendly or joke around with women, but they should be mindful about maintaining good boundaries.

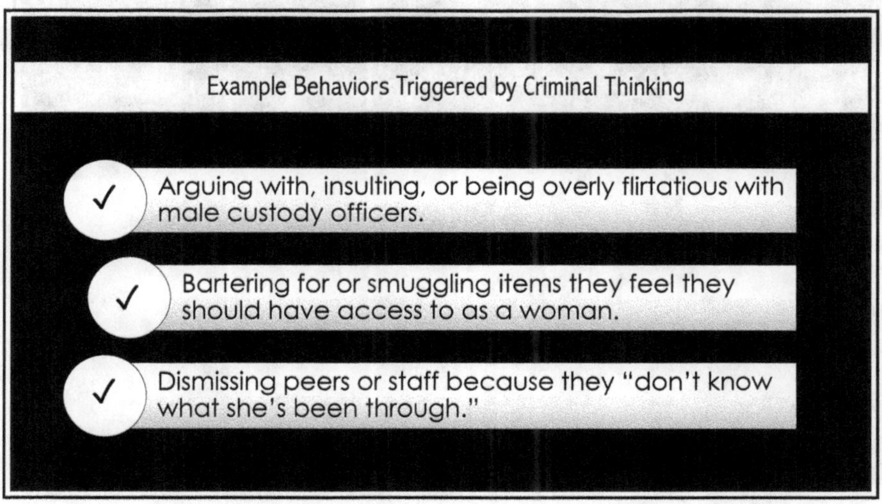

Slide 151 Can't have too much repetition of the three-step model! In this last iteration, we're separating out and acknowledging issues uniquely related to the person's gender or their gender-based experiences that are creating challenges before addressing the criminal thinking errors underlying their actions.

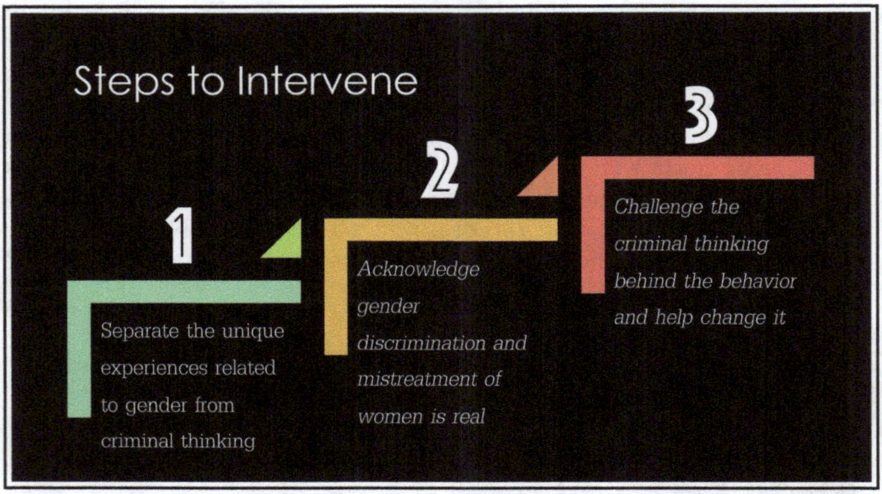

Slide 152 Remind trainees that gender differences can be inherent (e.g., biological needs) or system-created differences (e.g., viewing women as less intelligent or trustworthy). Either separately or in combination, these differences can create different routes to expressing criminal thinking. Given the higher prevalence of physical and sexual abuse against women and other gender minorities, especially among those who end up incarcerated, criminal thinking may be a manifestation of a trauma response. Therefore, to best engage women in the corrective process of changing their criminal thinking, correctional staff must first consider if and how gender-related experiences are connected.

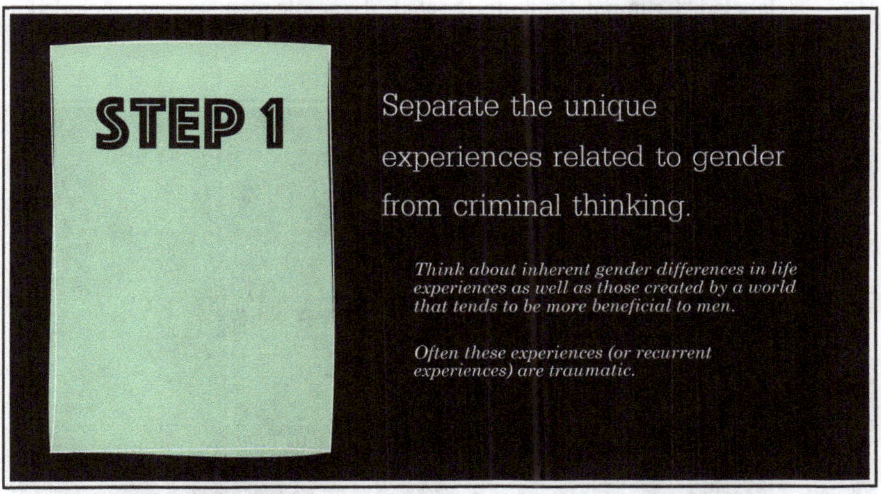

Slide 153 This slide introduces trainees to Regina H. and her story involving a history of traumatic experiences. The story illustrates how past traumas can lead to certain decisions to protect oneself that may not be the most useful or helpful and, in fact, may cause further harm to others or even themselves. Some of Regina's behaviors are not okay, but they do have a logical explanation that helps put her situation into perspective. To practice Step 1, have trainees separate the gender-related factors in the story from the criminal thinking-related outcomes or decisions. You may choose to write down responses on a whiteboard or paper pad. It may be useful to create two columns: one labeled "Gender-Related" and one labeled "Criminal Thinking-Related." Example responses are included in the slide notes.

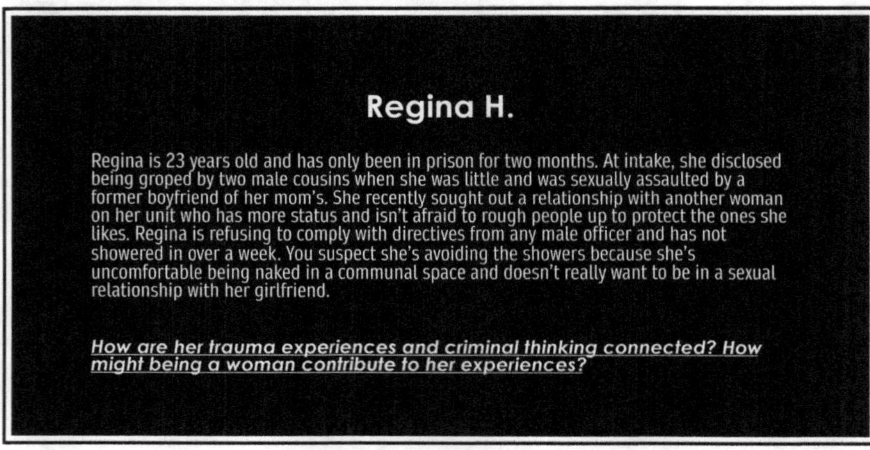

Slide 154 Because many correctional facilities are male dominated (including those housing women), blatantly acknowledging the realities of gender discrimination and sexism is not a common occurrence. But, as we know, women's behavior (which stems from their thoughts and feelings) can be influenced by their experiences as a gender minority. The purpose of Step 2 is to demonstrate compassion and understanding about these often unfair realities so trainees will have a better chance of addressing the criminal thinking. In this case, we're teaching trainees to empathize with the challenges of being a woman or other gender minority in a system built by and intended for men. In doing so, they will likely create a stronger sense of trust and respect.

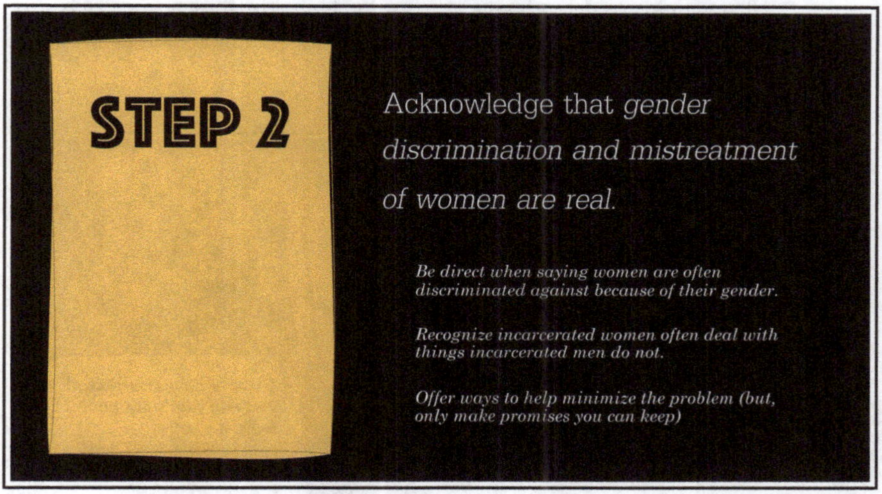

Slide 155 We return to Regina's story to practice applying Step 2. Two examples of how to acknowledge her experiences are provided on the slide. Prompt trainees to think of additional examples. Be sure to swiftly but constructively correct responses that play into gender stereotypes/ sexism, dismiss or minimize her issues, or are overly punitive. For example, telling Regina she "needs to shower for the sake of her personal hygiene" may sound empathic, but it ignores the reason she doesn't want to shower (i.e., she's avoiding sexual contact with her girlfriend likely because sex is traumatizing for her). This could be enhanced by saying, "I think I know why you're avoiding showers. It's understandable given your trauma history, but your hygiene is related to your overall health. What would need to change for you to feel safe showering?" Also, be attentive to answers that could exacerbate her trauma such as escorting her to a secluded area of the unit to talk.

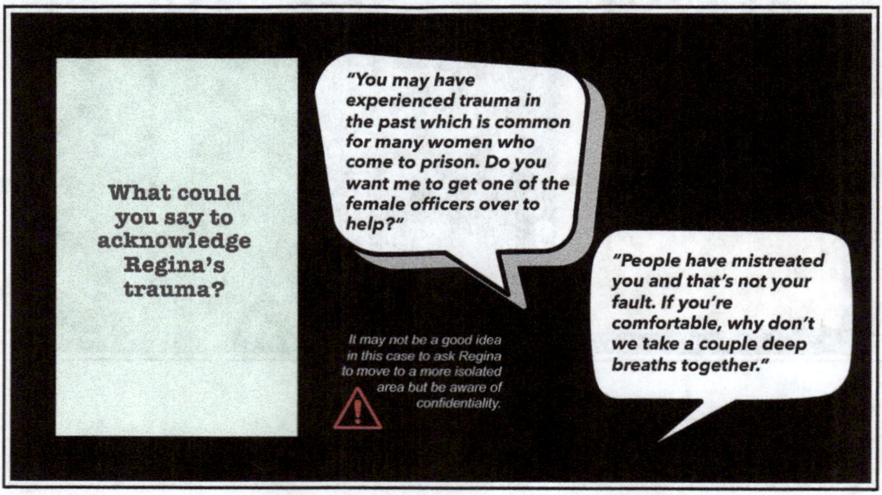

Slide 156 Just as we discussed in the section on serious mental illness, it's unproductive to argue the reality of a reported traumatic event with someone. For the purpose of acknowledging gender differences, it doesn't matter whether a traumatic event actually happened or not. Debating the facts reinforces the myth that women shouldn't be believed and will likely harm any rapport between the officer and the woman (thereby disrupting the ability to address criminal thinking). Even if there is clear and convincing evidence that the claim is false, it doesn't negate the fact that women face challenges related to their gender. If proven false accusations of victimization are determined to be a form of criminal thinking, this can be addressed in Step 3 with care. Remember, false accusations may still be rooted in a desire to avoid additional trauma.

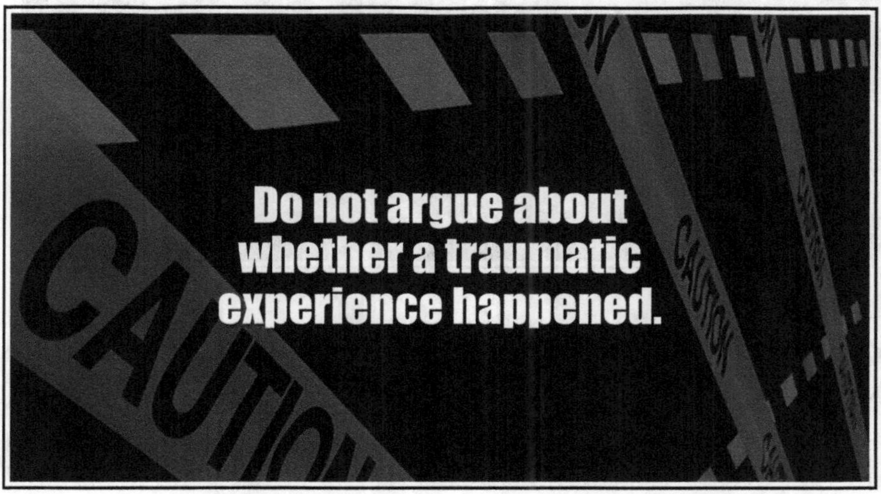

Slide 157 Gender-based discrimination, bias, and even trauma do not give people the right to do whatever they want or harm others. Women, other gender minorities, and people in general need to find more productive ways to process the events that happen to them and advocate for themselves or systemic changes.

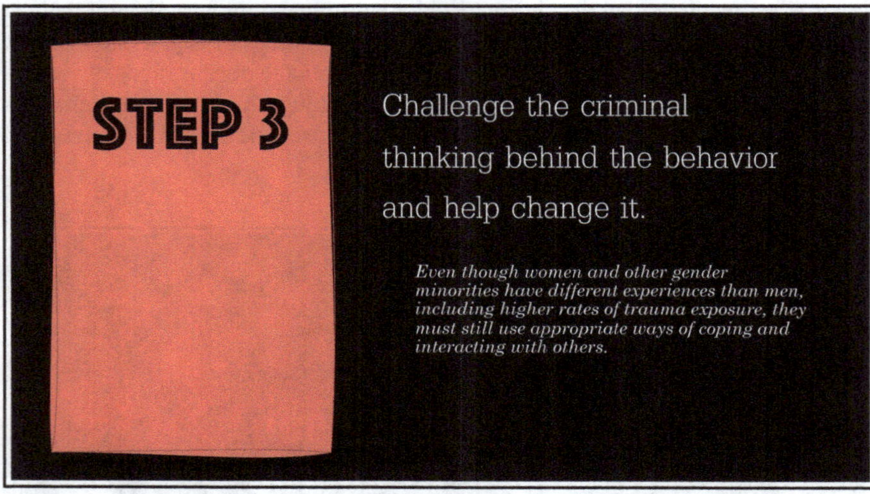

Slide 158 Thinking back to Regina, ask trainees to consider the types of criminal thinking errors that might have been active in Regina's mind at various points in her story. You may need to remind the group about the key elements (e.g., her history of sexual assault, relationship with another woman on the unit for protection, refusal to comply with directives or shower).

Slide 159 Now have trainees discuss hypothetical ways they could acknowledge and then help correct the criminal thinking. A few examples are on the slide to get the discussion started. Note that further support may be needed for someone like Regina, such as a referral to mental health or assisting Regina in requesting a unit change if she feels afraid in her relationship or reveals there's abuse going on.

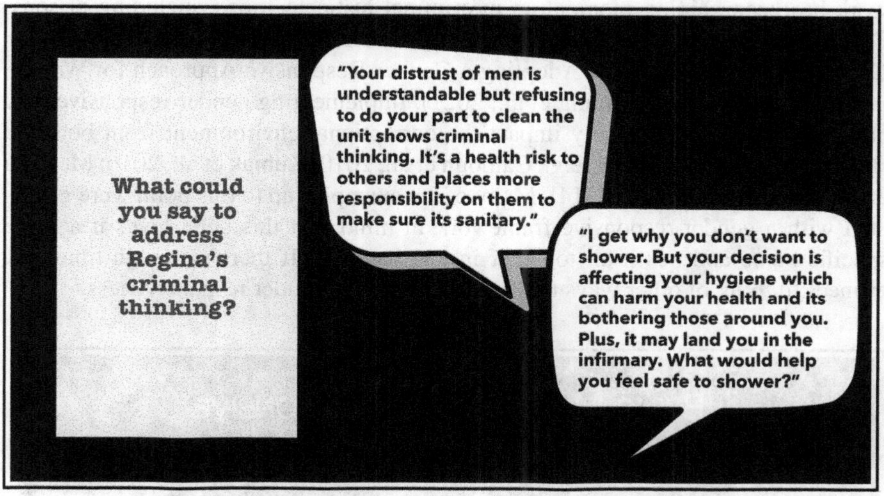

Slide 160 On this slide, trainees are introduced to a specific framework for working more productively and conscientiously with women and gender minorities. Gender-responsive approaches recognize gender inequalities and focus on meeting the unique needs of women and other gender minorities as well as overcoming challenges they often experience. Gender-responsive care can be applied to broader policies, programming, case management, and individual interactions. This framework has been gaining momentum in criminal justice settings, including prisons. For more information, we direct you to The Council of State Governments Justice Center's Resource Guide on Adopting a Gender-Responsive Approach for Women in the Justice System (Fleming et al., 2021). Implementing gender-responsive care has been shown to positively impact the correctional environment from both the staff and client perspectives (e.g., Calhoun et al., 2010; Kubiak et al., 2016; Messina et al., 2010; Saxena et al., 2014). Many of the examples up to this point were generated with a gender-responsive framework in mind, but this slide gives it a more specific name and ties it all together in one package. If there's enough time, ask trainees to think of other ways they can demonstrate gender responsiveness.

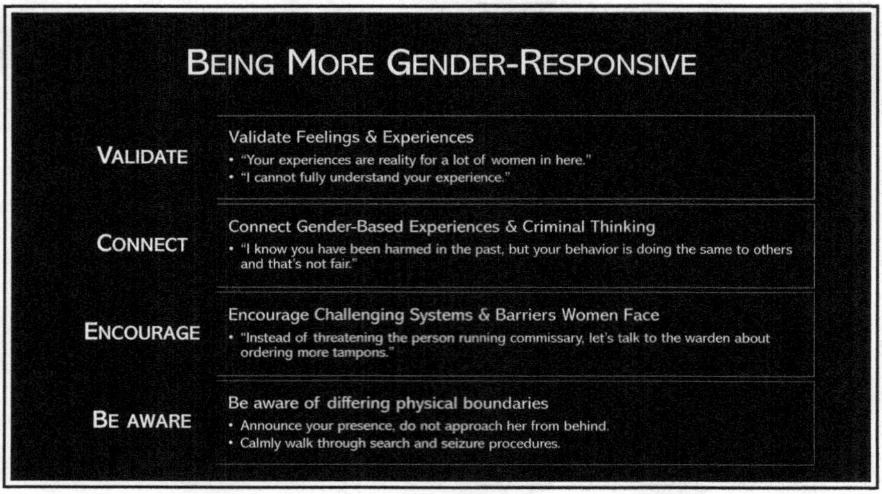

Slide 161 To gain more perspective, minimize frustration, and improve staff's ability to empathize, encourage them to consider how they would handle the situation if it were a woman in their personal life, such as their own wife, mother, daughter, or sister. Of course, we don't expect staff to treat the women on their unit like their spouses or other close family members, but it might help them stay more level-headed and remember the common struggles many women experience. The ones in our custody have simply learned different ways to prevent, cope, or work through those struggles. Our goal is to help them change the ways that are unhelpful and potentially harmful.

Slide 162 For the final time, you'll summarize the three-steps. This is also a good place to remind trainees about the Desk Reference guide they can use if they forget the steps while on the unit. These easy steps are one way staff can be an agent of change.

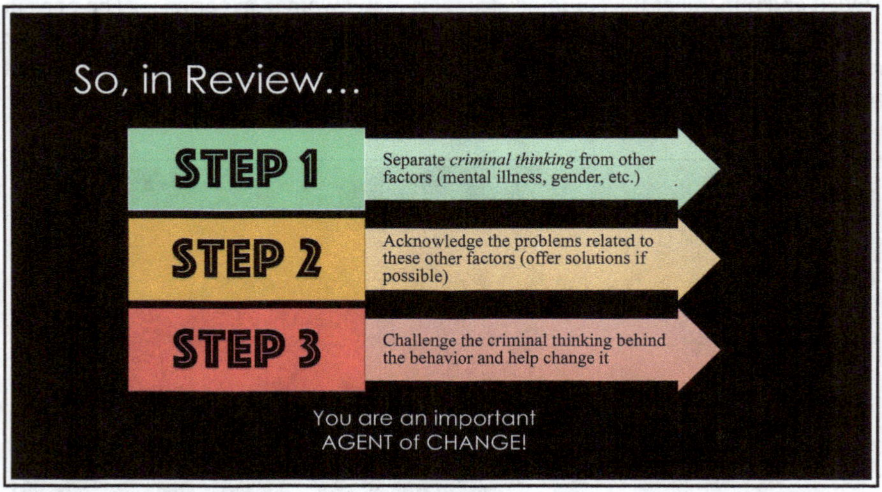

Slide 163 Give trainees about a 10-min stretch break. Encourage the group not to stray too far from the training room.

References

Arber, S., McKinlay, J., Adams, A., Marceau, L., Link, C., & O'Donnell, A. (2006). Patient characteristics and inequalities in doctors' diagnostic and management strategies relating to CHD: A video-simulation experiment. *Social Science & Medicine*, *62*(1), 103-115. https://doi.org/10.1016/j.socscimed.2005.05.028

Calhoun, S., Messina, N., Cartier, J., & Torres, S. (2010). Implementing gender-responsive treatment for women in prison: Client and staff perspectives. *Federal Probation*, *74*(3), 27.

Chapman, E. N., Kaatz, A., & Carnes, M. (2013). Physicians and implicit bias: how doctors may unwittingly perpetuate health care disparities. *Journal of General Internal Medicine*, *28*(11), 1504–1510. https://doi.org/10.1007/s11606-013-2441-1

Fleming, E., Upton, A., Wright, F. L., Wurzburg, S., & Ney, B. (2021). *Adopting a gender-responsive approach for women in the justice system: A resource guide.* The Council of State Governments Justice Center.

Karim, F., Islam, A. Chowdhury, A. M. R., Johansson, E. & Diwan, V. K. (2007). Gender differences in delays in diagnosis and treatment of tuberculosis. *Health Policy and Planning, 23*(6), 329-334. https://doi.org/10.1093/heapol/czm026

Kubiak, S., Fedock, G., Kim, W. J., & Bybee, D. (2016). Long-term outcomes of a RCT intervention study for women with violent crimes. *Journal of the Society for Social Work and Research*, *7*(4), 661-679. https://doi.org/10.1086/689356

Lamb, H. R., & Bachrach, L. L. (2001). Some perspectives on deinstitutionalization. *Psychiatric Services, 52*(8), 1039–1045. https://doi.org/10.1176/appi.ps.52.8.1039

Link, B. G., Phelan, J. C., Bresnahan, M., Stueve, A., & Pescosolido, B. A. (1999). Public conceptions of mental illness: labels, causes, dangerousness, and social distance. *American Journal of Public Health*, *89*(9), 1328-1333. https://doi.org/10.2105/AJPH.89.9.1328

Messina, N., Grella, C. E., Cartier, J., & Torres, S. (2010). A randomized experimental study of gender-responsive substance abuse treatment for women in prison. *Journal of Substance Abuse Treatment*, *38*(2), 97. https://doi.org/10.1016/j.jsat.2009.09.004

Morgan, R. D., Fisher, W. H., Duan, N., Mandracchia, J. T., & Murray, D. (2010). Prevalence of criminal thinking among state prison inmates with serious mental illness. *Law and Human Behavior, 34*(4), 324–336. https://doi.org/10.1007/s10979-009-9182-z

Morgan, R. D., Flora, D. B., Kroner, D. G., Mills, J. F., Varghese, F., & Steffan, J. S. (2012). Treating offenders with mental illness: a research synthesis. *Law and Human Behavior, 36*(1), 37. https://psycnet.apa.org/doi/10.1037/h0093964

Morgan, R. D., Kroner, D. G., Mills, J. F., & Batastini, A. B. (2013). Treating criminal offenders. In I. B. Weiner & R. K. Otto (Eds.), *The handbook of forensic psychology* (4th ed., pp. 795-838). Wiley.

Saxena, P., Messina, N., & Grella, C. E. (2014). Who benefits from gender responsive treatment? Accounting for abuse history on longitudinal outcomes for women in prison. *Criminal Justice and Behavior*, *41*(4), 417. https://doi.org/10.1177/0093854813514405

United States Census Bureau. (2019). *Table S2412: Occupation by sex and median earnings in the past 12 months*. https://data.census.gov/table?q=s2412&tid=ACSST1Y2019.S2412

Chapter 6
Module 5 Guide and Wrap-Up

Module 5. Pulling It into Practice

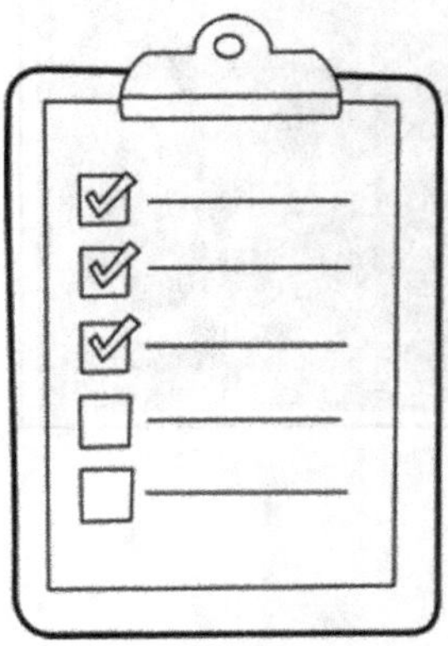

Materials:
1. *PowerPoint Slides 164-166*
2. *Practice Scenarios (Appendix or e-Resource 6.1)*
3. *Knowledge Acquisition Quiz Answer Sheet and Answer Key (Appendices or e-Resource 6.2 and 6.3)*
4. *Evaluation of Trainee Engagement Form (Appendix or e-Resource 6.4)*
5. *Completion Certificate (Appendix or e-Resource 6.5)*
6. *Training Evaluation Form (Appendix or e-Resource 6.6)*

The annotations below are intended to help you prepare for the content and discussions related to each slide. Remember, there are also presenter notes within the PowerPoint slide deck to help you along in real time.

Supplementary Information The online version contains supplementary material available at https://doi.org/10.1007/978-3-031-88404-7_6.

© The Author(s), under exclusive license to Springer Nature Switzerland AG 2025

A. B. Batastini et al., *Training Correctional Staff to Recognize Criminal Thinking*, https://doi.org/10.1007/978-3-031-88404-7_6

Slide 164 Now it's time to step away from the PowerPoint slides for a while and get into some hands-on practice. Refer to the Module 5 Practice Scenarios handout in e-Resource 8 and follow the instructions. The handout is divided into three phases: (1) instructor-led demonstration, (2) trainee-led demonstration, and (3) small group role-play. In the final phase, you will need to pre-cut each scenario on the last page along the dotted lines. You may want to make a few copies of this last page so everyone in the small group can have a copy of the scenario they will be acting out.

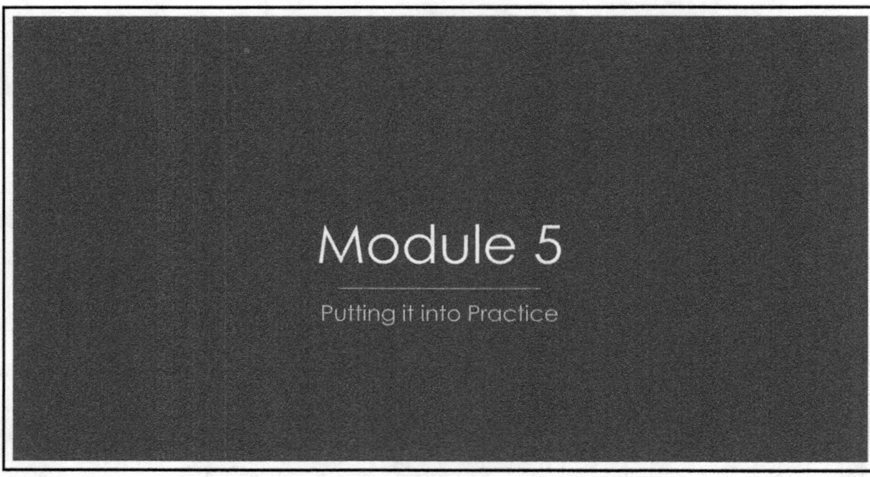

Slide 165 This slide allows the class to see each question relevant to each practice scenario. When it's one group's turn to share, have them read the script they were provided or summarize the scenario they were asked to act out. You can also print this slide to distribute to the class for their review. Or skip this slide altogether and go around to each of the groups and pose these questions to keep their discussions going.

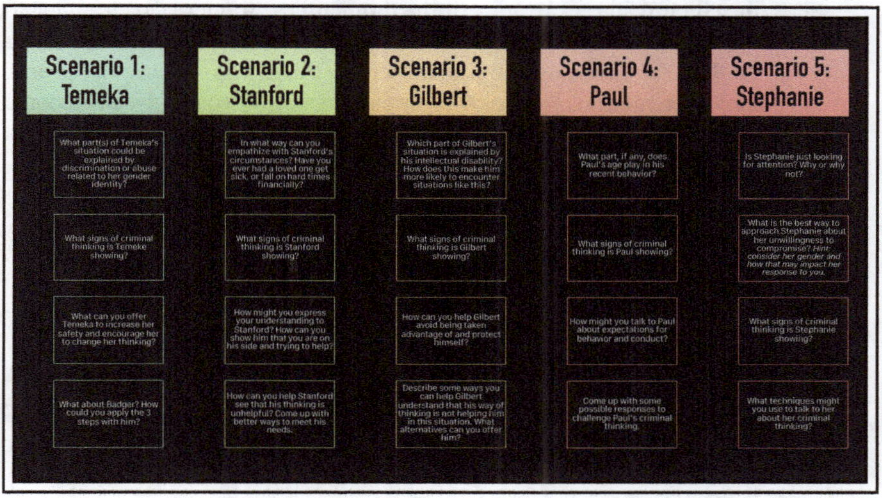

Slide 166 This slide marks the final portion of the training where trainees complete a multiple-choice knowledge acquisition quiz and an anonymous training evaluation form. An answer key for the quiz is in e-Resource 10. Remember, trainees need to earn a score of 75% or better to receive a completion certificate. For trainees who score below 75%, review their incorrect answers and ensure understanding before providing a completion certificate. Instruct trainees to complete the quiz before the evaluation form. Sometimes, trainees are hesitant to complete evaluation forms either because they're worried it won't really be anonymous or because their opinions won't matter in the end. However, getting feedback is important so the training can become more tailored to the needs of staff at your facility, and you can grow as an instructor. It may help to reiterate the importance of their experiences.

Wrap-Up

Assessing Pre-training Preparedness

By this point in the guidebook, you should feel more oriented to the structure, flow, and content of the training, and feel prepared to deliver the training to your colleagues, team members, or staff. Not sure how prepared you feel? Rate yourself on the following scale:

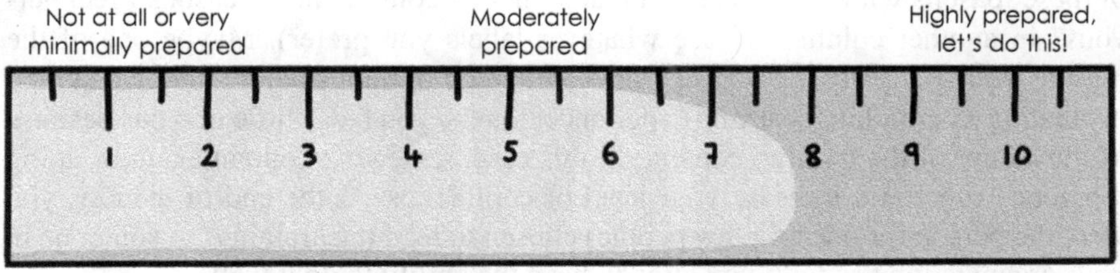

Why did you rate yourself the way you did? Is it because the material is new? Is it because there's a lot of stuff to cover? Because you have some general anxieties about presenting in front of an audience? Because you're expecting negative or uncooperative responses from trainees? Because you're not feeling excited about the training yourself? Or is it something else?

If you don't feel very prepared (self-ratings around 0–3), it might be a good idea to review the content again (including the tips discussed in Chap. 1), set up a time to practice with a trusted peer who can provide constructive feedback before the "real-deal," and/or make sure you have an experienced co-trainer to rely on during your first training session (co-trainers are encouraged for all sessions regardless of level of preparedness). If your concerns are more focused on presenting treatment-related content (e.g., reviewing components of cognitive-behavioral therapy, how to address criminal thinking in ways that match evidence-based practices), we recommend collaborating with mental or behavioral health staff at your institution to either help you prepare or co-lead the training alongside you.

If you're feeling a bit lukewarm about the training itself, think about the ways it may benefit you, your fellow staff, the incarcerated individuals you manage, or the communities most of them will return to one day. Prior to running your first training session, try integrating the techniques into your own interactions with others—use the three-step model with those you serve (both incarcerated individuals and fellow staff) and note any differences in their reactions or behavior toward you. Remember our discussion in Chap. 1; new techniques don't always land well the first time and it may take a few tries to see positive gains. Hopefully, you'll begin seeing evidence of how these new skills can improve the workplace environment! Using the techniques for yourself will also give you a better sense of the challenges or pushback that may emerge during implementation, as well as add to your credibility as a trainer (you're not asking people to try something you haven't tried yourself). You could also think about ways to make components of the training more interesting and engaging—is there somewhere you can insert an interesting case example or personal experience specific to your workplace (keeping the details de-identified, of course)? Are there any quotes or media clips you like that might really drive home key points for your particular audience (while being mindful of timing constraints)? Within reason, we encourage modifications to the training to best fit the needs of your environment and the populations housed there.

If you're feeling moderately prepared (self-ratings around 4–7), several of the actions listed above might likewise be beneficial, depending on the reasons you feel more vs. less confident in your ability to deliver the training. Consider making a list of these reasons with "reasons I feel ready" in one column, and "reasons I feel nervous" in another column (or use whatever labels you prefer). Maybe one of the reasons you feel ready is because you've delivered trainings before and feel skilled in creating an enriching learning experience; maybe you feel a little nervous because of the nature of the training content. In this case, reviewing content again or doing a practice run could increase your level of confidence. At the end of the day, you were the person (or one of a few people) chosen to lead this training, so someone in your organization has faith you already have the ability to do it well!

Although not a required pre-requisite for delivering the training, we also recommend the use of a train-the-trainer model as described in further detail in Fig. 1.1 of Chap. 1, especially if you and your training team feel less prepared or confident about your skills. To initiate a train-the-trainer session, please contact the authors at: [intheact.training@gmail.com]. Please note that expenses for time and travel will be charged and a retainer fee may be requested.

If you rated yourself in the upper range of the scale (around 8–10), that's great! We want you to have confidence in moving ahead with this training. We also want you to be realistic. Remember, there will always be parts of a training that don't go exactly as planned. It's a lot of work to keep your energy up, manage time, navigate various personalities in the room, and think on your toes when novel situations or questions arise. It also often takes multiple training sessions before delivery starts to feel easy and routine. Don't let any of that knock your confidence down. Go in there with the amazing talents you have, then reflect on what went well (and what didn't) so you can keep improving while maintaining a high level of confidence.

Assessing Post-training Performance

Already ran the training? How did it go? Rate yourself on the following scale:

Just like we did in the previous section, let's think for a moment about why you rated the training session the way you did. Is it related to your level of preparedness? It is because there were issues with timing or being able to cover all content? Because the group was disengaged or challenging to manage (or conversely because they were lively and positive)? Or did something else contribute to how well or not the training went?

We encourage you to revisit this scale after each training session to ground yourself and begin determining what (if any) improvements need to be considered for the next iteration. After each session, try setting aside some time to make a list of what aspects of the training went well and what you'd like to change next time. Taking notes of these soon after a training will help you remember the changes you'd like to make while it is fresh in your mind; it could be a long time before the next training session. Hopefully, your ratings are more consistently placed higher on the scale as you gain more experience, and your list of proposed changes gets shorter.

However, even seasoned trainers have "bad days"—sometimes there are things going on in our own lives that distract us from doing the best job we can, sometimes it's the dynamics of a given trainee cohort that present unique problems, or sometimes there's something larger looming across the institution or department that influences the "vibes" of the training room (e.g., shifts in management, policy changes, union negotiations, budgetary cuts, political division). The important thing is to reflect on each training session and take feedback from trainees seriously. Taking feedback seriously doesn't necessarily mean each point of criticism is applied. It's impossible to appease every person or make every recommendation; in fact, sometimes trainee recommendations are contradictory (e.g., one person may feel too much time is spent on a certain topic, while another person may feel not enough time is spent).

Instead, the idea is to think through the merit and feasibility of feedback, rather than dismissing what people have to say because it might hurt the ego or because it doesn't match your perceptions of the training day. By merit, we are referring to the quality and/or accuracy of the comment. Sometimes people say rude things that have very little to do with you or the training and, therefore, have minimal value for improving the training. Feasibility refers to the ease with which feedback can be implemented. For example, someone who comments that your voice was annoying is giving feedback that has no merit (it's not constructive) and is not feasible (you can't do much to change the sound of your voice). The person could have said this because they were disgruntled about having to attend the training and needed someone to project their frustrations onto. If, however, you received lower ratings on items related to your presentation style and/or comments such as, "I wish the trainer spoke up more" or "I think if the presenter moved around the room more often, my attention would have been held better" you can do something proactive with this feedback. These kinds of comments are fair and give you some concrete ideas for how to better engage your audience next time.

We recommend looking for patterns in the numerical ratings of the Training Evaluation Form (were some domains more consistently rated higher vs. lower across trainees?), as well as themes in any written comments to help you figure out how best to prioritize feedback. If multiple people are saying similar things, it's probably worth considering ways to address their feedback in the future. In some cases, feedback may have merit, but it isn't feasible. For example, suggestions to spread the training out over 2 days so there's more time to practice role-play scenarios is a nice idea, but it's likely not feasible, particularly when there are staffing limitations (i.e., staff are needed on the floor and can't be held up in training for 2 days). In other cases, there may be creative ways to address some aspect of the feedback without making drastic changes.

Again, keep in mind the possibility of needing to modify components of the training to align better with your institution's setting or population. For example, if your trainees won't ever work with incarcerated women, those slides could be reduced or eliminated and time could be allocated to another relevant subpopulation (inserting new slides as needed) or redistributed elsewhere (e.g., spending more time talking about serious mental illness, practicing role-plays). By knowing your audience and the settings where they work well in advance, such modifications can be made before administering the training, so you might avoid post-training feedback related to the relevance of these topics. However, if training material is modified or new content is added, it may be useful to explicitly ask trainees to provide feedback on these newer elements so you can further refine them.

On the flip side, it's not a good idea to dwell only on negative feedback or give too much power to these types of comments. We know this can be hard to do—even one nasty or unintentionally hurtful comment among a sea of praise can really dampen our spirits. In the first author's experience, one trainee commented on their dislike of the design of the slides, which was admittedly difficult not to take personally. Find ways to cope with the comments that "sting" a little and take in and appreciate the ones that support the good work you did!

Go get 'em! ☺

Appendices

Appendix 6.1: Practice Scenarios

Phase 1: Instructor-Led Demonstration

Instructors ***Request a volunteer to play Lorenzo, an adult who is in custody in your facility. Then, read the following scenario out loud to the training group. You will play the correctional officer interacting with Lorenzo. As you work through the scenario with the volunteer training, you will pause whenever you see "Prompt!" in the script. Follow the prompt to encourage audience participation.***

Scenario *Lorenzo is incarcerated on a medium security mental health unit. He regularly takes medications to help with symptoms of schizophrenia, including psychosis and agitation. He can become irritable and difficult to communicate with when his medications are not taken at the same time every day. Lorenzo is 45 years old and has been in prison for the past 5 years.*

Script:

Lorenzo (volunteer): (*in a moderately aggressive tone*) Hey! I still haven't gotten my fucking medications this morning. I've asked you three times now to figure out why these damn people haven't come over here yet.

Officer (instructor): Man, I told you already, the nursing station is short-staffed today. They'll be here when they can.

Lorenzo: Fuck, man. (*starts to walk away from the officer*). They won't be so short-staffed when I crack my head open on the floor.

Prompt!

Prompt the audience to recall the first step the officer should do in this scenario: Separate the symptoms of mental illness from the criminal thinking. Guide trainees to instruct the officer to tease apart which aspects of Lorenzo's behavior are likely related to his mental illness vs. criminal thinking. In this scenario, Lorenzo's frustrations are justified but his lack of medications may be making him more agitated than normal. However, Lorenzo's attempt to prompt a response by saying something shocking is an example of criminal thinking. He is trying to prioritize his needs over others such as other patients needing medical attention. The seriousness of his statement could also trigger unnecessary safety and security measures that will spread staff even thinner. He is allowed to be frustrated but can use better coping skills to help manage his symptoms until his medications arrive. Once audience members have worked through these distinctions, **prompt them to recall Step 2: Acknowledge the problems related to the person's mental illness.**

Officer: (*in a calm voice*) Hey, Lorenzo, come back over here for a minute. I know it messes you up when your meds don't get here on time. It sucks your symptoms can get worse because of staffing issues. I think that's what's happening now. You're right to be annoyed but not having your meds is making you feel this even more strongly.

Prompt!

Prompt the audience to recall Step 3: Challenge the criminal thinking behind the behavior.

Officer: (*in a calm voice*) The fact that nursing is held up isn't your fault. It also doesn't give you permission to take your frustrations out on other people or make threats to get what you want. That's an example of criminal thinking and you have to correct that. What could be the negative consequences of saying something like that?

Lorenzo: They might come strip me and put me on suicide watch. But I'd sure as hell get my meds then!

Officer: Maybe. But, you'll be in an uncomfortable place and, unless you are seriously wanting to harm yourself, you would be taking time and attention away from patients with more pressing medical needs or who are also waiting on meds like you. Staff are already spread thin. Your way of handling the situation is not very responsible and could make things worse not just for you but for others, too. What's your reaction to this?

Lorenzo: Yeah, alright. I get it. But sometimes there ain't no other choice.

Officer: I understand it can feel that way sometimes. Thinking about some coping skills you learned in treatment, what could you do to manage your frustrations until nursing is able to get to you?

Prompt!

This could be the end of the scenario, or the audience could discuss examples of coping skills such as making an entry in a thought log, deep breathing exercises, guided imagery, thought stopping, art therapy, etc.

Phase 2: Trainee-Led Demonstration

Instructors ***If possible, request one junior-level and one senior-level volunteer. The junior-level trainee will play Karla, an adult who is in custody in your facility. The senior-level volunteer will play the correctional officer interacting with Karla. Then, read the following scenario out loud to the training group. As you help the volunteers work through the scenario, you will pause whenever you see "Prompt!" in the script. Follow the prompt to encourage audience participation.***

Scenario *Karla, a 24-year-old woman, just graduated from the Alcohol and Drug program. She has been sober for 3 months now, and you have noticed big changes with her attitude and the way she spends her time. One night, you observe her sitting at a table with other people on her unit who are still struggling to stay sober. While at the table, you see Karla sharing food and cigarettes. Eventually, she goes back to her cell and hands a pair of her socks to another woman. After final count, you visit Karla at her cell to check in on her and make sure she is staying sober.*

Script:

Officer (senior trainee): Karla, how are things going? Still doing good?

Karla (junior trainee): I'm doing amazing! Tomorrow is 100 days sober. I started visiting the chapel. I'm even thinking about doing college classes.

Officer: Good for you. What was up with your friends out there earlier? They giving you a hard time?

Karla: Oh no, nothing like that. Everyone has been so nice since I got clean, now they come to me for advice. I feel like a sponsor, you know? It feels good to give back and help other women get their lives on track.

Officer: Yeah, I mean that's great you want to help people. From what I know about those programs, I think it can be pretty risky to spend so much of your time on other people. Maybe you should keep focusing on your work in the program and getting into classes.

Karla: Helping people is part of the 12 steps! I have not had any cravings in weeks, I'm not worried about staying sober. They do not even offer me anything anymore. I've got this, Officer!

Prompt!

Prompt the audience to recall the first step the officer should do in this scenario: identify the criminal thinking error. This is a hard one to pick out. But in this scenario, Karla's style of criminal thinking is keeping her from being realistic with herself about how hard it can be to stay sober, especially with friends who are still using drugs. She is becoming overconfident and dismissive of what she truly needs to do to stay clean. While she has not broken any rules at this point, she is at serious risk of relapse which could lead to disciplinary problems and other serious consequences. She should also know from previous attempts at sobriety that if she doesn't prioritize her recovery, she may jeopardize it. The officer needs to find a way to be supportive of Karla while still challenging her unhelpful and possibly dangerous thinking.

Officer: (*in a calm voice*) I'm so proud of you for the hard work you have put into getting clean. It's also good to have the support of friends in your recovery. I have just seen too many people get comfortable or overconfident in their sobriety and fall back into old habits, especially when they're not disengaging from other people who are still using. I want you to stay on this path of success—which means putting yourself first. The 12-steps also say something about this. In fact, I think not putting yourself first in this particular scenario is an example of criminal thinking because you're downplaying with the level of care and precaution you need to be taking. I'm wondering if you're starting to think relapse couldn't happen to you now that you've gotten this far.

Karla: Criminal thinking?! You people are all the same, just trying to bring people like me down. I've fought negativity my whole life! But I thought you were different. I thought you had faith in me.

Officer: Remember criminal thinking isn't always about breaking a rule or committing a crime. It's thinking that is irresponsible and *can* lead to unfortunate outcomes. I know you're sober, and I know you can stay clean. So, it's not a matter of not believing in you. It's a matter of keeping things real. Sometimes it's difficult to see how things could go wrong until it's too late. What do you think could go wrong in this situation? Have you ever been overconfident in your sobriety before and it caused you to misjudge a risky situation?

Karla: I guess someone could still offer me something even though I told them not to. And those were my last new pair of socks I gave away. The last time I relapsed it was because I thought I could handle being around my mom who still smokes dope. I thought she would change if she saw me happy, but instead, I started using with her again.

Officer: Exactly. So, having the overconfident mindset is a bit irresponsible when you know it's led to bad judgment, which can keep you stuck in this lifestyle. You worked too hard to get to this point. So, let's think about how you can start to distance yourself from those ladies, find other supports, and not feel pressure to give away your things. You can still be supportive of them and their sobriety during your Narcotics Anonymous (NA) meetings.

Prompt!

Discuss with the audience what coping skills or resources the officer could offer Karla to help her stay sober and keep healthy friendships.

Phase 3: Small Group Role-Play

Instructors ***Split groups into 2–4 people and assign each group 1–2 scenarios. Group members should rotate between playing the person in custody and the officer addressing their criminal thinking. In groups larger than two, members who are not directly participating in the role-play should offer suggestions or feedback. Use the three-step processes described in Module 4 to guide group conversations and possible strategies for redirecting behavior. Below are questions you can also use to direct the role-play or provide corrective feedback. On the next page, you can photocopy the scenarios, cut along the dotted line, and distribute to groups.***

Scenario 1: Temeka

1. What part(s) of Temeka's situation could be explained by discrimination or abuse related to her gender identity?
2. What signs of criminal thinking is Temeka showing?
3. What could you offer Temeka to increase her safety and encourage her to change her thinking?
4. What about Badger? How could you apply the three-steps with him?

Scenario 2: Stanford

1. In what way can you empathize with Stanford's circumstances? Have you ever had a loved one get sick, or fall on hard times financially?
2. What signs of criminal thinking is Stanford showing?
3. How might you express your understanding to Stanford? How can you show him you are on his side and trying to help?
4. How can you help Stanford see that his thinking is unhelpful? Come up with better ways to meet his needs.

Scenario 3: Gilbert

1. Which part of Gilbert's situation is explained by his intellectual disability? How does this make him more likely to encounter situations like this?
2. What signs of criminal thinking is Gilbert showing?
3. How can you help Gilbert avoid being taken advantage of and protect himself?
4. Describe some ways you can help Gilbert understand that his way of thinking is not helping him in this situation. What alternatives can you offer him?

Scenario 4: Paul

1. What part, if any, does Paul's age play in his recent behavior?
2. What signs of criminal thinking is Paul showing?
3. How might you talk to Paul about expectations for behavior and conduct?
4. Come up with some possible responses to challenge Paul's criminal thinking.

Scenario 5: Stephanie

1. Is Stephanie just looking for attention? Why or why not? What real issues or needs could be explaining her behavior?
2. What is the best way to approach Stephanie about her unwillingness to compromise? *Hint: consider her gender and how that may impact her response to you.*
3. What signs of criminal thinking is Stephanie showing?
4. What techniques might you use to talk to her about her criminal thinking?

Scenario 1: Temeka *Temeka is a transgender woman who was recently denied her request for additional estrogen injections to assist in her gender-affirming transition. She is currently housed in the male prison where you work waiting to transfer to a female prison. Temeka has been in a pretty consistent bad mood over the past few days, getting an attitude with officers and refusing to attend program activities. While walking over to the showers, another male known as Badger, yells "get out the way, here comes that nasty-ass she-man!" Temeka turns around and shoves Badger into the wall, saying "I'll fuckin' show you nasty ass, you little bitch!" Officers break up the altercation and Temeka is escorted to a holding cell. She's back on the unit the next day, and you approach her to check in and have a chat.*

Scenario 2: Stanford *During routine cell searches, you find a stash of cell phones behind Stanford's bedframe. Another officer tells you Stanford must be trading contraband on the yard. You were told by Stanford's psychiatrist last week that his mother was diagnosed with an aggressive form of cancer and his family is having difficulty paying for her treatment on top of keeping money on his books. You assume he's trading contraband for things like soap and toothpaste while his family pays for her treatment; you decide to confront him about the cell phones.*

Scenario 3: Gilbert *Gilbert is 32 years old and has a diagnosed intellectual disability. He seems to rotate frequently between the special needs unit and general population. You try to keep a closer eye on Gilbert when he's in the general population, as he can be naïve and easily taken advantage of. You see him eating at a table with some younger guys on the unit who are known gang affiliates. The next day, you see Gilbert lunge toward Jeremiah, who is known on the yard to have mental health issues of his own. You see Gilbert take a swing at Jeremiah and the gang-affiliated guys laugh and cheer him on. While other officers break up the fight, you pull Gilbert aside later and ask him, "what's gotten into you?" He says "well, they told me if I help them keep people in line, they'd make sure no one took my stuff."*

Scenario 4: Paul *Paul just turned 18 years old. He was tried as an adult in court and placed in a facility for youthful offenders. He was recently transferred to your facility after his birthday; he's never been to an adult prison before and is still learning the ropes. He tries to impress people with his stories and jokes. His behaviors are sometimes a little over-the-top. This week, Paul began pulling pranks on other people on his unit, such as coming up behind them while sitting at tables and startling them. Some of the guys brush him off, but others get really pissed and threaten to hurt him. Paul doesn't seem to get that many people in prison have a history of trauma, violence, and impulsivity. Today, he thought it would be funny to clog the toilet in his cell so when his cellmate uses it, it backs up and floods their cell. After Paul is made to clean up the flooded cell, you sit him down to talk about his recent behavior.*

Scenario 5: Stephanie *Stephanie was recently transferred to your high-security unit after several fights and disciplinary infractions on a general population unit. Other officers have told you she is a restrictive housing and psych "frequent flyer," and that she is attention-seeking. Upon arriving on the unit, she tosses her cell-mate's belongings off the top bunk and puts her pillow there. They start to yell at each other, and you try to de-escalate the situation. You say to Stephanie, "you just got here, what's your problem?" Stephanie responds by saying "I don't give a shit about none' a y'all, this is my home and I'm not sleeping nowhere but the top."*

Appendix 6.2: Quiz Answer Sheet

The following questions test your knowledge of the material you learned today. Try your best. You need to earn at least a 75% or 12 out of 16 correct. Read each question carefully.

1. ***Which of the following was NOT a goal of this training?***
   a. *Help incarcerated persons change their behavior*
   b. *Replace the need for long-term therapy*
   c. *Learn strategies to address criminal thinking in the moment*
   d. *Create continuity between correctional officers and therapists in supporting behavior change*

2. ***What is "criminal thinking"?***
   a. *A pattern of thinking that is impulsive, irresponsible, and helps justify criminal behavior*
   b. *A style of thinking that originates from the criminal part of the brain*
   c. *Thinking about committing a crime*
   d. *A technique used by therapists to understand why people violate rules and laws*

3. ***What is one of the benefits of becoming an agent of change in correctional settings?***
   a. *Increase negative interactions between correctional officers and the people in custody*
   b. *Getting more vacation days and job perks*
   c. *Learn how to change your own criminal thinking*
   d. *Reduce feelings of burnout and mental exhaustion*

4. ***Criminal thinking is a risk factor for future offending that CANNOT be changed.***
   a. *True*
   b. *False*

5. ***Which of the following is NOT one of the Central 8 Risk Factors for offending behavior?***
   a. *Age*
   b. *A history of criminal activity*
   c. *Drug or alcohol misuse*
   d. *Poor work or school performance*

6. ***People with a mental illness or cognitive impairment are incapable of engaging in criminal thinking.***
   a. *True*
   b. *False*

7. ***When addressing criminal thinking with people in custody.***

   a. *The same three-steps should be used in exactly the same way with everyone.*
   b. *You should tailor how you apply the three-steps depending on different factors or characteristics of the person (e.g., mental illness, gender, etc.)*
   c. *There are no specific steps to address criminal thinking, as long as you address it in some manner early on.*
   d. *You shouldn't address it until mental health staff are available to assist you.*

8. ***Which type of criminal thinking is more impulsive and unplanned?***

   a. *Proactive*
   b. *Hyperactive*
   c. *General*
   d. *Reactive*

9. ***Which type of criminal thinking is more planned and calculated?***

   a. *Proactive*
   b. *Hyperactive*
   c. *General*
   d. *Reactive*

10. ***How should correctional officers respond to instances of criminal thinking?***

    a. *Degrade or shame the person*
    b. *Give a sanction or increase the person's security level*
    c. *Acknowledge the criminal thinking and redirect the behavior*
    d. *Use criminal thinking to get a step ahead of the person*

11. ***Which of the following is the best example of a behavior rooted in criminal thinking?***

    a. *Moderately increasing the speed of your car to pass the vehicle in front of you*
    b. *Scanning the barcode of a coupon you found in the checkout line so you can get a discount on the potato chips you want to buy*
    c. *Breaking one of the mugs in the staff kitchen and blaming it on a co-worker when your boss asks how it broke*
    d. *Submitting your request for time off to your supervisor via email rather than through the official process on the human resources website*

12. ***In what order should you use the following steps to address criminal thinking with someone who has a serious mental illness (SMI)?***

    a. *Acknowledge the mental illness; challenge criminal thinking; separate mental illness from criminal thinking*
    b. *Challenge criminal thinking; acknowledge the mental illness; separate mental illness from criminal thinking*
    c. *Challenge criminal thinking; separate mental illness from criminal thinking; acknowledge the mental illness*
    d. *Separate mental illness from criminal thinking, acknowledge the mental illness, address criminal thinking*

13. ***To address criminal thinking, a correctional officer needs to argue with the person about the appropriateness of their behavior.***
    a. *True*
    b. *False*
14. ***Which strategy can help ensure older people and those with cognitive disabilities understand attempts to redirect their criminal thinking?***
    a. *Speak faster, using shorter words*
    b. *Repeat each sentence at least three times*
    c. *Look for head nods, eye contact, and verbal agreement*
    d. *Offer free commissary items when they change behavior*
15. ***What can officers do to be more gender-responsive when working with women?***
    a. *With permission, attending meetings with women and encouraging them to appropriately assert their needs that are not being met on the unit*
    b. *Tell women there is nothing you can do about their victimization*
    c. *Question the facts surrounding their report about what happened*
    d. *Explain that criminal thinking happens when women are mistreated*
16. **Diego, one of the youth in custody on your unit, asked to change the channel on the television earlier than the scheduled time. When you told him no, he called you a pig and knocked a chair over before crawling underneath his bunk and refusing to come out. Which of the following statements would be the best way to address Diego's behavior?**
    a. *You're acting like a child. Come out from under there.*
    b. *No wonder you're here in prison, only criminals throw fits when they don't get their way.*
    c. *If you don't come out from under your bunk, I'm writing you up.*
    d. *I know this kind of stuff was probably okay at home or with your friends, but it's not helpful here. Getting upset, calling names, throwing stuff when things don't turn out the way you want is criminal thinking.*

Appendix 6.3: Quiz Answer key

The following questions test your knowledge of the material you learned today. Try your best. You need to earn at least a 75% or 12 out of 16 correct. Read each question carefully.

1.

   a. *Help incarcerated persons change their behavior*
   b. ***Replace the need for long-term therapy***
   c. *Learn strategies to address criminal thinking in the moment*
   d. *Create continuity between correctional officers and therapists in supporting behavior change*

2.

   a. ***A pattern of thinking that is impulsive, irresponsible, and helps justify criminal behavior***
   b. *A style of thinking that originates from the criminal part of the brain*
   c. *Thinking about committing a crime*
   d. *A technique used by therapists to understand why people violate rules and laws*

3.

   a. *Increase negative interactions between correctional officers and the people in custody*
   b. *Getting more vacation days and job perks*
   c. *Learn how to change your own criminal thinking*
   d. ***Reduce feelings of burnout and mental exhaustion***

4.

   a. *True*
   b. ***False***

5.

   a. ***Age***
   b. *A history of criminal activity*
   c. *Drug or alcohol misuse*
   d. *Poor work or school performance*

6.

   a. *True*
   b. ***False***

7.

   a. *The same three-steps should be used in exactly the same way with everyone.*
   b. ***You should tailor how you apply the three-steps depending on different factors or characteristics of the person (e.g., mental illness, gender.)***
   c. *There are no specific steps to address criminal thinking, as long as you address it in some manner early on.*
   d. *You shouldn't address it until mental health staff are available to assist you.*

8.

a. *Proactive*
b. *Hyperactive*
c. *General*
d. ***Reactive***

9.

a. ***Proactive***
b. *Hyperactive*
c. *General*
d. *Reactive*

10.

a. *Degrade or shame the person*
b. *Give a sanction or increase the person's security level*
c. ***Acknowledge the criminal thinking and redirect the behavior***
d. *Use criminal thinking to get a step ahead of the person*

11.

a. *Moderately increasing the speed of your car to pass the vehicle in front of you*
b. *Scanning the barcode of a coupon you found in the checkout line so you can get a discount on the potato chips you want to buy.*
c. ***Breaking one of the mugs in the staff kitchen and blaming it on a co-worker when your boss asks how it broke***
d. *Submitting your request for time off to your supervisor via email rather than through the official process on the human resources website*

12.

a. *Acknowledge the mental illness; challenge criminal thinking; separate mental illness from criminal thinking*
b. *Challenge criminal thinking; acknowledge the mental illness; separate mental illness from criminal thinking*
c. *Challenge criminal thinking; separate mental illness from criminal thinking; acknowledge the mental illness*
d. ***Separate mental illness from criminal thinking, acknowledge the mental illness, address criminal thinking***

13.

a. *True*
b. ***False***

14.

a. *Speak faster, using shorter words*
b. *Repeat each sentence at least three times*
c. ***Look for head nods, eye contact, and verbal agreement***
d. *Offer free commissary items when they change behavior*

15.

a. ***With permission, attending meetings with women and encouraging them to appropriately assert their needs that are not being met on the unit***
b. *Tell women there is nothing you can do about their victimization*
c. *Question the facts surrounding their report about what happened*
d. *Explain that criminal thinking happens when women are mistreated*

16.

a. *You're acting like a child. Come out from under there.*
b. *No wonder you're here in prison, only criminals throw fits when they don't get their way.*
c. *If you don't come out from under your bunk, I'm writing you up.*
d. ***I know this kind of stuff was probably okay at home or with your friends, but it's not helpful here. Getting upset, calling names, throwing stuff when things don't turn out the way you want is criminal thinking.***

Appendix 6.4: Evaluation of Trainee Engagement

Date of training: __________

Trainee name: ____

For trainer use only *Please answer the following using the five-point scale to the right of each question.*

Criterion	Strongly disagree	Disagree	Neutral	Agree	Strongly agree
This trainee was attentive throughout the training	1	2	3	4	5
This trainee participated adequately throughout the training	1	2	3	4	5
This trainee seemed invested in learning the skills taught during this training	1	2	3	4	5
This trainee appeared to give their best effort on all training activities	1	2	3	4	5
This trainee demonstrated a high level of professionalism with the trainer and their peers	1	2	3	4	5
I feel confident this trainee has sufficiently met all learning objectives	1	2	3	4	5

Additional comments or feedback:

Appendix 6.5: Completion Certificate

CERTIFICATE OF COMPLETION

Presented to:

For successfully completing the "In the Act: Recognizing Criminal Thinking" training course.

Trainer Signature

Date

Appendix 6.6: Training Evaluation Form

Date of training: __________

Presenter(s):____

Please answer the following using the five-point scale to the right of each question.

Learning objectives	Strongly disagree	Disagree	Neutral	Agree	Strongly agree
I can define "criminal thinking errors" and their effects on people's behavior while in prison	1	2	3	4	5
I feel like I could identify criminal thinking errors when I see evidence of them in other people's behavior	1	2	3	4	5
I feel like I could intervene when I see evidence of criminal thinking errors in other people's behavior	1	2	3	4	5
I feel I could identify special populations within a prison setting and adjust my approach to addressing criminal thinking to fit their needs	1	2	3	4	5
I can identify several benefits to addressing criminal thinking	1	2	3	4	5

Program content and delivery	Strongly disagree	Disagree	Neutral	Agree	Strongly agree
The content presented met the stated objectives	1	2	3	4	5
The content was relevant to my job and can be applied to my daily work	1	2	3	4	5
The information I learned will enhance my work	1	2	3	4	5
The course material was appropriate to my education and experience	1	2	3	4	5
The skills and principles taught in this training are generally in line with what I believe and practice as a professional	1	2	3	4	5
The course material was current	1	2	3	4	5
The course material presented the content effectively	1	2	3	4	5
The handouts and teaching aids enhanced the content of the course	1	2	3	4	5
The location was suitable	1	2	3	4	5
The facilities were conducive to learning	1	2	3	4	5
The instructions for requesting accommodations for a disability were clear	1	2	3	4	5

Program content and delivery	Strongly disagree	Disagree	Neutral	Agree	Strongly agree
Program administration questions or concerns were addressed effectively and in a timely manner	1	2	3	4	5

Presenter	Strongly disagree	Disagree	Neutral	Agree	Strongly agree
The presenter demonstrated superior knowledge in the content area	1	2	3	4	5
The presenter's pace was easy to follow	1	2	3	4	5
The presenter conveyed knowledge clearly and effectively	1	2	3	4	5
The material was well organized	1	2	3	4	5
The coverage was thorough	1	2	3	4	5
The presenter provided information regarding the scientific basis for the material presented	1	2	3	4	5
The presenter incorporated questions, group discussions, and interactivity well	1	2	3	4	5
The presenter conveyed a balanced coverage of the training material	1	2	3	4	5
The training material demonstrated respect for various relevant aspects of cultural and individual diversity	1	2	3	4	5
The training was free of commercial bias	1	2	3	4	5
The instructor presented the subject matter clearly	1	2	3	4	5
The instructor was responsive to participants	1	2	3	4	5
The instructor used technology effectively	1	2	3	4	5

General training administration	Strongly disagree	Disagree	Neutral	Agree	Strongly agree
I learned a lot from this training course	1	2	3	4	5
I would recommend this training course to others	1	2	3	4	5
Our facility could easily implement the skills and techniques taught in this training program	1	2	3	4	5
I would like to see the training program continue at my facility	1	2	3	4	5
Overall, the content of this training course was useful for my work and professional development	1	2	3	4	5

Please tell us anything else you'd like us to know about your experience or how to improve the experience for future participants:

Appendices

The Work Stress Scale-Correctional Staff

Please indicate the level to which you agree with each statement as it relates to your current work as correctional staff on a scale of 0 to 4 (0 = Strongly disagree, 4 = Strongly agree).

	Strongly disagree	Disagree	Unsure	Agree	Strongly agree
1. When I'm at work, I often feel tense or uptight.	0	1	2	3	4
2. A lot of the time my job makes me very frustrated or angry.	0	1	2	3	4
3. Most of the time I am at work I feel that I have a lot to worry about.	0	1	2	3	4
4. I am usually not calm nor at ease when I am working.	0	1	2	3	4
5. I usually feel that I am under a lot of pressure when I am at work.	0	1	2	3	4
6. There are a lot of aspects about my job that can make me pretty upset about things.	0	1	2	3	4

© The Author(s), under exclusive license to Springer Nature Switzerland AG 2025
A. B. Batastini et al., *Training Correctional Staff to Recognize Criminal Thinking*, https://doi.org/10.1007/978-3-031-88404-7

How to determine your score:

1. *Add up your scores on each item.* __________
2. *Mark your score on the number line below. This is the range of possible scores.*

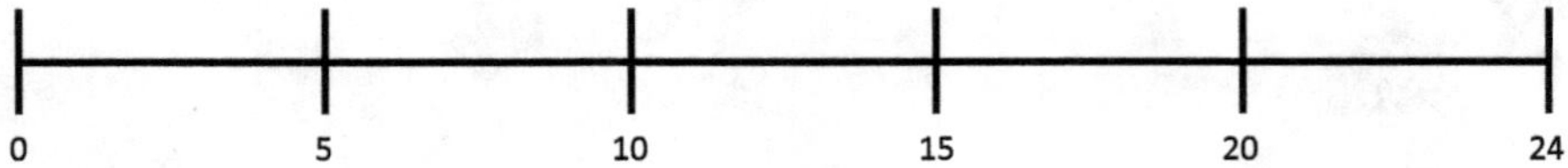

3. *Where your score is on the number line tells you how anxious and/or pressured you feel while at work. Scores between 0 and 12 suggest lower work-related stress. Scores between 12 and 24 suggest higher work-related stress.*

Self-Efficacy-12

Please indicate the level to which you agree with each statement by circling a number on the five-point scale (1 = Strongly disagree, 5 = Strongly agree).

1. How certain are you that you are able to successfully identify the issues the inmate wishes to address during the conversation?

0	1	2	3	4	5	6	7	8	9

2. How certain are you that you are able to successfully make an agenda/plan for the conversation with the inmate?

0	1	2	3	4	5	6	7	8	9

3. How certain are you that you are able to successfully urge the inmate to expand on his or her problems/worries?

0	1	2	3	4	5	6	7	8	9

4. How certain are you that you are able to successfully listen attentively without interrupting or changing the focus?

0	1	2	3	4	5	6	7	8	9

5. How certain are you that you are able to successfully encourage the inmate to express thoughts and feelings?

0	1	2	3	4	5	6	7	8	9

6. How certain are you that you are able to successfully structure the conversation with the inmate?

0	1	2	3	4	5	6	7	8	9

7. How certain are you that you are able to successfully demonstrate appropriate non-verbal behavior (eye contact, facial expression, placement, posture, and voicing)?

0	1	2	3	4	5	6	7	8	9

8. How certain are you that you are able to successfully show empathy (acknowledge the inmate's views and feelings)?

0	1	2	3	4	5	6	7	8	9

9. How certain are you that you are able to successfully clarify what the inmate knows in order to communicate the right amount of information?

0	1	2	3	4	5	6	7	8	9

10. How certain are you that you are able to successfully check the inmate's understanding of the information given?

0	1	2	3	4	5	6	7	8	9

11. How certain are you that you are able to successfully make a plan based on shared decisions between you and the inmate?

0	1	2	3	4	5	6	7	8	9

12. How certain are you that you are able to successfully close the conversation by assuring that the inmate's questions have been answered?

0	1	2	3	4	5	6	7	8	9

13. How certain are you that you are able to successfully cope with emotional inmates?

0	1	2	3	4	5	6	7	8	9

14. How certain are you that you are able to successfully handle angry inmates?

0	1	2	3	4	5	6	7	8	9

15. How certain are you that you are able to successfully communicate difficult news to inmates?									
0	1	2	3	4	5	6	7	8	9
16. How certain are you that you are able to successfully manage your time with inmates?									
0	1	2	3	4	5	6	7	8	9
17. How certain are you that you are able to successfully involve the inmates in the decisions being made?									
0	1	2	3	4	5	6	7	8	9

How to determine your score:

1. *Add up your scores on each item.* __________
2. *Mark your score on the number line below. This is the range of possible scores.*

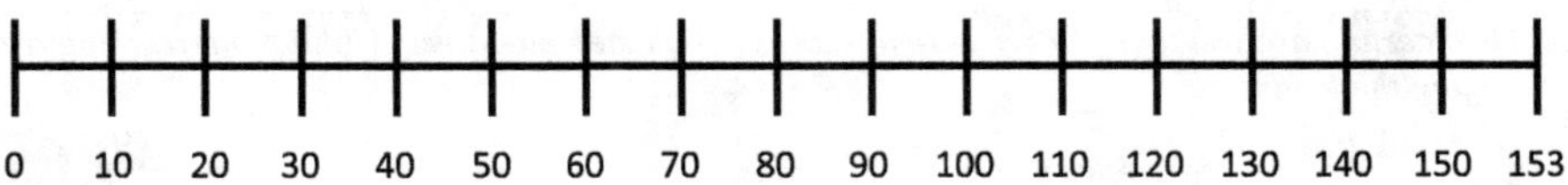

3. *Where you score is on the number line tells you your confidence in your ability to successfully do your job. Your confidence in your ability is also known as self-efficacy. Scores between 0 and 77 suggest lower self-efficacy, while scores between 77 and 153 suggest higher self-efficacy.*

Psychological Inventory of Criminal Thinking Styles–Simplified Version

Please indicate the level to which you agree with each statement by circling a number on the four-point scale (1 = Disagree, 4 = Strongly agree).

	Strongly agree	Agree	Not Sure	Disagree
1. I won't allow anything to get in the way of getting what I want.	4	3	2	1
2. I blame other people and situations for the problems I have had in life.	4	3	2	1
3. Change can be scary.	4	3	2	1
4. Even though I start out with good plans, I can't stay focused and keep "on track."	4	3	2	1
5. I can do anything if I try hard enough.	4	3	2	1
6. When problems build up, I say "the hell with it" and use drugs or commit a crime.	4	3	2	1
7. I get worried when I don't know what's going to happen.	4	3	2	1
8. I thought the victims of my crimes deserved what they got or should have known better.	4	3	2	1
9. One of the first things I check out about someone is if they look strong or weak.	4	3	2	1
10. I sometimes think of things too awful to talk about.	4	3	2	1
11. I am afraid of losing my mind.	4	3	2	1
12. The way I look at it, I've paid my dues and have the right to take what I want.	4	3	2	1
13. The more I got away with crime, the more I thought there was no way the police would ever catch me.	4	3	2	1
14. Breaking the law is no big deal as long as you don't really hurt somebody.	4	3	2	1
15. I have helped out friends and family with money I got doing crime.	4	3	2	1
16. I don't stop and think about the problems I could cause until it is too late.	4	3	2	1
17. It's not fair that I got locked up when bank presidents and lawyers get away with crimes every day.	4	3	2	1
18. I often argue with others over pretty small things.	4	3	2	1
19. I can honestly say when I did my crime, I thought about the well-being of my victims.	4	3	2	1
20. When I get fed up I say "fuck it" and then do something careless, wild, or just plain stupid.	4	3	2	1
21. New problems and new situations make me nervous.	4	3	2	1
22. Even when I got caught, I told myself that there was no way they'd send me to prison.	4	3	2	1

	Strongly agree	Agree	Not Sure	Disagree
23. I take the easy way out, even if I know it will get in the way of something bigger I may want later.	4	3	2	1
24. When I'm not in control of something, I feel weak, and I want to get control.	4	3	2	1
25. Deep down I am basically a good person.	4	3	2	1
26. Many times, I start something but never finish it.	4	3	2	1
27. I hear voices and see visions that others do not hear or see.	4	3	2	1
28. When it's all said and done, society owes me.	4	3	2	1
29. I have said to myself more than once that if it wasn't for someone "snitching" on me I would have never gotten caught.	4	3	2	1
30. I don't have to work so hard, things will work themselves out.	4	3	2	1
31. I have used alcohol or drugs to calm my nerves before committing a crime.	4	3	2	1
32. I have made mistakes in life.	4	3	2	1
33. On the streets I told myself I needed to rob or steal in order to continue living the way I deserve to live.	4	3	2	1
34. I like to be right in the middle of things, in control as much as possible.	4	3	2	1
35. When people ask me why I did my crime, I point out how hard my life has been.	4	3	2	1
36. I want to do the right thing, but I have trouble making it happen.	4	3	2	1
37. After doing a crime or hurting someone, I act kind to animals or little children to make myself feel better.	4	3	2	1
38. There have been times in my life when I felt the law didn't apply to me.	4	3	2	1
39. I have trouble focusing, even on easy things.	4	3	2	1
40. I tend to act without thinking when I'm under stress.	4	3	2	1
41. I have done crimes so that I would not look worthless in front of my friends and family.	4	3	2	1
42. If I'm afraid I might fail, I don't even try.	4	3	2	1
43. I tend to put off until tomorrow what I should do today.	4	3	2	1
44. Although I always knew that I might get caught, I told myself that there was "no way they would catch me this time."	4	3	2	1
45. I feel better about my crimes when I tell myself that if I didn't do it, someone else would.	4	3	2	1
46. When I try something new, it's hard to stick with it because I get scared and I don't know how it will turn out.	4	3	2	1
47. People have trouble understanding me because I talk about lots of things at the same time.	4	3	2	1
48. There is nothing more frightening than change.	4	3	2	1

	Strongly agree	Agree	Not Sure	Disagree
49. Nobody tells me what to do, and if they try, I threaten them or I might even hurt them.	4	3	2	1
50. After I break the law or hurt someone, I do a "good deed" or something nice to make up for the bad things I did.	4	3	2	1
51. I have a hard time thinking through the good and bad things that could come from my plans.	4	3	2	1
52. Nobody can do something better than me because I am stronger, smarter, or slicker than most people.	4	3	2	1
53. I have thought, "everybody else is doing it, so why shouldn't I?"	4	3	2	1
54. If someone is wrong, I saw "yeah, you're right," because it's easier than arguing with them about it.	4	3	2	1
55. Being afraid of change makes it hard for me to be successful in life.	4	3	2	1
56. The way I look at it I'm not really a criminal because I never meant to hurt anyone.	4	3	2	1
57. I saw to myself, "the hell with working a regular job, I'll just take what I want."	4	3	2	1
58. I sometimes wish I could take back things I said or did.	4	3	2	1
59. Looking back over my life I can see now that I didn't have clear goal.	4	3	2	1
60. Strange smells, that I can't explain, come to me for no apparent reason.	4	3	2	1
61. On the streets, I thought I could use drugs and not get addicted.	4	3	2	1
62. I am easily sidetracked so that I almost never finish what I start.	4	3	2	1
63. If there is a short-cut or easy way around something I will find it.	4	3	2	1
64. I have trouble controlling my angry feelings.	4	3	2	1
65. I am a special person, so my situation usually needs special attention.	4	3	2	1
66. There is nothing worse than being seen as weak or helpless.	4	3	2	1
67. The good things I have done for others make up for the bad things.	4	3	2	1

	Strongly agree	Agree	Not Sure	Disagree
68. When I set goals I often do not reach them because I am sidetracked by things going on around me.	4	3	2	1
69. There have been times when I tried to change but stopped because I was afraid of what might happen.	4	3	2	1
70. When I get fed up, I say "fuck it" or "the hell" with it.	4	3	2	1
71. I have told myself that if I had a good job, I wouldn't need to do crime.	4	3	2	1
72. My life would be better if I could learn to make better decisions.	4	3	2	1
73. There have been times when I felt I had a right to break the law so I could pay for something I wanted.	4	3	2	1
74. I never thought about the end result of what I did before I got locked up.	4	3	2	1
75. A lot of my life on the streets was spent trying to control people and situations.	4	3	2	1
76. When I first started breaking the law I was very careful, but after I didn't get caught, I believed that I could do just about anything and get away with it.	4	3	2	1
77. as I look back on it now, I was a pretty good guy even though I was doing some crime.	4	3	2	1
78. I broke plans with my family so that I could hand out with my friends, use drugs, or do crimes.	4	3	2	1
79. I tend to push problems to the side rather than deal with them.	4	3	2	1
80. I have used good behavior (like not doing crime for a while) or bad situations (like a fight with a girlfriend) as an excuse to commit a crime or use drugs.	4	3	2	1

How to determine your score:

To determine your score, contact the creator of the measure at ________. In the first worksheet copy the answer circled in this packet to the corresponding item number. Then, go to the second worksheet. The column labeled *Raw Score* indicates what the individual's score is on several various criminal thinking styles. Higher scores indicate higher levels of that type of thinking style.

Burnout Assessment Tool

The following statements are related to your work situation and how you experience this situation. Please state how often each statement applies to you.

Section A: Exhaustion	Never	Rarely	Sometimes	Often	Always
1. At work, I feel mentally exhausted.	0	1	2	3	4
2. Everything I do at work requires a great deal of effort.	0	1	2	3	4
3. After a day at work, I find it hard to recover my energy.	0	1	2	3	4
4. At work, I feel physically exhausted.	0	1	2	3	4
5. When I get up in the morning, I lack the energy to start a new day at work.	0	1	2	3	4
6. I want to be active at work, but somehow I am unable to manage.	0	1	2	3	4
7. When I exert myself at work, I quickly get tired.	0	1	2	3	4
8. At the end of my working day, I feel mentally exhausted and drained.	0	1	2	3	4

Section B: Mental distance	Never	Rarely	Sometimes	Often	Always
9. I struggle to find any enthusiasm for my work.	0	1	2	3	4
10. At work, I do not think much about what I am doing and I function on autopilot.	0	1	2	3	4
11. I feel a strong aversion towards my job.	0	1	2	3	4
12. I feel indifferent about my job.	0	1	2	3	4
13. I'm cynical about what my work means to others.	0	1	2	3	4

Section C: Cognitive impairment	Never	Rarely	Sometimes	Often	Always
14. At work, I have trouble staying focused.	0	1	2	3	4
15. At work I struggle to think clearly.	0	1	2	3	4
16. I'm forgetful and distracted a work.	0	1	2	3	4
17. When I'm working, I have trouble concentrating.	0	1	2	3	4
18. I make mistakes in my work because I have my mind on other things.	0	1	2	3	4

Section D: Emotional impairment	Never	Rarely	Sometimes	Often	Always
19. At work, I feel unable to control my emotions.	0	1	2	3	4
20. I do not recognize myself in the way I react emotionally at work.	0	1	2	3	4
21. During my work I become irritable when things don't go my way.	0	1	2	3	4
22. I get upset or sad at work without knowing why.	0	1	2	3	4
23. at work I may overreact.	0	1	2	3	4

How to determine your score:

1. *Add up your scores on each item in Section A.* __________
2. *Mark your score on the number line below. This is the range of possible scores for Section A.*

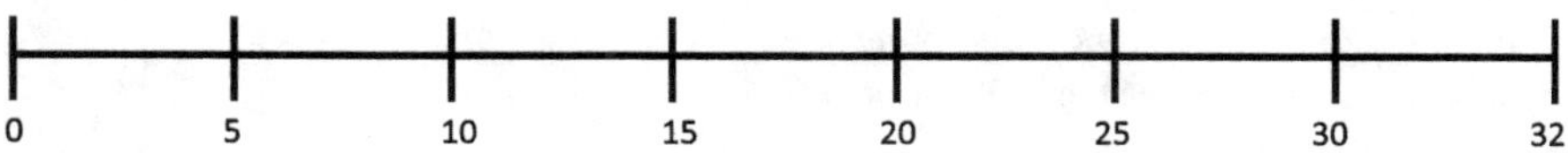

3. *Where your score is on the number line tells you how emotionally and physically exhausted you are right now because of your work as correctional staff. This is one of the signs of burnout. Scores between 0 and 16 suggest low levels of exhaustion. Scores between 16 and 32 suggest higher levels of exhaustion.*
4. *Add up your scores of each item in Section B.* __________
5. *Mark your score on the number line below. This is the range of possible scores for Section B.*

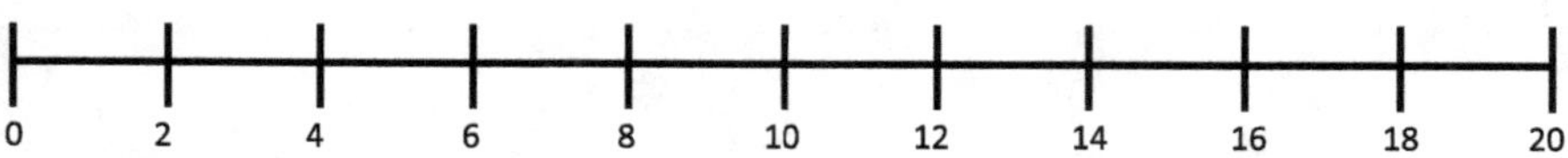

6. *Where your score is on the number line tells you how much you have detached yourself mentally and emotionally from inmates and co-workers (i.e., mental distance). This influences burnout and could be a result of burnout. Scores between 0 and 6 suggest you create low mental distance. Scores between 7 and 13 suggest moderate mental distance. Scores between 14 and 20 suggest high mental distance.*
7. *Add up your scores for each item in Section C.* __________

8. *Mark your score on the number line below. This is the range of possible scores for Section C.*

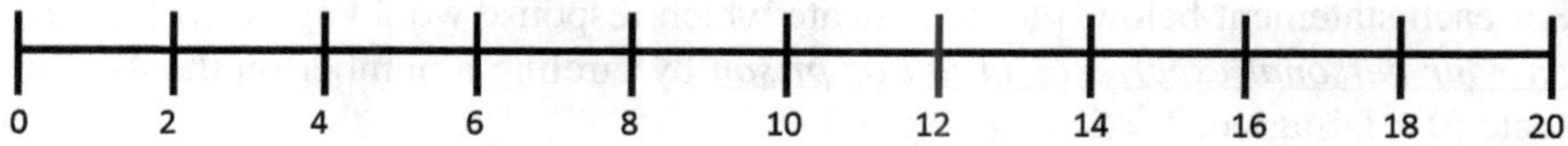

9. *Where your score is on the number line tells you how much you experience cognitive difficulties at work. Scores between 0 and 6 suggest few cognitive difficulties or low distress related to your cognitive difficulties. Scores between 7 and 13 suggest moderate cognitive difficulties/distress. Scores between 14 and 20 suggest you experience many cognitive difficulties/distress at work.*
10. *Add up your scores for each item in Section D.* __________
11. *Mark your score on the number line below. This is the possible range of scores for Section D.*

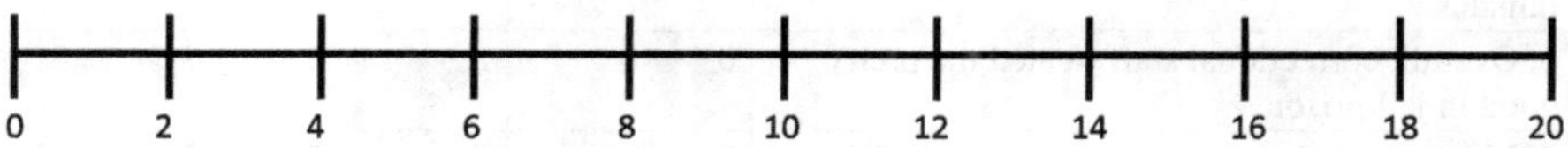

12. *Where your score is on the number line tells you how much you experience emotional distress/your emotions interfere with your work. Scores between 0 and 6 suggests little emotional distress and/or interference. Scores between 7 and 13 suggest moderate emotional distress/interference. Scores between 14 and 20 suggest much emotional distress/interference.*
13. *Now, add up your scores for all items (Sections A-D).* __________
14. *Mark your total score on the number line below. This is the possible range of scores overall.*

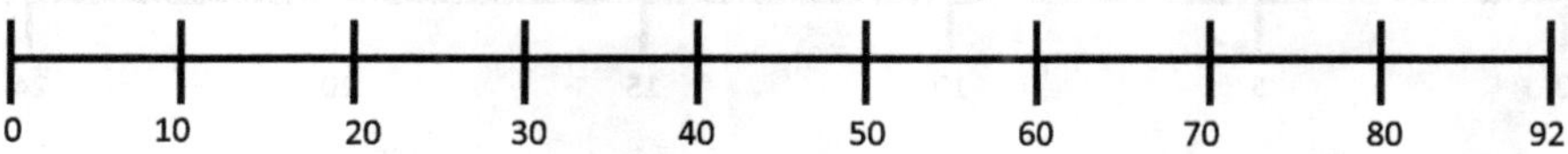

15. *Where your score is on the number line tells you how much burnout you are experiencing and how much it is impacting your work. Scores between 0 and 30 indicate no/low levels of burnout. Scores between 31 and 61 suggest moderate levels of burnout. Scores between 62 and 92 suggest high levels of burnout. Please remember that burnout at any level is serious and taking care of yourself physically, mentally, emotionally, and reducing stress can help to reduce and prevent burnout.*

Attitudes Toward Correctional Staff—Inmate Version

For each statement below, please indicate which response would agree with *based on your personal experience in jail or prison* by circling a number on the 4-point scale (0 = Disagree, 3 = Strongly agree).

	Strongly disagree	Disagree	Agree	Strongly agree
1. The legal system is just as tough on offender today as it used to be.	0	1	2	3
2. I have very few problems with correctional officers.	0	1	2	3
3. Female correctional officers do their jobs as well as male officers.	0	1	2	3
4. The quality of new guards entering jail/prison today is as good as it ever was.	0	1	2	3
5. Jail/prison staff often act fairly toward inmates.	0	1	2	3
6. Overall, correctional staff treated me pretty good in jail/prison.	0	1	2	3
7. Most guards in jail/prison treat inmates like they are humans.	0	1	2	3
8. Correctional officers often use the right about of force on inmates.	0	1	2	3

How to determine your score:

1. *Add up all your scores on each item.* ___________
2. *Mark your score on the number line below. This is the range of possible scores.*

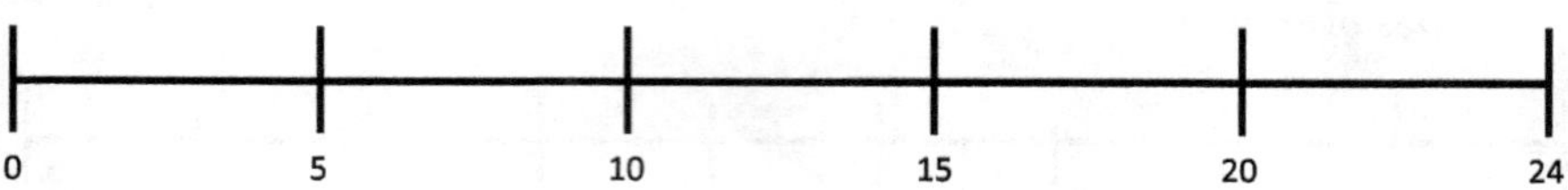

3. *Where your score is on the number line tells how positively or negatively you view correctional staff. Scores between 0 and 12 suggest more negative views toward correctional staff. Scores between 12 and 24 suggest more positive views.*

Index

© The Editor(s) (if applicable) and The Author(s), under exclusive license to Springer Nature Switzerland AG 2025
A. B. Batastini et al., *Training Correctional Staff to Recognize Criminal Thinking*, https://doi.org/10.1007/978-3-031-88404-7

GPSR Compliance
The European Union's (EU) General Product Safety Regulation (GPSR) is a set of rules that requires consumer products to be safe and our obligations to ensure this.

If you have any concerns about our products, you can contact us on

ProductSafety@springernature.com

In case Publisher is established outside the EU, the EU authorized representative is:

Springer Nature Customer Service Center GmbH
Europaplatz 3
69115 Heidelberg, Germany

www.ingramcontent.com/pod-product-compliance
Lightning Source LLC
Chambersburg PA
CBHW070804171025
34092CB00051B/24
9783031884030